Survivin

Surviving Theresienstadt

A Teenager's Memoir of the Holocaust

Revised Edition

VERA SCHIFF

Edited by CHERYL A. FURY

McFarland & Company, Inc., Publishers

Jefferson, North Carolina

This is a revised and expanded edition
of *Theresienstadt: The Town the Nazis Gave to the Jews*
(Toronto: Lugus, 1996).

All photographs are from the author's collection
and the Schiff family unless otherwise noted.

LIBRARY OF CONGRESS CATALOGUING-IN-PUBLICATION DATA

Names: Schiff, Vera, 1926– author. | Fury, Cheryl A., 1966– editor.
Title: Surviving Theresienstadt : a teenager's memoir of the Holocaust /
Vera Schiff ; edited by Cheryl A. Fury.
Other titles: Theresienstadt
Description: Jefferson, North Carolina : McFarland & Company, Inc.,
Publishers, 2021. | "This is a revised and expanded edition of
Theresienstadt : the town the Nazis gave to the Jews (1996)"—Title page verso.
Identifiers: LCCN 2021017745 | ISBN 9781476685557 (paperback) ∞
ISBN 9781476643304 (ebook)
Subjects: LCSH: Schiff, Vera, 1926– | Jews—Czech Republic—Biography. |
Holocaust, Jewish (1939–1945)—Czech Republic—Personal narratives. |
Theresienstadt (Concentration camp)—Biography. | Czech Republic—Ethnic
relations. | BISAC: HISTORY / Holocaust
Classification: LCC DS135.C97 S35 2021 | DDC 940.53/18092 [B]—dc23
LC record available at https://lccn.loc.gov/2021017745

BRITISH LIBRARY CATALOGUING DATA ARE AVAILABLE

ISBN (print) 978-1-4766-8555-7
ISBN (ebook) 978-1-4766-4330-4

Front cover image: Vera Katz, 1941; Theresienstadt gate
(author photographs)

Printed in the United States of America

*McFarland & Company, Inc., Publishers
Box 611, Jefferson, North Carolina 28640
www.mcfarlandpub.com*

To My Sons

The events in this book
are as the author remembers them.

Acknowledgments

The author would like to acknowledge Cheryl Fury who has breathed new life into this tragic story that offers insight into the darkness of the Shoah. It is because of her selfless work and energy that this memoir is offered to the public in this confusing time of 2021.

The editor would like to acknowledge the author whose words and insights into life and death not only during the Holocaust but in our current times have been life changing. It has been an extraordinary journey and a privilege to work with Vera Schiff as an historian and as a friend.

The author and the editor would like to thank Dr. Carson Phillips, Michael Rajzman and Roy Danics for their assistance with photographs for this book. They wish to thank the University of New Brunswick (Saint John) and Stephanie Adams.

Table of Contents

Preface

This book is a result of much thought, soul searching and wrestling with conflicting aspects, to once more reflect upon the worst chapter of our lives—the Holocaust. In the end, I decided to document my experiences for several reasons. First and foremost, it is a work dedicated to my family. I believe that they have a right to know the truth—our truth.

Another powerful reason was to contest the ever-repeated arguments of those who wish to deny the Holocaust or downplay the enormity of the crimes perpetrated upon the Jews. Not only did six million Jews perish, among them my entire family, but to add insult to injury, more than seventy years later arguments are being put forward denying the Holocaust itself. That is a posthumous slaughter of their memory.

The third reason is the wide-spread misunderstanding of the very nature of Theresienstadt: a camp in which my parents, sister and grandmother perished and where I spent three years of my life, fending off my own demise. Theresienstadt, although not a death camp, was just as horrible and lethal as other concentration camps designed for the Jews by the Nazis. The statistics of the harvest of death tell the story in incontestable numbers. The fallacy of "Spa Theresienstadt" was one of the Nazi deceptions. It was designed to extort hidden money from the old, once affluent Jews of Germany under the guise of them purchasing space in a spa-like old-folks home—Theresienstadt.

For the thousands upon thousands of innocent Jews who perished in this infamous place who could not tell their story, I believe we, the survivors, owe it to them to relate our own experiences. The fate of every survivor is different, unique but also typical of the horrid times of the Nazi rule of Europe.

Introduction

In 1939 I was a teenager with an extended family of fifty, counting relatives on both sides. In 1945 I was still a teenager, a sole survivor of the Holocaust, the only person in my entire family who was not destroyed, turned into ashes.

I write so that our children will continue to learn something about the Holocaust. We survivors were initially silent, and only with the passage of time we began to share our experiences. It seems that in the 1950s no Jew could talk about German concentration camps. Our wounds were open, we bled, but we could not discuss or analyze what was—and still is—beyond the pale of human understanding. We feared that few, if any, could grasp it and most of us felt that there were ultimately no words for the indescribable. We did not discuss horrific Nazi atrocities; we hoped that our children would grow up happier and would be better adjusted if they were sheltered, spared—if you will—the truth of our history.

And the younger generation did not ask; perhaps they guessed our pain. We tacitly embarked on a conspiracy of silence. It was more comfortable and painless, but also more mistaken and unjust. The topic became a taboo between the survivors and their children. Today that taboo is no longer tolerable. The Holocaust should serve as a warning to humankind. It should caution us that the fight against evil is not yet won. Even an educated nation like Germany was capable of indescribable atrocities and genocide.

We, the vanishing survivors of Nazi concentration camps, have not always fulfilled our obligation toward the millions whose voices were silenced forever. It is our solemn duty to record our personal stories as only we knew them.

Although Theresienstadt was not an extermination camp, it was a place of infamy where thousands upon thousands of Jews from all over Europe perished. It was also a place where thousands of inmates struggled to bring some light into the darkness, resisting the Nazi efforts to dehumanize us.

I feel that I too have a duty to fulfill on behalf of my family. Belatedly, I am recording my experiences of life with those whom I loved and lost.

For those I love, I hope to inform about the past.

1

Beginning

Supposedly it was a beautiful day, May 17, 1926, the date I was born in Prague, the capital of Czechoslovakia. I was the second and last daughter of a middle-class Jewish family. My parents married rather late in their lives, my mother in her early thirties and my father in his late thirties. Their first child, my sister Eva, was born mere 17 months before me. Though our nuclear family was a small one, we had a large, extended and harmonious family, and better yet, most lived in the same part of Prague, so we enjoyed an intense daily interaction.

The Republic of Czechoslovakia was carved out from the Austro-Hungarian Empire which was defeated in World War I. The Empire had fallen apart under the weight of its numerous problems: the ossified bureaucracy administered from Vienna, the lack of understanding of the needs of the dissimilar nationalities living under Austrian rule, and, last but not least, the humiliating defeat in World War I. The war, initiated by Austria and its ally Germany, exacted not only a horrendous cost in human lives but also brought Austria to the brink of bankruptcy. The varied nationalities of the Empire, sickened by the imperious concentration of power in Vienna, perceived themselves as the ones to foot the bill for the bloody war. The Czechs, Slovaks, Hungarians, the assorted nationalities of Yugoslavia, all wanted to shake off the rule of the Habsburg dynasty that had lost touch with its assorted subjects a long time ago. The monarchy was ousted by the indignant subjects and the imperial family was sent into exile.

The man who fought for the independence of the Czechs and Slovaks had impressive credentials. Thomas Garrigue Masaryk taught philosophy at the famous Charles University and actively participated in public as well as political life. He was well known in the academic circles of Europe as the author of many works and essays which dealt with a broad range of subjects from suicide to humanism and from national self-determination to women's rights. He was a resolute proponent of democracy, firmly believing that this was the best form of government.

Masaryk was a staunch defender of all human and civil rights. He believed passionately in the equality of women, a doctrine that enjoyed, in the days preceding World War I, lip service at best. The Jewish minority in the Czech lands embraced Masaryk as the champion of human rights of all minorities. The history of Jews in the Czech lands was a tattered one, marred by many tragedies. Though Jews settled in Central Europe early on, their history can be traced back to the 10th century. They were never fully accepted into the mainstream or offered equal rights by the Czech or German majorities. The Jewish destiny depended on grace or the needs of the powers that be, and thus Jews were alternately expelled from cities and invited back later to help restore the faltering commercial establishment. The Middle Ages were punctuated by bloody pogroms, many of which were orchestrated by the clergy or the ruler. Many times Jews were used as scapegoats for whatever ailed society—even natural catastrophes were blamed on Jews. For example, Jews were accused of spreading the Black Death by poisoning the wells and of starting the big fires of Prague's old city in the 16th century.

The end of the 19th century was a time of rampant anti–Semitism, including a sensational ritual-murder case. Leopold Hilsner was accused of killing Agnes Hruza, a girl barely known to him. He was charged with ritual murder, allegedly killing Agnes for the purpose of obtaining blood of a Gentile virgin. Rumors persisted that Jews needed the blood of a Gentile virgin for baking matzoth, the unleavened bread traditionally a symbol of the Passover holiday. Although there was evidence that she may have been killed by her brother, the charge against Hilsner was allowed to stand.

Not only did local officials not intervene when Hilsner was accused of the murder, but Vienna tacitly approved of the outrageous allegation in the hope that the trumped-up charges would distract the restive nation. Although most intelligent Czechs knew that the charges were falsely concocted, no one would publicly dare to challenge the sensational indictment. Only Thomas Masaryk rose to the occasion. Using his university platform, he declared that the ritual-murder charge was a superstition taken straight from the Dark Ages and insisted that the Czech nation should be ashamed to even consider such an atrocious slander. Masaryk was accused of being bribed by the Jews. He was expelled from the university lecture circuit and the newspaper that he edited, the *Athenaeum*, was closed down. Eventually, however, Masaryk prevailed, substantiating his lifelong motto, "The truth wins, even if at times suppressed."

At the outbreak of World War I, Masaryk arrived at the conclusion that the battle for the independence of the Czechs and Slovaks should be waged from within as well as from abroad. As a result, he left the country and traveled to Western Europe and the United States, organizing the successful campaign for independence of the Czechs and Slovaks.

The Czechoslovaks obtained their liberty on October 28, 1918. The new republic was comprised of four provinces: Bohemia, Moravia, Slovakia and Ruthenia. The most affluent, Bohemia, had long been industrialized, was once known as the "Engine of the Empire," and was also the most advanced politically and educationally. Moravia closely resembled the Czech lands. Agriculturally-based Slovakia was much poorer and less educated and developed. The neglect of the past overlords, the Hungarians, was legendary. Ruthenia, the easternmost tip of the new state, was even worse off. The heterogeneity of the new state greatly reflected the Jewish minority.

The Jews who lived in the west—Bohemia and Moravia—were mainly assimilated, slowly drifting away from the orthodox practice of their ancestral faith. Some went so far as to accept baptism as a passport to full acceptance, while others intermarried and relinquished their heritage. For many ambitious assimilated Jews, affiliation with Judaism became a distinct liability which had to be shirked one way or another. The Jews of the Eastern provinces maintained their Jewish identity and adherence to the traditional faith. A number of them found strength in this reliance to inherited tenets of Judaism.

Czechoslovakia, then the only true democracy in heart of Europe, was sandwiched between five neighboring countries, none friendly to the new state. To the north and west was Germany, which insisted on maintaining contact with the considerable ethnic German minority in the Czech lands. To the south was Austria, the remnant of the disintegrated Habsburg Empire, and on the southern Slovakian border was Hungary, which cultivated ties with Slovakia's sizable Hungarian minority. Likewise, Poland, in the northeast, nursed territorial demands. The most eastern tip of Czechoslovakia shared borders with the Soviet Union, an enigmatic giant, hardly to be trusted under the convulsive, communist dictatorship. Thus, the new republic was not located in a very propitious environment.

The Czechoslovak Republic's ruling party, the Social Democrats, provided security and equality to all minorities and guaranteed education and health care to all citizens. The legislative branch codified all these principles into a constitution. The provinces and municipalities enjoyed independence but the vast economic disparities between the more affluent west and the much poorer east could not be evened out quickly enough. While the thriving industrialized west prospered, exporting and maintaining business ties with many countries, the agricultural east limped slowly behind, never quite catching up in prosperity, education and culture.

The first seeds of discontent were planted and with the passage of time they turned into serious, divisive issues. These disparities made the Slovaks bitterly resentful of the Czechs. Still, there was hope for a safe and lucrative future. The new state's constitution guaranteed freedom and protection to all citizens. The representatives of the state elected Thomas G. Masaryk as their first president.

The new head of the state returned home from his four-year stint abroad in 1918, a man of 68 years of age. Unfortunately, the Czech presidency is void of any real power as the role is largely ceremonial. Nevertheless, the two decades between the two wars was but a brief interlude of civilized conditions provided by the Czechoslovak government in the very heart of Europe. It was a great place and time to be born and live in, and it was one of the short moments in history which later prevented many from despairing over humankind. Unfortunately, in the 1930s, dark clouds began to gather in neighboring Germany in the form of a new far-right movement, initially seemingly insignificant in numbers but menacing in its dogma.

Our family, the family of my father, the Katzs, had lived in southern Bohemia's townships for as long as anyone could remember. Prior to the 19th century, however, the archives provide only scant information. Their livelihood was based on small-scale businesses such as trading in grains and dry goods; some even owned a pub.

My mother's family, the Taussigs, hailed from Ricany, a town close to Prague. They were also engaged in small business ventures, as were most Bohemian Jews until the end of the 19th century. In those days many professions were inaccessible to Jews so that trade remained one of the few ventures to which they could apply their talents and make a living.

My parents were married in Prague in 1924. Their marriage was a harmonious one. Although they had different dispositions, they complemented each other well, and their mutual respect was obvious. My father was a lawyer, a calling he loved and for which he had sacrificed a great deal to achieve. He had to work through his high school and university years as my grandmother, who was widowed in her young years, was unable to help him financially. In those days, before implementation of any welfare measures, a fatherless home suffered a great number of economic deprivations. Moreover, my father had to study in Prague, far from his home in southern Bohemia, and the cost of rent, food and tuition was steep. In those days, it was mainly the privilege of the wealthy families to send their sons to university. My father must have been strongly motivated to study under such difficult circumstances and follow his dream for a number of years. Nevertheless, in due time, he graduated with a degree in law bestowed upon him by the prestigious Charles University.

The outbreak of World War I interrupted his career. He was recruited for military service to join the army of Emperor Franz Joseph. For some time, he was assigned as a field court judge, but his heart was not with the Habsburgs or their war efforts which, four years later, resulted in Austrian defeat.

Vera's parents, Elsa and Siegfried Katz, 1924.

Upon demobilization, my father returned to Prague and accepted a position at the Finance Ministry of the new government. He loved his work there, and he seemed fulfilled and content. He must have been appreciated, for he was regularly promoted, and soon he was assigned to a position overseeing the distribution of tobacco at wholesale and retail outlets, then a government monopoly.

My father was a tall, slim man of unusual intelligence whose hard work lifted him from a necessity of eking out a living to a gratifying, challenging job. He was also actively involved in politics, social studies, economics and its resulting consequences on society, and he imparted those interests to us. He was an avid reader and probably would have wanted nothing more than to be a lifelong student.

He firmly believed that the future of the Jewish minority would be best served by assimilating into the mainstream of Czech society as long as Jews were granted religious freedom. He placed his trust in the leadership of Thomas Masaryk, the first president of the Czechoslovak Republic, and he remained his lifelong ardent follower.

From our young years Father would talk to us, his two daughters, about topics not covered in our school curriculum. He discussed l9th-century philosophers such as Karl Marx, whose works my father studied with great interest, but doubted their practical or universal application. Father would also select books for us to read, and later we would discuss the content, acted out as a debate of equals. The flip side of the coin was his limited interest in money. Unlike my maternal uncles, he did not acquire great wealth. Money was not a major issue in our family.

The only sore point was the pro–German stance of my uncles, including their use of the German language and support of German cultural institutions such as their subscription to a German stage theater, opera and philharmonic orchestra. I remember a few heated discussions between my father and his brothers-in-law in which my father attempted to convince my uncles of the need of Jewish loyalty and support for the newly established republic. Perhaps my father hoped that the nonviolent brand of Czech anti–Semitism would vanish, if only the Jews would wholeheartedly commit themselves to the Czech cause. Much later he revised his opinion of a possible eradication of anti–Semitism.

Because my father supported not only us but also his mother and widowed sister, he took another job, besides the one in the Finance Ministry. He regularly contributed articles and essays to a financial magazine and freelanced for other publications.

We enjoyed a very good living standard. We lived in a spacious apartment in a nice residential district of Prague and our home was exquisitely furnished and maintained. My father's study was lined with bookshelves which were filled to capacity. We had a live-in servant and hired outside help for cleaning and laundry washing. My parents entertained frequently and in an elegant style.

The better part of my parents' time, money and interest was invested in the education of their two daughters, their pride and joy. Our days were filled with learning both from our school curriculum and diverse private lessons—music and languages among them. While we were still preschoolers my parents hired a French-speaking mademoiselle who taught us French, the only language she knew. Later, singing lessons and art appreciation classes were deemed important for our education. Religious classes were also incorporated into our day, sometimes late in the afternoon. Little time, if any, was left for sports. Although my father loved to play tennis, we never got around to acquiring the skill. On occasion, we would swim or skate and sometimes attend gymnastic events, but athletics were always subordinate to academic pursuits.

My mother was not really an intellectual, but she wholeheartedly supported her husband's planning of our education. They both shared the belief in the importance of learning to the best of one's ability. Had my mother lived in different times when there were more opportunities available to women, she would have probably turned out to be a successful businesswoman. She was involved in the business ventures of my uncles, and they in turn repeatedly solicited her advice. They trusted her natural talent for commerce. She also loved people. She needed companionship more intently than my father ever did. She was very interested not only in her own family but also in scores of friends and acquaintances. One of her gifts was a tactful ability to handle people and get along with one and all. It is evident that my parents had different temperaments and interests. If these differences caused difficulties between them, they must have managed to work them out in private. Most middle-class families resolved their disagreements peacefully, without contemplating drastic measures. A middle-class woman, no matter how gifted, if she had no family of her own, would spend her life with one of her close relatives and would be more or less aimlessly shifted within the extended family, a fate few women wished for. As a result of so few options for a single woman, most couples worked out their differences by accommodating the husband's wishes. Perhaps it was a credit to my father's tolerance and flexibility that my parents' discrepancies were often resolved in my mother's favor because our lifestyle reflected her sociability and activities arising from it.

Our summer holidays were spent in one of the popular resorts in the company of relatives or friends whose mundane interests were hardly shared by my father. But he did his best to fit in and my mother, in turn, would never disturb my father when he was involved in reading or his studies. Because my father's work took up most of his time, his vacations were rather short. He would spend a week or two with us at the lake or in the mountains, perhaps in some spa, and return to Prague. He would then rejoin us only on weekends. Life was pleasant, carefree and full of joy. We girls had many friends, and I was particularly fond of one of them, Hanna Freimuth. She lived in the same high-rise as we did, and we shared a lot of time and activities together. But the best and most intimate friend of mine was always my sister. I cannot think of a more amicable relationship than the one shared by Eva and me.

Eva was only 17 months older, and we did everything together and were extremely compatible. She was a tall, slim, attractive girl, unusually gifted in languages, and excelled in a host of academic disciplines. Unlike me, she achieved outstanding results in subjects like mathematics, algebra and geometry, all of which were my Achilles' heel. I banked on the kindness of my inordinately generous sister who often re-did or completed my homework or projects when I had all but despaired over some insurmountable problem. But we also had a lot of fun together, laughing and giggling about some secrets and exchanging comments about boys whom we professed to ignore or hate. Neither of us would ever admit to any interest in those pimply members of the opposite sex, who were, of course, the focus of our curiosity.

Eva was born on the 24th of December 1924. I always remember my mother relating an event etched in her memory. It happened on the day when she first returned from the hospital with the newborn Eva in her arms. The concierge of our building, a simple, uneducated and superstitious woman, accosted my mother with an announcement that children born on Christ's birthday live a short life and die tragically. My mother used to describe this story to illustrate the ignorance and tactlessness of the woman, but somehow later, the concierge's story became a dark reality—for Eva lived a short and tragic life. Although Eva was the older, more mature and generous sister who indulged many of my caprices, I believe that we were both good children, trying hard to accomplish what our parents expected of us. Later, when German persecution made life an arduous and trying experience, Eva and I would do our utmost to help in the daily chores, trying to mitigate the growing hardships of our day-by-day existence.

I would say that we had a happy childhood although it was brief and somewhat crammed with duties. Most Jewish families set similar expectations for their children including a firm commitment to duty and achievement and devotion to family. Success, accompanied with at least some affluence, would guarantee a certain degree of security and comfort. Most middle-class families were small, hardly exceeding one or two

Baby Vera with her sister, Eva, and their mother, circa 1926.

children—perhaps the urban lifestyle was not conducive to large families. Or was it foreboding of the impending disaster?

More than half of Prague's Jews had German acculturation and their adaptation to the Czech cultural lifestyle was slow in coming. Somehow everything German seemed to have higher class or value. This was a lingering hang-up from the 300 years of rule emanating from Vienna where all intellectual, business or artistic pursuits were conducted in a German environment and language. Jews, forever anxious about the fickle swings of goodwill, taken and withdrawn rather capriciously from the government officialdom, tried to please the ruling class by any means including accepting their language and values. The central European Jews loved Germany with a kind, albeit unrequited, affection.

Our adaptation to the novel realities, mandated by the establishment of Czechoslovakia, made only reluctant progress. Also, the idea of Zionism did not meet a ready acceptance. The Jews of Prague had too good a life to wish to move to Palestine. At that time, it was perceived as a distant, hot, poor, sand-filled country, punctuated periodically by rioting Arabs and infested by malaria-carrying mosquitoes. Most Czech Jews contributed financially to the cause of Zionism, believing that a Jewish homeland would help to resolve the problem of the Eastern European Jews whose existence was always teetering on the brink of disaster. Jews there had to put up with a lot of hostility by their Polish, Ukrainian or Russian host nations.

A caustic joke made the rounds in Prague at that time. It went something along these lines: "A Zionist is a man who raises money from another man to send a third man to Palestine." The Eastern Jew, who had far fewer opportunities to advance himself (Poland and Russia practiced "Numerus Clausus"), became a cause of embarrassment to his more fortunate Western brothers and sisters. The Eastern Jew, secluded and segregated, remained more religious and traditional. Some of them wore black kaftans (overcoats), streimels (wide hats), pajot (side locks) and other outer signs of Jewish orthodoxy. If and when some of the Eastern Jews visited the Czech lands, the local Gentile population would stare and watch with amazement at these different, highly visible Jews, while Czech Jews would recoil with horror, fearing resurrection of more intense anti–Semitism.

When I was six years old, I began my school years in a public institution near our home, where Eva was already two years ahead of me. While Eva loved and excelled there, I did not enjoy going there at all and, following a few miserable days, I decided that school was not for me. I simply refused to go. This decision of mine was met with little approval by my parents who tried very hard to persuade me to change my mind, at first kindly, and then later, less so. Caving under the pressure, I agreed to try one more time to fit in among the first-graders. The next day, right when I entered my class and hesitantly searched for my bench, the homeroom teacher gave me a rough push hoping perhaps to speed up my decision to sit down. Her none too gentle transgression did it. I decided never to return, and I meant it. My parents realized that they had a real problem at hand and they quickly transferred me to a private school. There, all seemed to be just right for me. I loved the school, and the friendly homeroom teacher and I got along really well practically from the first day on.

When I reached the third grade, my parents began to have some serious discussions about my father's transfer to Caslav, a smaller city in Bohemia. There, he was to become the director of the financial district office. This relocation was crucial for his career. It was expected of those who had the ambition to reach the top position in the public service to demonstrate their leadership qualities by serving, for a while, outside of the capital.

The projected move became a source of much pain to my mother. She would have to be separated from her brothers' families. From then on she would only see them several times a year—and for my mother this was a nearly unimaginable hardship. She cared little for the small-town lifestyle with its petty gossip and the scarcity of most musical and stage performances she so enjoyed. Even the prospect of an eventual return to Prague to the position my father coveted did not seem like a redeeming feature for her. Eventually, of course, she went along with the move, and faithful to her energetic disposition, she began to organize our transfer to Caslav, a medium-sized Czech provincial city. Caslav was an unappealing town, with only a smidgen of industry, but it was home to a large military base. The city's elite (the mayor, the judge, the priests, the base's commanding officers) was expanded by yet another member, a Jewish finance director.

Dutifully my parents socialized with the city's notables, but they hardly fit in and were neither happy nor comfortable in Caslav's environment. My father liked his work and in turn was respected and accepted by people there, but my mother, though fond of the big, spacious house we rented, waited for the hour we could transfer back to Prague. Eva and I were fond of our stint in Caslav. Our school there was much less demanding and life seemed laid back in this drab garrison town. We continued with our piano, French and religious instructions, all at a noticeably less hectic pace.

Our religious instruction was provided by Rabbi Dr. Richard Feder from nearby Kolin, who came once a week. He taught a group of children of varying ages together as one group. His instructions were punctuated by much mischief. Some of the older boys made it their business to shoot small paper balls at him, a prank we thought of as uproarious fun. Evidently we could not learn much about our religion in Dr. Feder's classroom. Somehow we sensed that religion was not the top priority of our elders, an attitude prevalent in the Czech Jewish community of the 1930s. Although we must have been a difficult bunch, Rabbi Feder was never angry with his unruly class. He was a wise and kind man indeed.

At that time we knew little about the anxiety dampening the spirit of our parents. They watched the growing economic shadows of the Depression years anxiously, and the strange, rapidly spreading phenomenon of the Nazi movement in Germany. However, most Czech Jews dismissed the Nazi party as a temporary oddity. Was not Germany, after all, an educated and cultured nation? The 20th-century Germans could not possibly accept a long-term government based on the primitive and brutal principles of blood purity and racial superiority. All that seemed absurd. Most smiled condescendingly when watching Hitler, whose appearance reminded them of Chaplin and whose oratory resembled more an epileptic attack than a political statement. Well, the Jews were not the only foolish ones in their unrealistic appraisal of the new wave sweeping Germany. Many men, including Masaryk himself, dismissed Hitler as a clown, a passing aberrant product of an economic depression.

In 1936, following five years of primary school, I passed the exams required for entering high school. At the age of 11, students in Czechoslovakia were separated between those who were to attend academic centers and those who were to go into vocational schools. Eva and I were included in the group destined for academic, liberal arts education. This year also marked our move back to Prague, a transition that made my parents happy. Father got his promotion, and Mother returned to the fold and the lifestyle of Prague she loved so much. We children also looked forward to the move with enthusiasm. We were ready for a new life and new challenges. It was possibly the last happy year enjoyed by the Katz and Taussig families. We rented a beautiful apartment in the same district of Prague where our entire family lived. It was a well-established tradition to rent apartments in near proximity, permitting daily interaction. Besides, there were two lovely parks surrounding the residential area, an ideal place for play, walks and pure fun.

School went well for us. Our private lessons kept us busy and we seemed to progress well at all our endeavors. If only the shadows cast from the north were not getting heavier and darker. New experiences entered our lives. Initially, there was a trickle, then a steady stream, of Jewish refugees from Germany. They related terrible stories of persecution and discrimination against Jews in Germany. Initially what they had to share with us was not quite believed. Their stories were not dismissed outright but perceived as somehow exaggerated. The Czech Jews had a hard time accepting that Germany was governed by a bunch of thugs who mostly behaved like loose cannons. Perhaps the refugees hoped that by

Vera (left) and Eva with their mother in the Letna park in Prague, early 1930s.

magnifying their suffering, they could obtain more support, money or better shelter from their Czech brethren. Was it possible that the Germans who styled themselves as a flagship of culture and progress had turned into barbarians? But with the passage of time the abhorrent happenings in neighboring Germany became an indisputable reality. By that time we adopted a daily ritual of listening to radio broadcasts. All that was discussed was politics and related implications. We were rapidly recognizing the impending danger and with it the need for some contingency plans.

In 1938, we spent our summer holidays at a spa in Marienbad where the mood was much influenced by its proximity to the borders with the German Reich. The frame of mind of the spa's guests, mainly Jewish, was somber, intimidated by the many vocal members of the local Nazi party. Their motto was loudly proclaimed: "Back to the Reich." They quite openly voiced their longing for unification and annexation by the Nazi Third Reich. They were united under the leadership of Konrad Henlein, a one-time physical education teacher whose violent anti–Semitic and anti–Czech exhortations were only minimally, if at all, curbed by the Czech administration. After all, the little Czechoslovak Republic was a perfect democracy, guaranteeing the right of free speech. This privilege was much abused by the Nazis who did their best to undermine the existence of Czechoslovakia. In retrospect, it is easy to see that individual freedoms should have been curbed, considering the dangers emerging from those hate mongers who used and abused the privilege of freedom of expression.

In that frame of mind we spent our last holidays. I remember one event which I did not then and still do not understand because what I did was so out of character, but those were strange times. One morning, my mother announced that we were to attend a lecture by Theodore Lessing, a renowned writer and Jewish refugee from Germany. It was offered at Miramonte, a nearby coffee house located in the forest. At the appointed time we all walked through the thick pine woods to the coffee house. The scenery was beautiful, the air exuded fragrances of the fir trees, the birds were chirping and the world seemed at peace. As we entered Miramonte we were ushered to our table. I noticed that there was much less laughing and joking than customary during these afternoon teas. Gloom and sadness seemed to cloud the place. Normally I would have behaved properly, but for some reason, I decided on mischief, perhaps to lighten the oppressive mood or have some fun? On an impulse, just as we were about to sit down at our table, I pulled the chair from under my mother and she crashed down, landing on the white pebbles covering the ground of the outdoor coffee house. For a moment she was shocked, while people curiously turned their heads in our direction, but a prompt waiter helped her to her feet. His presence saved the day. Luckily nothing happened to her. As befitted the manners of those days, she only fleetingly and disapprovingly glanced in my direction and

Eva (left) and Vera on vacation with their nanny, chauffeur and a mascot in costume, 1933.

continued her conversation as if no interruption had occurred. Dr. Lessing delivered his ominous message, warning of the Nazi rule which would drown European Jewry in an ocean of its own blood.

We returned home, saddened and distraught by the speech that we had just heard. My bizarre behavior was forgotten, trivialized by the dismal message carrying a dire prognosis for our future.

2

Time Is Running Out

No sooner had we returned to Prague than our family gathered to forge plans for an escape out of the burning soil of Europe. Finally, we all came around to accept the possibility that we might have to leave Europe and resettle far from the danger looming just around the corner. The decision we arrived at was to immigrate to Curaçao, the home of my Aunt Irma. The Gerstl family had built in the Dutch West Indies a prosperous export-import business, encompassing holdings in Aruba and Curaçao. We were all well acquainted with Irma's family. Some visited Europe yearly, and they were all very generous, friendly and elegant.

We, the children, were delighted with the prospect of living on the warm island, sunlit year-round. Our elders were less enthusiastic, each for a different reason. My mother did not enjoy the idea of the monotonous heat and less cultured life of the West Indies. My father loathed the thought of giving up his work, well aware of the fact that a European lawyer had no chance of being engaged in a similar calling in another country. My uncles, in turn, felt badly about leaving their wealth in Europe, for the monetary restrictions would have permitted them only a fraction of their assets. Uncle Adolf had opened, some time ago, an account in Switzerland, as a precautionary measure, into which he channeled some of the outstanding foreign payments of the Glaser and Taussig export-import business. The sums were minuscule in comparison to the fortune which had to be abandoned in case of departure. The Swiss accounts were numbered only; no names or any closer identity of the owner was involved, providing complete discretion. During the years of persecution, it was an immeasurable advantage but later that proved to be a great detriment, for after the war, I could not come up with the numbers of any account my uncles opened during those critical years. Unfortunately, nobody informed me, then a 12 year old, about financial transactions, but then no one had foreseen the mass destruction of the Nazi era. As many others, I lost my claim to the money deposited in Switzerland.

Time was running out on us very, very fast. The restive German minority in Czech lands was becoming more and more aggressive. Their grumbling for unification with Nazi Germany was getting increasingly louder. Goaded by their leaders and incited by other Germans, they staged provocations on an ever-increasing scale.

All this unrest grew exponentially from the year 1933 when in Germany proper the Nazi party assumed power. Elected by popular vote, Hitler was legally appointed to the position of chancellor. The aging and senile president Paul Von Hindenburg who hated the "mob orator," Hitler, caved under the pressure of popular vote, hoping that Hitler might be easier to restrain within the channels of legislative office. Hitler had, of course, different ideas and he had public support. Germans came to idolize the comical figure who spewed his speeches with the anger of a deranged man. It was of no importance that the content of his speeches was almost identical, always belaboring the "stab in the back" theory, that the Germans did not really lose the war. They were betrayed by Communists and Jews into surrendering at the 1918 armistice. The continuing harangue reiterated the injustice of the Versailles treaty and the need for Germany to take its rightful place in the world community. Germans exulted in listening to Hitler's diatribes and applauded his every lie, rising to a feverish pitch when his tirades reached his favorite topic, the hated Jews—the cause of all evil, "Germany's tragedy." The world watched this spectacle with disbelief, unable to take such exhortations seriously, for they were out of touch with reality. The Germans, however, liked what they heard and admired and applauded his oratory even more. Somehow, Hitler struck a chord with the Germans, tapping into their innermost passions, and they responded to him and his biding with enthusiasm and devotion. Every one of these speeches was accompanied and often drowned out by applause that escalated to a high pitch of hysteria.

Hitler not only re-armed Germany in violation of the Versailles treaty, he also failed to pay reparations owed to the Allies, practiced the most violent anti–Semitism and abused human rights. All this happened with the tacit acquiescence of the world at large—a world that failed to grasp the threat in front of its eyes.

Hitler used the primitive maneuvering method of a carrot and a stick. Each time he transgressed on some major issue, he proffered a hand of peace, promising that this was his last demand, bringing Germany to its rightful position in the European community. The seemingly impotent Western democracies, namely France and Britain, would, amidst some protests, acquiesce to the new realities.

Hitler offered another prospect for the future: Germany's "master race" would rule Europe and eventually the world. His rabid anti–Semitism was enthusiastically accepted by his followers whose numbers grew by leaps and bounds.

Soon Hitler's madness reached another pinnacle. He began to kill those deemed unworthy of life, namely the mentally ill and the disabled. This experiment was his first gassing humans "unworthy" of life. Here, however, he ran afoul of German clergy and due to public outcry this operation had to be abandoned.

In 1935, the Nazis promulgated what became to be known as the Nuremberg racial laws. These abominable laws laid the foundation for the Nazi concept of who was a Jew. Any individual who had at least one grandparent of Jewish descent was to be considered Jewish. This categorization hit even some members of the Christian clergy including Catholic nuns and quite ironically some fiery anti–Semites who no longer perceived themselves to be affiliated with Jewish communities.

With hindsight it is incredible that a charlatan like Hitler, uneducated and primitive, succeeded in attracting a large body of followers. The electorate that considered him a man of providence stood by him until the bitter end. The later assassination attempts of Hitler stemmed from the upper echelon of officers who had concluded that the west would not negotiate a separate peace with Germany as long as he stood at the helm. One of the most famous attempts on his life took place on July 20, 1944, and it miraculously missed Hitler. Count von Stauffenberg, once a devoted Nazi, hoped to remove Hitler, convinced that the führer's presence was the obstacle to peace negotiations.

It has often been credited to Hitler that he relieved Germans of the curse of unemployment, inflation, and inferiority complexes, that he restored their pride in Germany's greatness and gave them a reason to hope. If this was indeed the case, I believe that Germans will pay for the ephemeral 12 years of Nazi euphoria until the end of time. The further we move away from the horrors committed by Germans in the name of Hitler, the worse the outrage. Hitler and his cohorts came to symbolize wickedness incarnate. It casts a giant shadow over the German nation for notionally they did elect him and continued to support him in his crimes.

Some later defended Hindenburg who had agreed to appoint Hitler as chancellor. He believed that Hitler would mellow and drop his radicalism and his murderous anti–Semitic views. Marshall von Hindenburg's only absolution was his senility, which was quite obvious. He was then a man of 85 years and visibly suffering loss of his mental faculties.

Hitler never showed the slightest inclination to modify his extremism in order to reach the pinnacle of power. In 1933, the Nazis decided to destroy the Communist party of Germany, the most powerful Nazi foe and the only credible contestant for electoral majority. The plan was sinister and crude and it brought about the physical destruction of the Communist party, allowing no recourse to the law. The plot called for arson of the state legislature, the Reichstag building. Less than one month after Hitler became chancellor, the Reichstag building was set ablaze.

The Nazis chose a patsy, a young, near-blind street vagrant named Marinus Van der Lubbe who was placed in the vicinity of the legislative assembly by Göring's political police. The "arson" was blamed on the Communists. On the night of the fire, the Nazis suspended Article 48, abrogating all civil rights, declaring it a Communist insurrection and an attempt to overthrow the government. The crime was the pretext for the creation of the Gestapo's (Geheime Staatspolizei) concentration camps and also marked the gradual extinction of the Communist party whose members were either murdered, chased out of the country or incarcerated indefinitely in concentration camps.

Later on, this recipe was repeated, with slight variations, several times. Whenever the Nazis wished to ruin some faction of society, they would create an incident or find a ploy to raise public anger which would result in a "spontaneous" murder spree. The Reichstag fire created a precedent.

Hitler's brazen and lawless bestially stunned the world into near paralysis. Emboldened by the dumbfounded acceptance of his rampage, he decided the time was ripe for larger territorial expansion. In 1938, the Austrian Nazi party began to instigate social unrest and street brawls. Their leader, Seyss-Inquart, fully cooperated with his German puppeteers, bringing about another crisis. The Austrian chancellor, von Schuschnigg, was an unpopular man. Hitler summoned him to Germany and simultaneously arranged for an unceremonious removal of Schuschnigg from power.

High on his success, Hitler annexed Austria, his homeland where he was greeted as a savior. The Austrians rejoiced hysterically at their reunification and "return to the Reich." As usual, following a major violation of an international treaty, Hitler declared that he had no further territorial demands. Within a few months of Austria's annexation, the führer turned his sights on Czechoslovakia.

Our anxiety rose. We continued to pay lip service to the unlikely hope that perhaps Czechoslovakia would not be overrun or appended to the Third Reich. Perhaps the Nazis really only wanted to reunite all Germans. We knew that we were clinging to a breaking straw. To exacerbate tensions, the local Nazis committed many provocations egged on by Germany. Czechoslovakia had several treaties that were designed to protect its safety. For example, the foreign policy agreement with France and Britain called for mutual assistance in case of aggression. As well, there was a conditional treaty of assistance with the USSR as well as a strong bond of shared support with Yugoslavia and Romania. Furthermore, Czechoslovakia's statehood and borders were defended by a well-trained army, an excellent air force and a well-developed munitions industry. All would fall into the hands of the Nazis if the west conceded to Hitler's aggression.

The Czechs had high expectations of the international conference even though no Czechoslovak representatives were invited. The meeting convened in September 1938 in Munich. The Czechoslovaks hoped that if not justice, decency or common sense, pragmatic considerations would prevail. The world would not permit the strengthening of the Nazi military machine by the addition of Czech military hardware. Unfortunately, they were proved wrong. The outcome of the Munich conference showed that the west was willing to pay any price to avoid conflict. The sacrifice of a small central European country was but a minor inconvenience. Disclosures later revealed that in 1938 Hitler was bluffing. He may well have lost a major armed conflict as he was still under-armed.

Chamberlain, then the British prime minister, was not the only British politician to misread the writing on the wall. He was preceded by Lord Runciman who headed a fact-finding mission to Czechoslovakia. He unwisely suggested acceptance of the demands made by Konrad Henlein and the local Nazi party. The Munich conference concluded with the intimidated Western leaders (including Neville Chamberlain and Edouard Daladier, the French prime minister) caving in under the threats and intimidation of the fuming Hitler. The Czech government received an ultimatum from its allies ordering a retreat from the Sudeten, the disputed north Bohemian territory inhabited by the German minority. Thereby they relinquished all the heavy artillery built into the frontier mountain range, the natural borders between the two countries. These massive fortifications, dubbed the Czech "Maginot Line," were planned to halt the first onslaught by the Germans. They were now to be vacated without a shot. Within a year the Allies found themselves locked in a mortal struggle with Nazi Germany.

The cession of the Sudeten to Germany and the betrayal by the admired and trusted Allies left the Czechs bitter, bewildered and disillusioned. The Jews were absolutely frantic. No one believed that Hitler's territorial demands were satiated although he once more announced that he had no plans for further expansion. No one doubted that the Nazis' next target would be the defenseless remnant, the crippled rump of Czechoslovakia. Panic-stricken Jews wanted to leave at all costs. But few countries were willing to take us in: almost all slammed their gates shut. Jews were trapped in countries which could not protect them and exposed to the approaching Nazi terror because no country offered a haven. The rest of the world seemed to look at the unfolding drama with total indifference. At that point, my uncle realized that time was running out. Even so, the family underestimated how little of it was left. They were captives of their assets, devoting a great deal of time, imagination and energy trying to salvage at least a sizeable part of it.

Prague also changed. It was now a city blanketed in fear, a city expecting a calamity. Jews scrambled for visas to anywhere. Every day at dawn, or earlier, long queues formed in front of every embassy. Prague fed on rumors. Everyone had some reliable information about this or that embassy that might issue visas. Mostly, it was just wishful thinking and unsubstantiated gossip. Jews continued to line up and wait for hours on end, only to find out that no visas would be granted. Our family still had the potential haven in Curaçao—or so we hoped. Hurriedly we purchased a large crate, obtained an export permit, packed our most valuable possessions and sent the crate to Curaçao. This was done under the lenient scrutiny of the Czech custom officials, susceptible to bribery through money and alcohol, both of which we supplied.

Another catastrophe befell the Jews of Europe shortly after the Munich debacle: there was a pogrom of unparalleled proportions in Germany and Austria. Kristallnacht, the "Night of the Broken Glass," took place on November 9, 1938. The Nazi Party was behind the outrageous fury of this infamous night. The Nazis had shown they had no scruples when they set fire to the Reichstag building; this was true of Kristallnacht as well.

The aim of the former act was to smash the support for the Communist party of Germany. Now, the Nazis' outrage was directed against the

Eva (left) and Vera and their dog, Jerry, 1936.

Jewish community that they wished to decimate. At the same time, the Nazis wanted to seize Jewish emigration funds. Van de Lubbe, a pathetic patsy, was used as the stooge for the Reichstag fire in 1933. The Nazis now had a real crime as the pretext to attack the Jews.

A young 17-year-old émigré, Herschel Grynszpan, was a desperate and misguided young man. His family hailed initially from Poland but had immigrated to Germany at the beginning of the 20th century to escape the ever-increasing wave of persecution and violence perpetrated by the Poles against the Jewish minority. Grynszpan went to school in Germany but was later sent to study in Paris. The Nazis stripped the Grynszpan family, along with other Jews who had moved to Germany from the east, of their citizenship and evicted them immediately. A train full of these tragic, stateless Jews reached the German-Polish borders but the Poles refused to accept any of their Jewish ex-nationals. Neither the Germans nor the Poles would budge. The train remained motionless on the border, packed with people who received no food or were not allowed to leave the car—even for basic hygiene.

Herschel Grynszpan's parents wrote to their son, detailing their plight and misery. He decided to attract world attention and provide a wake-up call to the world's conscience. The naïve boy conceived an idea of killing the German ambassador to Paris. In his mind it seemed an ideal way to gain the world's attention. The world would take notice and act on behalf of the Jews, abandoned and left to rot at the border. At least this was how young Herschel reasoned. He bought a gun and went to the embassy where he was prevented from reaching the ambassador. Desperate and determined, he settled on the third secretary—ironically, a man known for his anti–Nazi sentiment. Herschel shot Ernst vom Rath. No sooner had the news reached Hitler than the Nazis made the decision to exploit the desperate act of a Jewish youth by claiming it was a conspiracy of international Jewry.

The Nazi party instigated an onslaught upon the Jews. Orders were issued that the "spontaneous outburst" was not to be hindered by police. The spree of violence was well orchestrated, whether it was the burning of synagogues, shattering of windows, merchandise thrown into the streets, or the wide-ranging looting and scavenging. Under the cover of darkness, illuminated by the many raging fires, the looters poured gasoline, while the firemen stood idly by their engines, making sure they contained the fires to Jewish targets.

The night of savagery was justified as the manifestation of the people's ire against the Jews of Germany. Nearly thirty thousand Jews were sent to concentration camps. More than one hundred were murdered, many were plunged into the ice-cold river where they drowned, and scores died as a result of maltreatment and injuries sustained in the course of the ghoulish night.

The Night of Broken Glass was so-called because of all the shattered windowpanes but Kristallnacht also shattered the remnants of the Jewish community. One hundred synagogues were burned down, 76 others were demolished, and some 7,500 Jewish stores were ruined. It was a night of indescribable orgies of hatred, even when considering the long history of infamies perpetrated against the Jews.

When the smoke had cleared and the extent of the damage evaluated, it was obvious that the Jewish community lay in ruins. The German government imposed a fine of one million Deutsch Marks for "cleaning of the mess caused by Jews." The funds once earmarked for Jewish emigration from Europe were confiscated by the Nazis, and the Jewish community was left penniless. Why did the Germans do it? Perhaps to offer a night of looting and violence to their followers, and to demonstrate to the world at large that Jews were unprotected by law.

All this alarmed Aunt Irma's family greatly and they sent an emissary, Irma's brother, Otto Gerstl, who was determined to bring his mother, sister and her family to the safety of the Dutch West Indies. Aunt Irma's family was frustrated by the slow progress of their European relatives. Otto Gerstl left Czechoslovakia even angrier than when he had arrived, for only his mother agreed to leave with him. His sister, my aunt, refused to consider leaving without her husband who still was not finished with the transfers and consolidation of the family assets. Viktor, their only son, also remained behind with his parents and the rest of the family in the insecurity of the truncated republic of Czechoslovakia.

No one in our family seemed to rush to emigrate, as if everybody was paralyzed by fear. We read in German newspapers the hateful propaganda against Jews, displaying ugly, mean-looking, long-hooked-nosed Jewish faces for public ridicule. At times I would look in a mirror trying to find similar features in my face or I would scan the features of my relatives, never finding any of the repulsive traits. Were there really individuals somewhere with such ugly countenances or were they just figments of Nazis' hateful imaginations?

Indefatigably, the Nazis reiterated the worst insinuations about Jewish crimes against humanity and slanders of every possible nature. No lies were vile or mean enough. Often the Jews were portrayed as vermin requiring extermination. Even the fictitious "Protocols of the Elders of Zion" was unearthed, pulled out from the czar's archives and published as proof of the conspiracy of a Jewish cabal aiming to rule the world and destroy humanity. We lived through all that, somehow hoping for a miracle which might keep Hitler out of the mutilated remnant of the Czechoslovak Republic. But miracles do not happen!

3

German Invasion
and Occupation

The events we had dreaded for so long came to pass. Still, when they finally happened, they came as a shock that stunned us. I woke up to the familiar sounds of the daily ritual, the voice of the anchorman reporting the morning news. The monotonous voice informed us that the German army had just crossed the border and was in the process of occupying Bohemia and Moravia. The broadcast continued with the report that Hitler had granted independence to the Slovaks and had installed a fascist government there. I glanced at the calendar; it was March 15, 1939. Outside a snowstorm raged, quite unusual for this time of year in Central Europe.

The adults huddled around the radio, apparently listening to the exhortations about the need to maintain calm and not to offer any resistance. Indeed, it would have been sheer madness to stand up and fight at this stage. I was then almost 13 years old, mature way beyond my age. I still remember the feeling of foreboding that I had on that day. There are some days that I seem not to be able to forget, and one of those is March 15, 1939.

During the broadcast, I suddenly got the feeling that I might suffocate if I did not get a breath of fresh air. I decided to get out of the apartment. Everybody was totally wrapped up in listening to the continuously repeated news. No one noticed me sneaking out. Outside everything seemed very still, as is often the case during heavy snowfalls. Then, suddenly, I heard right behind me a powerful roar of many heavy motors, quickly gaining in volume. I turned back and saw a military column, the first German unit I met. They were coming down a street where in other times endless annual fairs were held. The columns moved quickly, effortlessly, and, of course, unopposed. That was the day my adolescence ended although it really never began, the one I had to skip in order to survive.

I hastily beat a retreat, getting home at double time, finding all our relatives already gathered there. They tried to reassure one another about our chance for a fast departure from this part of the world. Curaçao suddenly seemed very, very attractive.

The Germans declared Bohemia and Moravia the Protectorate of Germany and imposed a government of quislings, headed by an old jurist, Emil Hacha. The real authority was vested in the office of the German protector, and the first one to be appointed was an old German aristocrat, Konstantin von Neurath. Bad as he was, by German standards he was considered a moderate, rather conservative in his political orientation.

Not a day went by that some new laws and regulations were not issued but there was no violence against those Czechs who did not put up any resistance. Not yet, anyway.

The fact of the matter was that the Czech population proved to be not only docile but also responsive to monetary stimuli. So enticed, they excelled in production of exemplary quality of wares destined for the Germans. It got so bad that Hitler called the Czechs "Meine Gute Tchechen" (My good Czechs). This attitude proved to be a great embarrassment to the government in exile, headed by the last freely elected president, Edvard Beneš.

In the early days of the occupation, the Czechs were not subjected to brutal treatment, there were no appalling food shortages, and consequently most of the nation settled into a rather willing cooperation with the occupiers. As for the Slovaks, they rejoiced in their independent government headed by a fascist priest, Father Tiso. They had never been fond of the union with the better-educated Czechs. They had always felt shortchanged economically, inferior culturally, and alienated religiously. Whereas the Slovaks were and still are devoted Catholics, the Czechs were a rather lukewarm mixture of Protestants and Catholics. The Slovak autonomous government had to toe the German line but it was granted some latitude in local decisions, a fact that initially benefited the Slovak Jews. The government of Father Tiso, though rabidly anti–Semitic, was more interested in the economic profit it could reap by confiscating Jewish properties. Worse was to come later.

The Czechs did not seem unduly perturbed by their puppet government. The situation of the Jews was entirely different. We immediately became the defenseless target of German hate and persecution. Every day would bring new restrictions, making our day-to-day existence more precarious and complicated. The lives we had a few years previous seemed to have vanished forever. It appeared incredible that only a brief while ago our lives were enjoyable, a smooth flow of seasonal pleasures.

Often I would close my eyes, trying to remind myself of our past. I would try to remember that in days bygone, school would begin in the fall, soon interrupted by Rosh Hashanah—the Jewish New Year. Eva and

I, dressed in new outfits chosen with a great deal of care, would attend the services in the synagogue where my parents worshiped (with the men and women still separated). Ten days later on Yom Kippur, the Day of Atonement, we girls would be preparing apples, garnished by cloves, which exuded a pleasant scent. Our mother and our childless Aunt Irma would each receive a small bouquet of flowers and an apple that exuded the fragrance of the spices. Ostensibly the fragrance was to help them with their fast but I suspect that it was more a gesture of love and appreciation.

Autumn would fill the air with the acrid odor of the decaying yellow leaves; the parks became bare and drab as Mother Nature was readying herself for winter. Actually, fall was the saddest season of the year. It was chosen as a special time to remember the dead by visits to the cemeteries, where chrysanthemums were placed on the graves.

I always felt a sense of relief when fall switched into winter. I welcomed the change, though I disliked the bitterly cold weather. We always delighted in the times spent together at home, particularly during the winter season. It was cozy in our well-heated apartment which was filled with the fragrance of baked goods. Although we did not observe the religious aspect of Christmas, we still were caught up in the mood of partying and gaiety. The festival of lights, Chanukkah, frequently overlapped or coincided with Christmas so that we also lit candles and received gifts. Our winter break would be spent at times in some mountain resort or we would remain in Prague, which I much preferred. We attended theaters, concerts or other performances. In the days of my childhood Prague was a city buzzing with artistic activities. There was always a wide choice of large or small stage performances, most of the highest quality. The secular new year was always celebrated with a lot of good cheer. February brought a whirlwind of parties, mostly costumed, for this was the time of carnivals. What a great month that was! We never heard of the "February blahs"; it was one of the merriest months in a series of joyful ones.

As the year continued, we welcomed the first signs of spring, which ushered in the Passover holidays. The entire family gathered in our place for the traditional Seder, presided over by our grandfather. I still see his tall and stately figure at the head of the table. Directed by him, we would take turns reading from Haggadah, the story of the exodus from Egypt, pondering the cruelty visited upon our ancestors. A few short years later, we envied them and wished to have their plight instead of our destiny. The Passover meal, long and delicious, was preceded by the traditional questions asked by the youngest of the family, the Ma nishtana, all of which would be answered in the course of the festive reading. Much later in the night each child would get a gift to complete the happy occasion. In the concluding days of winter we began to sift through fashion journals in search of the new spring outfits and matching accessories. Having settled on a design, we would buy material and everything would be sewn at the dressmakers' fashion house. For the more casual wardrobe, a seamstress would come to our home and spend a few days sewing, repairing and taking care of our clothing.

Twice a year we would bring home our report cards. Again the family would gather while Uncle Adolf would ceremoniously put on his glasses and read our grades out loud, commenting enthusiastically and benevolently about our success, impressing on everyone that this was the most important event in our family. Though my businessman uncle never studied psychology, he knew how to motivate his nieces and nephew.

Once the school year was completed, we left Prague for our annual summer holidays, at times spent at Macha Lake, perhaps some spa, or in the mountain resorts. Frequently we would be joined by our relatives; at times family members from Curaçao would come or assorted friends would join our summertime fun.

In 1939, all the pleasant times of our youth seemed an eternity away, the days when our worries consisted of when to practice piano to the sounds of the metronome or fret over our inability to convince Mother that Eva and I need not wear identical clothing, a practice Mother loved and the both of us loathed. Gone were the days when we watched the daily work on Eva's trousseau—the artistic embroidery and monogramming of linens, towels, tablecloths and other items, deemed imperative for a young lady's future. Eva had an impressive amount completed for these preparations began early, way before the teenage years, and involved a lot of artistic handicraft.

All these memories seemed remote now that we were living under German occupation. Even in the early stages, our lives were consumed by anxiety and awareness; we sensed the sinister nature of this regime. No longer did we dismiss or minimize the perilous evil. All our thoughts were directed toward finding a potential escape. But now the situation changed; the Germans would not let us. Even those of us who had foreign visas were refused permission to leave. Whereas a short while ago our main consideration was how to arrange for the transfer of our assets, the invasion made us focus all our efforts on how to slip out of the country. All Jews within the territories occupied by Germans panicked, concerned with the threat to their safety and indeed physical survival. The Germans encouraged this anxiety by allowing a trickle of rumors about the impending doom planned for the Czech Jews. The rumors were often the Nazis' trial balloons to observe the reaction to some of their proposed bans.

Few of us had read the only book Hitler had written, *Mein Kampf* (My Struggle). Those of us who got hold of this demented book had a hard time taking it seriously, and we found it incomprehensible that any nation would elect a government on a platform that combined poisonous hatred towards some with delusive aggrandizement of the Germans, the Teutonic race. At times we hoped that all this was an insane nightmare, one from which Europe must awake and restore itself to some semblance of sanity. It was inconceivable that the Western world would not assume its moral responsibility, steeped in Judeo-Christian ethics, and overthrow the Nazis. This form of fascism became a cancerous growth on the body of European civilization, spreading fast into its healthy tissue. The civilized world needed to take notice and realize that only radical surgery could restore societal values Europeans used to live by. These were the only hopes we had, and we nursed them diligently amidst hectic plans for an escape, hiding our possessions and adapting to a life of ever-growing deprivations.

Father became the first professional casualty. At this stage of his career he was nearly the top-ranking government official in the Finance Ministry and thus highly visible and vulnerable. Immediately following the German occupation, he was sent into mandatory retirement and his pension payments were transferred to a closed bank account, inaccessible to him. All Jewish accounts were ordered shut, immediately preventing access by the lawful owner. All our stocks, bonds, savings, and safety deposits were out of our reach. That meant that my father was kicked out of office after 20 years of service, at the age of 53, without so much as a penny to live on. Later, he could withdraw a small monthly allowance from our own accounts but it was wholly inadequate.

The first things to be sacrificed were our private lessons and the household help. We no longer had the money to pay for them. The Nazi occupiers planned to strip us of everything we owned and change our daily lives; more and more, we were to be set apart from the Gentiles. Almost daily, new decrees were promulgated, all directed against Jews; they demanded full obedience and were enforced with the never-ending harangues. We were ordered to turn in our jewelry and bring it to the closest police station. A few days later, our electrical appliances went the same way, and then it came time to confiscate our furs, radio, collectibles, stamps and coins. The Nazis allowed only one watch per family. We duly received a detailed official receipt for all items.

Early on, among the orders passed that curtailed our freedom was a ban on the use of city parks and recreational facilities. We were restricted to the back of the streetcars and we were only allowed to use them for few hours in the afternoon. Daily more and more stores posted signs announcing that "Jews and dogs are unwanted." The Jewish minority was forbidden any social, business or sexual contact with the Gentiles. Jewish businesses were expropriated, taken out of the hands of their owners and transferred to Gentile managers and, later, to some "deserving Germans." Before long, we were not only impoverished materially, we were also stripped of all civil and human rights. Any aggression or insult was commended and rewarded by the occupiers. We became *personae non gratae.*

Perhaps it is a credit to the Czechs that there were few bodily attacks against us; anyone kicking or maiming a Jew would ingratiate himself and would be singled out for praise by the Nazi authorities. Luckily the Czechs had queasy stomachs for blood and violence.

Early in the war the Germans ordered food rationing. Every citizen obtained a ration card, stipulating the kind of ration and quantity allotted to the holder. The whereabouts of all eligible citizens was easily established, for in the Czech lands everyone had to be registered with the police. Even in the good old days, if a citizen remained anywhere for more than 24 hours, police had to receive a form filled with all particulars relating to the traveler. All hotels or guesthouses had to comply with these rules.

Food rations allotted to Jews were to be much reduced compared to other citizens, and our ration cards were therefore stamped with a capital "J" for "Jude," the German word for Jew. Our identity cards bore the same stamp so that we could not try to pass ourselves off as regular citizens. Our new masters decreed that Jews, lower race that we were, would receive only about one-third of the food rations of other citizens.

While the general population could get by, our allotment was totally insufficient. A new phenomenon entered our lives: hunger. Though we were not famished, not yet—that came later in the camps—we often had too little food to satisfy our hunger. We were forbidden to use the trains, so even if we had some money left, we could not travel to the countryside to purchase food there. We were relegated to the flourishing black market but the prices went through the roof, out of reach for us. We had to adjust to poverty and hunger.

A new and distasteful phenomenon crept into Czech society: using the Nazi laws to settle old grievances. One often-chosen method was to accuse a disliked individual of violating a German rule. The accusation most frequently made was that another person had listened to radio broadcasts from Western Europe (a serious crime by Nazi laws). These accusations could be neither proven nor verified and the accused was always punished with utmost severity. I doubt that anyone had an idea of how many lives were destroyed by this ugly tactic. Another trumped-up charge involved the Nuremberg racial laws. Jews and Gentiles were forbidden any interaction and sexual relations were deemed an outright felony. According to German racial theories, steeped in the belief of Aryan blood purity, any sexual interaction of Gentiles and Jews would defile the pure Nordic race. Consequently, any interracial couple accused of miscegenation was punished with utmost severity, Jew and Gentile alike. These crimes were hardly ever investigated but were always prosecuted with great harshness. Those couples in "mixed marriages" were encouraged to divorce, with the Gentile retaining all the assets. Most of the wives swore that the children were not begotten by their nominal Jewish father but by an illicit Gentile lover. Children thus "purified" were granted the status of Aryans and could continue their schooling, retain jobs and generally live a normal life. The Jewish partner in the marriage was kicked out of the marital abode and had to fend for himself as best he could. Large numbers of intermarriages collapsed under the pressure of those times. Czech interracial marriages consisted mainly of a union between a Jewish man and a Gentile woman. Strangely, few Jewish women entered this type of union. (I only mention this because I referred to the Jewish spouse as "he.") So much for love and devotion under the litmus test of hard times!

We were ordered to observe curfew according to which we had to be at home by 8 p.m. at the latest and remain confined there till the next day. Often we were obliged to stay overnight at some friend's place when we realized that we could not return home on time. The curfew remained in place till the end of the war, long after the last Jew had been deported.

The Germans deliberately instilled fear not only in the Jewish population but in the Czech majority as well. Any violation of their orders would routinely result in brutal punishment for all or part of the offender's family. This technique was later refined to include the entire street, district or village, people who had nothing to do with the arrested transgressor. Fear of bringing other people, even children, into trouble prevented many a brave man from sabotaging German ordinances. The steady diet of threats of deportation to concentration camps forced many antagonists of the Nazis to have second thoughts about engaging in some acts of sabotage. In reality we did not know exactly what these dreaded concentration camps were all about, but rumors reaching us suggested that they practiced medieval methods, back-breaking work of endless duration in quarries, mines or factories, supervised by guards who brutalized or killed inmates for little or no reason at all. We heard that the medical help and housing that existed there was not fit for human beings. Hearsay had it that in some of the camps in the east people were left in the open, exposed to the elements in fields or marshes, just to accelerate their demise. Yes, we knew enough to dread the deportation order to one of those infamous places.

In the early days of the German rule, the main victims of deportations were political opponents, mostly Communists. Eventually the ranks of the deportees swelled to include Jews and later homosexuals, Jehovah's Witnesses and whatever other group the German courts defined as habitual criminal and antisocial elements. For those interred, usually after a short stint in a concentration camp, the family would receive a brief notification of the inmate's death due to illness, accompanied with a small parcel containing his last worldly possessions. After a while, even this courtesy was stopped.

While the mood of those under Nazi control turned distrustful and somber, the Jewish population began its descent into a different category of citizenship. We were treated as lepers and we began to reflect on our humiliating station. Around us the Czechs looked on mostly with indifference, with the exception of those who had some close personal friends among the Jews. The Czech Jews, like my father, who thought that they were accepted and integrated, awoke to new realities. The Gentile Czechs worried about themselves; their hearts did not ache for the Jews in their midst.

Perhaps the Czechs' less bloody version of anti–Semitism was not a matter of less hatred but only a reflection of the Czech temperament which had little predilection for violence. In those days my father began to reevaluate his position which culminated in the reversal of his lifelong philosophy of assimilation into the mainstream, in everything except religion. Later, he shared with me the result of his soul-searching. Assimilation was not an option; the Jewish destiny could only be fulfilled in an independent Jewish state. The Zionists were on the right path; the Gentiles could only sympathize with either dead or absent Jews. It had to be a painful reversal for him for he strove and worked all his life for Jewish integration. He fully trusted that the Czechs could and would rise to the occasion. Now, occupied by the Nazis, we were abandoned and left alone with little, if any, show of sympathy.

The fall of 1939 was a gloomy and gray season, melancholy and pain seared into the prevailing mood. October 28 marked the anniversary of the establishment of the Czechoslovak Republic. Students marched through Prague, trying to create a semblance of a festive celebration. They were dispersed by the Germans, assisted by the local police. One student was shot and killed. His subsequent funeral was an expression of sorrow and also a protest against the senseless violence. The Germans were infuriated. They broke up the funeral procession with force. In a mop-up operation, the German forces encircled and invaded the Masaryk home in Prague. The students were brutalized, trying to escape, routed in the middle of the night. Some fled over the roofs—clad in pajamas—but scores were injured or killed. Only a few managed to escape. The residences were ransacked.

The next day the Nazis declared martial law in the Czech lands. All universities and centers of higher learning were closed immediately and indefinitely. There was to be no higher education for the low-born Slavs. As it was, the Nazi blueprint called for the use of the Slavs as laborers, followed by their eventual extermination. There were exemptions on the

German books for those Czechs deemed capable of German acculturation (Germanization). As for the rest, those deemed unfit for absorption, these were earmarked for liquidation. What comes to mind are the words of a famous German author, Thomas Mann, who observed that until Germany was fenced off from the rest of Europe, the world would not be safe from its crazed aggression. Interestingly, Mann was not a Jew.

The year of 1939 was also the last year of our regular school attendance. In the fall of 1939, the Germans issued a ban barring all Jewish youth from learning centers. From then on we were not allowed to attend schools at any level. The Jewish community did not have a schooling system in place; there was little support for separate Jewish education in pre-war Czechoslovakia. There was one Jewish high school in Brno but none in Prague. Hastily the Jewish community scrambled to fill in the gaps, preparing teaching instructions and facilities but the obstacles were insurmountable. Most of the parents began to teach their own children. Luckily, our father was very learned, not only by the regular educational system, as any lawyer would be, but also by his extensive reading and interest in politics, history and philosophy. From the fall of 1939, he taught Eva and me the regular high school material pertinent to our levels in all academic subjects. Thanks to him, even during this phase, we developed many new interests.

Mother still attempted to advance our chances for emigration at all costs, but she also began to adapt to the grim outlook that we might not be able to leave Europe. With the passage of months the whispered hearsay had it that Jews would be removed from all cities and countryside into some unspecified "resettlement areas." Prodded by these uncertainties, Mother decided that my sister and I needed some practical skill which might prepare us for earning a living somewhere in one of those much-dreaded resettlement areas.

She came to the conclusion that all the classical education was more or less a luxury for a Jew who would have to adapt to life in some distant camp. We had to master a useful craft. As a logical consequence, she enrolled us as apprentices with our one-time dressmaker who was to teach us the art of sewing. My sister grasped it quickly, but I never showed much enthusiasm. Perhaps I lacked the needed manual dexterity. My mother, keeping an eye on us, noticed my dislike of sewing and was on the lookout for an alternative. One day she surprised me by telling me that the Jewish community was hastily arranging courses in nursing and would admit girls of my age since there were only a few interested candidates. The Jewish community was in dire straits as no Jewish patient was granted admission to a public facility. While the small Jewish hospital in Prague boasted many physicians, there were few nurses. Somehow medicine always attracted many Jewish students, all of whom wanted to be physicians; nursing was not a popular calling.

In spite of my age (14), I was accepted for the two-year program. The assumption was that within the two years much would become resolved or conversely get worse. We matured fast under the German boot; there was no time for childhood or adolescence. My sister did not enroll because she loathed hospital work. The hospital and all related odors made her queasy. She continued her work as a seamstress and advanced her skills.

In course of the years 1939 and 1940 Mother must have begun to doubt if we would ever get out of the trap to the "promised land of Curaçao." No sooner had we arranged for the mandatory documents than the Germans would add some new demands, stalling our departure. Even before the Nazi occupation we thought of purchasing the Capitalist Certificate, the only legal entry to Palestine, but we could not afford the price. Britain held control over Palestine and attempted to appease the hostile Arabs who vehemently opposed Jewish immigration. The cost of a certificate was hitched sky high and even under those circumstances wasn't always attainable. The only concession the British were willing to consider was to take in a few thousand Jewish youngsters and offer them a temporary haven. With a heavy heart my mother registered the two of us but we were not among the chosen ones. It must have exacted a heavy price on Mom to consider parting with us. It seemed that everything conspired against our efforts to escape from the clutches of the Germans.

One day, a young friend of my sister, a non–Jew who had been seeing her for a while, came to our apartment and suggested, after a lengthy hesitation, that he would marry her to protect her from deportation. In those stages of the German rule the Jewish partner bound in an existing interracial marriage would not be subjected to deportation. However, my parents were not even willing to consider it. With hindsight, this was a very unfortunate error of judgment.

The winter of 1939–40 brought many problems. There was little food or coal to heat the apartment, we were stalled in our efforts to leave, and we were shunned by most of our Gentile

Eva Katz, 1936.

friends who began to treat us as lepers. Worse yet, in the year 1941, the deportation of Czech Jews was initiated en masse. The resettlements (as the Germans euphemistically called our deportations) meant that Jews were sent to some unknown destination somewhere in the east. All we knew was that those called up could take with them about 50 kilograms of personal items only. Everybody dreaded that call. These summonses were always carried out at night, and we got into the habit of waiting and listening intently for any sound on the stairs or the crackle of the old-fashioned elevator, night after night after night. With first shadows of twilight we began our vigil. We sat near the door, listening in silence. When someone walked past our door, we all stopped breathing and only when the steps continued did we let out a sigh of relief. Then we exchanged a quick, furtive glance— one more night of reprieve.

Two episodes happened in the fall of 1940. One kept us busy for a few months in the early hours of the morning; the other was of an immense significance in our later years, although we did not recognize it at the time. (It was this event that much later saved my life.) By the time the deportations began, we all knew that our attempts to escape failed. Mother, true to her practical and realistic disposition, decided that we had to hide our possessions, jewelry that we had not turned in, Eva's trousseau, and even original paintings and carpets. Some of these items we bartered for food, but many were left, some of which we did not want and others we could not sell on the black market. My father had many Gentile friends and colleagues and a few agreed to take some of our gold, paintings and even carpets for safe keeping. They would come and spirit them out in crates, boxes or luggage. The smaller items (clothing, linens and less expensive jewelry) were taken to the apartment of the porter of the Ministry of Finance.

Also, less expensive china sets, cutlery and our family photographs were to be hidden at the flat of the friendly Vrzak family. There was one hitch, though: Mr. Vrzak was unwell. He could not carry the many items nor did he have a car. An alternate plan had to be worked out, and as expected, Mother had an idea. Her plan called for Eva and me to get up at 4 a.m. three times a week and carry a piece of luggage filled with valuables to the flat of the Vrzak family. They did not live too far away, perhaps half an hour at a brisk walk, but to us it seemed a dreadful distance. First, there was the danger of being arrested or caught on the street for violating the curfew; second, walking through the dark, deserted, and freezing streets of Prague in winter was quite frightening; and third, the luggage was heavy. We seemed to have a never-ending amount of silver, jewelry, linens, towels and other commodities. But somehow we always succeeded and, following a brief pause at the Vrzaks, we returned home with the empty suitcases.

Today I wonder why my mother was not worried to let her two

daughters—Eva was then 16 and I was 14—walk the deserted streets alone but she was convinced that two teenagers walking the streets in the early hours of the morning would not arouse anyone's suspicion. The only other people on the streets at that time of the night were either the cleaners who swept the sidewalks, usually absorbed in their unappreciated activity, or the occasional drunk or perhaps a member of the oldest profession, none of whom paid any attention to us. It fell upon my mother to resolve all the practical problems of our family; my father was always interested mainly in intellectual pursuits and he did not have the knack of adapting to our new situation. The invasion of the Nazi hordes into his homeland, the loss of work he loved, the distancing by almost all of his friends—all these occurrences weighed on him. The cruelty which surrounded and threatened us was beyond his understanding; it was in such contradiction to everything he believed in. He tried hard to come to terms with it and cope under the challenge of these difficult times. His genuine attempts were not very successful.

From the fall of 1939, we were in a tailspin. Barely five months had passed since the occupation of Bohemia and Moravia; Hitler continued with his policy of an eastbound expansion. He issued an ultimatum to Poland to evacuate the Danzig corridor, territory which, according to him, belonged to Germany. At long last, the Western democracies decided to stand firm by their commitment to Poland and contain Hitler's aggression. None of this intimidated, or even impressed, the Nazis.

Hitler gave the go-ahead and the armored units crossed the border, ferociously attacking the Poles. Under air force cover,

Vera Katz, 1940.

they quickly advanced into the heart of the country, crushing all resistance. The Poles were so misinformed that they sent cavalry to confront the heavy armor! The military action against Poland was concluded in less than three weeks, and another three million Jews fell under Nazi rule, targeted for annihilation.

The defeat of Poland was followed by a lull in hostilities. Then, in early spring 1940, Hitler invaded Denmark and Norway. The Danish military resistance crumbled, but the Norwegians fought valiantly. Nonetheless, they too were defeated. Although the Danes could not resist the superior German armed units, they were heroic in their defense of their Jewish fellow citizens. As a nation, the Danes rose to the challenge of rescuing an endangered minority. Sadly, their actions were unprecedented. When the Danish Jews were ordered to attach the yellow star to their outer garments, most of the citizens of Copenhagen threatened to do likewise. Later, when rumors had it that the Jews were to be deported to concentration camps, the Danes organized a mass rescue. The small Jewish community (about 7,000 people) was spirited away on boats and ships to neighboring Sweden, all in the course of one night. The handful of Jews who could not be taken to safety were deported under a special set of rules negotiated by King Christian X. Few perished and most returned to Denmark after the war.

Shortly after the conquest of the Scandinavian countries, the German army invaded Holland and Belgium. Although both countries tried to mount a meaningful defense, they were swept out of the way of the quickly advancing German army. Hitler relied heavily on his sudden and fast attack, the "Blitzkrieg." His armies would descend in vast numbers, supported by the air force. They would crush all in their way, advancing with lightning speed to a pre-determined goal.

With Belgium and Holland out of the way, Hitler tightened his grip on France. He would not attack the famed Maginot Line, the heavily fortified first line of defense. He chose an alternate route to penetrate the French countryside. Tragically, the French were taken by surprise and were defeated within days. Hitler and his chiefs of staff were deliriously happy and enthusiastic about their victories. His "Blitzkrieg" worked!

France was forced to sign a surrender agreement in the same railroad car in which the 1918 German defeat was ratified in Compiegne. Hitler fulfilled his promise to the German people. He rendered null and void Germany's humiliating defeat in World War I. If his nationals adored him before, now they were swept off their feet, their infatuation escalating into deification of their führer.

Hitler divided France. The east, including the "City of Lights," Paris, was occupied and administered by Nazis. The west remained nominally self-governing with an appointed head of state, Marshal Henri Phillippe

Pétain. Pétain was an old man but a respected and much-decorated World War I hero. As elsewhere, the role of the appointed puppet of the collaborating administration would be to rubberstamp the orders of the real masters: the Nazis. Petain had no option but to do Hitler's bidding and "Vichy France" would dutifully and respectfully toe the line. For the free-loving nations of Europe it spelled disaster; to the Jews the significance was clear: doomsday was rapidly approaching. In 1940, Hitler seemed unstoppable to us. Was he really the superman he styled himself to be? Was a new dark era being ushered in?

Although we no longer had radios, we used some of the little money we had left to buy the early morning papers which informed us of the rapid victories of the Nazis. Gradually we came to believe that the hour of Jewish doom was just around the corner. Hitler believed Providence guided him. We began to accept that Fate blessed his nefarious deeds.

Later, when we no longer had access to newspapers, the fortunes of the war began to turn with the defeat of the Nazis at Stalingrad (1942–43). In 1940, however, the turning point seemed nowhere in sight. Then it seemed that the dark forces of the Teutonic rulers, descended straight from Valhalla, would subjugate the world. Under the stress of German persecution, our nerves became strained to the point of snapping at any time. The least provocation was unbearable.

My father was the one who was visibly declining. He felt that his world had collapsed, that he no longer could provide for his family. He felt badly for he had not been able to convince his brothers-in-law to forsake their attempts of financial transfers and leave Europe. With the outbreak of the war, the borders became tightly sealed, and barring perhaps an illegal nighttime escape (something which only a young and strong person could pull off), we were all trapped in the Nazi cage. My once self-assured father became insecure, aware that the formidable odds we faced exceeded his mental and physical prowess. My mother, my sister and the rest of our family coped somewhat better, retaining some optimism, hoping for a reversal of German fortunes. It was my father's ill luck that he realized early on that the sweeping victories of the Nazis would result in a long war. He did not nurture the unlikely hope of some miracle which might save us. He alone knew from the very beginning that doomsday was fast approaching and would engulf us all.

Sometime in the summer of 1941 there was a knock on our door. In those days we feared all uninvited visitors, for they rarely bore good tidings. I went to answer the call with considerable trepidation and I bolted the door carefully before looking out through the small peephole. Outside I saw a friendly face with a shy smile. Clearly this man was no threat nor an official emissary bringing bad news. When I opened the door, he introduced himself as Mr. Bleha and he asked to talk to my father, who stood right behind me. The two men exchanged warm greetings and our visitor was amazed at how much my father had aged since their last encounter. The man walked with considerable difficulty; his missing leg had been replaced by a poor prosthesis. My father invited the man to share a cup of coffee with us—all chicory, no real coffee anymore—and while the friendly conversation continued, I gathered that the man was disabled, a victim of World War I. When my father used to head the distribution of tobacco warehouses and tobacconists, he had helped this man to understand the red tape and procedures required to become an administrator. My father had appointed him administrator of a tobacco warehouse in a small city in north Bohemia: Theresienstadt.

Mr. Bleha remained grateful to my father who had helped him to unravel the bureaucratic maze, and he used to be one of the many who would occasionally send small gifts or cards. Only slowly did Mr. Bleha share with us the reason for his unexpected visit. He became privy of an unconfirmed report that Theresienstadt (Terezín, in Czech) had been designated as a future Jewish ghetto or some kind of a camp for important Jews. He offered us his help and promised he would do his level best to avert our starvation or worse. We did not hear about any future formation of a ghetto but there was a maximum-security jail near Terezín, and we therefore decided to give some credence to his story. We gratefully accepted his offer and asked him to take some of our concealed money and jewelry to use for our needs, just in case we were to be deported to this camp. Mr. Bleha promised to return and keep us posted.

When he left, we discussed the surprise visitor and, while my father was convinced that he was genuinely trying to help us, my mother and I remained skeptical. Since when did anyone help Jews lately? More likely, he was one of the gold diggers who remembered that he once knew a nice enough Jew to whom he could tell a few lies and relieve him of his valuables. But we thought that the risk was worth taking, and besides, we did not stand to lose a great deal.

In September 1941 the Germans issued another order. As of September 1, we would have to wear a yellow, six-pointed Star of David, displaying the inscription Jude (Jew) on all outer clothing. Disobedience or failure to comply would result in the harshest penalties. Nobody had to explain what this stood for under German rule. It was such a desecration of the Star of David which in other times had been a proud badge of Jewish identity. The Jewish community of Prague distributed the shameful pieces of yellow cloth. We stitched in the edges and then attached it to our meager wardrobe.

The first time I went out on Prague's streets marked like that I felt self-conscious, treading on eggshells, but a short time later I got used to it, reminding myself that this was the result of the Germans' shameful behavior, not ours. Every now and then I even noticed that some of the passersby inconspicuously averted their eyes so that they would not have to look and make me feel worse. I sensed that some people disdained the marking and stigmatizing of Jews, bringing back the evil custom of the Middle Ages. There were still some decent people left in the country who felt uncomfortable watching their Jewish nationals being branded like cattle. Far from returning home depressed, I was somehow exhilarated.

In 1941, many of our friends were deported to camps and ghettos in the east, and we dreaded the day when our turn would come. The Germans began to squeeze several Jewish families into one apartment to vacate flats which were always scarce in metropolitan Prague. The crowding, the tensions and the shortages frayed the nerves of many, even the most resilient among us. Often we tried to imagine what kind of life awaited us in those concentration camps. Hearsay had it that there was great suffering from hunger, exposure to cold, being forced to perform hard labor; all these deprivations usually resulted in assorted illnesses. The uncertainty lent itself to all kind of speculations, most of which frightened the daylights out of us. But as bad as we thought it would be, the reality turned out to be much worse.

When any family was deported, the empty apartment was sealed to prevent an unauthorized theft. To this end the Jewish community was ordered to provide a group of young, able-bodied Jews who would remove the contents to the local synagogues. Most houses of worship were converted into warehouses. The man in charge of this operation was a certain Salo Kraemer who was awarded a temporary stay of deportation for himself and his workers for as long as their services were needed. There was never a shortage of volunteers for this assignment—one of the most coveted by the petrified Jews of Prague. Any delay of enrollment into a transport was the best that the beleaguered Jews of Prague could hope for.

Once the contents of an emptied apartment had reached the synagogue, items were sorted according to their specific usefulness, classified, registered and stored. Different synagogues were assigned to hold various items (e.g., furniture, paintings, linens, clothing, medications, musical instruments, and so on). These were kept on hold and made available to "deserving Germans," mainly SS or members of the military who were eligible to choose what they wanted—all for free. Helping themselves to stolen goods only deepened the love and admiration of these "deserving Germans" for Hitler who showered them with such exquisite gifts. Lesser items were transported to Germany and offered to Winterhilfe (winter relief agency) or assorted charities.

The Nazis decided to remove the relatively benevolent protector, von Neurath, and appoint in his stead Reinhardt Heydrich, a high-ranking SS officer and a particularly sadistic killer—even by Nazi standards! He became known as "the butcher of Prague." He was disliked and feared even among his own ranks. His zeal was renowned; his fanaticism led him to hunt and prosecute less fiery SS men. Dark rumors implied that Heydrich's monomaniacal fanaticism had roots in a secret; there was an unthinkable blot on Heydrich's genealogy—one of his ancestors was a Jew! To cover up his family "shame," his fervor exceeded that of any SS man. This story was likely a figment of someone's imagination because even the SS could not understand what drove Heydrich; puzzled by his violence, they invented a plausible explanation—he was not of pure blood. Be that as it may, he was a loose cannon.

Today, it is difficult to describe the emotional climate of the trapped Jews. We knew that the laws of the land did not protect us; we lived in a tense anticipation of new, stringent restrictions; we were aware that we would be deported to unknown places where survival might not be feasible. I am certain that for most people this is next to impossible to imagine but we had to adapt and adjust and to retain some hope for a better tomorrow. We had to cultivate faith that, ultimately, justice would prevail and the Germans would be crushed. This belief gave us some fortitude to face yet another day. We cultivated this conviction with all the might and power we could generate.

Even as we tried to hope in the future and forged plans to hide some of our valued possessions, there did not seem to be even a faint chance for some light at the end of the tunnel in 1940. The Germans were strong, victorious and powerful, and they were sworn to the destruction of all Jews. There were those among us who despaired, opting for the more comfortable exit by their own means, will and timing. Thus, suicide became an option and many Prague Jews found their release in a barbiturate overdose or some similar means. If my parents ever considered such steps, we never heard about it. They never gave us a hint. On the contrary, Mother fiercely insisted on the continuation of our attempt to salvage all we could from the grabbing hands of the Nazis.

Even though our situation was constantly deteriorating, we continued to stash away our possessions. The tailor once responsible for my father's sartorial elegance volunteered to keep our fur coats safe; a longtime friend of my father took the best china and some jewelry. Another friend of long standing hid more jewelry and cash. All lesser valuables we planned to bring to the Vrzaks. My father vehemently opposed all these salvaging transactions. He was convinced that the risk incurred by hiding our possessions with Gentiles was not worthwhile. But my mother prevailed; she made up her mind that the Nazi swine would not put their grubby hands on the trousseau of her daughter.

Next, we began to devise plans how to smuggle some money or jewelry with us into the camp. We decided to sew some money and small pieces of jewelry into our shoulder pads and skirt hems. We heard rumors that nothing should be concealed in toothpaste because it was usually taken away from the inmates while they were screened and processed at the gates. Also, we did not hide anything in the soles of our shoes; searchers often cut the leather searching for contraband. We had to divide the items between the four of us in case we were to be separated during some selection. In addition, we had to cope with the management of our household that became increasingly complex.

My sister and I shared the heavy physical work. One of us brought coal from the cellar and prepared wooden shavings to start the fire in the kitchen stove. We heated only the kitchen, as the scarcity of coal supply did not allow for more. Also, cleaning the apartment was backbreaking labor, especially considering the standards of my mother which she was unwilling to lower, regardless of the circumstances. Shopping was yet another ordeal; there was next to no merchandise left by the afternoon when we Jews were allowed to shop. Washing laundry on the washboard, then the only way to do it, required a lot of muscle and energy.

In spite of all this trouble we still enjoyed some of our days for we were young and wanted to have some fun. We had many friends among other Jewish youth and we would meet at improvised home parties, dance a little, form groups and have our little romances. We would meet at the only gathering place at our disposal, the Hagibor, a meadow where we exercised, ran around, played games and for a few moments forgot that we were the pariahs of humankind.

There I encountered my first puppy love. Bobby was a charming, handsome boy, about 19 years old, and he had already completed high school. He could not pursue his ambition to study chemistry; therefore, he joined his father who was winding down his business. He would come to see me and we would go for long walks, accompanied by his cute dog, Knirac. We let our imagination run free, spinning many glorious plans for our future. Every single one started with the words "Right after the war, when the Nazis are gone, we will…." Well, we never did—Bobby did not survive the concentration camp to which he was soon deported. Our romances then were entirely innocent; at the most we would steal a kiss, anything else was unthinkable before marriage. Even our kissing was so harmless, none of the passion-arousing, sex-stimulating kind. Good God, when I think of it today, I only wonder about our naiveté. Not only did we believe in some positive outcome, disregarding the vicious reality, but even socially and

Vera (second from left) and Eva (right) with friends in Hagibor, a group which organized Jewish youth activities during Nazi occupation, 1940.

Vera exercising with Hagibor, 1940.

privately we adhered to the behavioral code of yesterday, convincing ourselves of a brighter tomorrow.

In fall 1941, the Nazis dispatched the first transports of Prague Jews to Poland. They were sent to an overcrowded ghetto in the city of Lodz or, in German, Litzmanstadt. This was short-lived as before long the ghetto there was packed beyond capacity. In addition, the Nazis realized that they had another major difficulty on their hands. There was a conflict of priorities. The same trains transporting the doomed Jews to their death were requested by the military, the Wehrmacht, to supply the German army, locked in battle with the Soviets in the east. In order to solve the dilemma of logistics, and still continue to remove the Jews from their homes, the Nazis had to find an alternate solution. Hoping to improve efficiency, the Nazis decided to open an interim camp, a transit camp in the Bohemian heartland. The choice fell on a one-time fortress of Theresienstadt.

The winter of 1941–42 was to be the last one our family spent in Prague. We all sensed it but never mentioned it, not even in a whisper or a hint. It was a taboo to discuss but we anticipated the heartbreak of our separation. Faithful to our tradition, we kept on visiting daily with our extended family; only the topics we chatted about were different.

Another topic that was never broached was our fateful mistake of having dilly-dallied and missed the opportunity to leave Europe for the safety of the Dutch West Indies. Our hopes were pinned now on the outlandish opportunity of being resettled together, to pool the items we wanted to include in the 50 kilograms of belongings that we would be allowed to take with us. We debated our chances of eking out a living with no trade or vocational skills. We pondered which blanket would be the warmest, which should be the one single dish we could include among our belongings we were about to take to the camps. Finally, we opted for the dish routinely used by Czech army: a round tin container with a cover that could be used as a plate. A lot of thought was invested into the choice of the few warm pieces of clothing we could take with us; we knew only too well that winters in Eastern Europe were bitterly cold. We, the youngsters of the family, were included in most of those debates but we were automatically excluded when money transactions were debated. We were never made privy to dangerous, surreptitious information that could have endangered the family. The Nazi interrogation methods were known to be brutal and much harm was wrought on families when one member disclosed secrets under duress. Interrogations of those accused of some infraction took place at the Gestapo headquarters, in the confiscated castle of the onetime most prominent Czech Jewish banker. The castle was located in a handsomely landscaped garden in the middle of one of the largest parks. This elegant piece of architecture, at one time a place of much merriment, became the most dreaded place in Prague. It was said that the Nazis' means to extract confessions were so sadistic and brutal that medieval torture or the Spanish Inquisition was almost a friendly encounter by comparison.

In those lonely months we had only one friend left but at the time we did not fully appreciate what an unselfish soul he was. Mr. Bleha really remained a loyal friend to my father and wanted to help us to survive the persecution. He would drop by every now and then, in itself a feat, for it was punishable by death to socialize with a Jew. With hindsight, I am glad that he never knew that we did not have full confidence in him, which he certainly deserved. But we were skeptical and embittered after having been abandoned by most of our former friends who had been so close to us before the Nazi takeover.

In the fall of 1940, Prague buzzed with rumors of a new ghetto-camp that might be opened in Bohemia. There the Czech Jews would be segregated and taught to fend for themselves "by labor of their own hands." We welcomed that gossip which said we would not be deported east, but instead we would remain in the country we called our home. This was by far the best news we had received of late. It almost seemed too good to be true. But it was more than a rumor. Before long the Germans issued orders to call up 400 young, healthy Jewish men for a transport named AKI for Aufbau Kommando Eins, which was followed by 1,000 more men labeled AK2. These were the men who were ordered to prepare and build the camp. They hammered together barracks and made the place ready for a mass arrival of inmates. When we finally began to believe this latest piece of news, we felt much relieved. The site of the new internment center was Theresienstadt, a town some two hours away from Prague. For our family it was almost a miracle; it was the town where Mr. Bleha lived and had his warehouse. The members of the working commandos AK1 and AK2 sent rather reassuring postcards to Prague during the winter of 1941–42 which gave rise to cautious optimism.

Late one afternoon, when dusk began to settle on Prague, we heard the doorbell ring quickly three times, a signal agreed upon beforehand for us to know that Mr. Bleha was at the door. As usual, he entered, greeted my father deferentially, winked vaguely to us girls, kissed my mother's hand and sat down to share his latest information with us. He knew this peculiar catacomb-surrounded town like the back of his hand. He gave us a rather detailed description of the place to which we might be deported, and then he assured us that he would do his level best to alleviate our starvation, generally rumored to be one of the worst afflictions of day-to-day life in the camp. To this end he would try to meet one of us in the underground passages. We would be informed of all the technical details by his friend inside the camp. Mr. Bleha assured us that the logistics were not at all complex. He also indicated that even when all the valuables we had given him to barter for food ran out, he would not leave us without assistance. Then he intimated that only a few Jews might stay a longer period of time in Theresienstadt, for it should become a special kind of a camp where most deportees would be gathered, and following some brief stint, would be deported farther east to extermination camps in Poland. We must have shown our misgivings about all this, but our friend explained to us that his information was reliable because one of his close friends, an inmate and a member of AKI, was a physician in charge of the camp's hospital. He treated the Elder of the Jews, Jakob Edelstein.

Vera Katz, 1941.

Mr. Bleha's intimate friend was none else than Dr. Robert Tarjan. Tarjan would also be the one who would try to guarantee our stay in Theresienstadt for as long as he could pull the necessary strings. Dr. Tarjan and Mr. Bleha were friends of long standing, and currently they were engaged in clandestine assistance to as many inmates as they could. They also seemed to entertain regular contact in some covert way, meeting in the catacombs, ramparts and underground passages of this garrison town. Mr. Bleha informed us that the 1,400 men who adapted the garrison town into a concentration camp were awarded the temporary privilege of being allowed to stay there (instead of being deported east) and sheltered their families along with them. Dr. Tarjan, a bachelor, had no one on his list, and he gave his sacrosanct promise to Mr. Bleha that he would use his special status to shield us. Mr. Bleha made a rough sketch of the camp, told us to commit all details to memory, not to leave any incriminating papers lying around. Furthermore, he told us that unless changes were to occur, he would not come again for it could endanger all of us. I watched my parents following his departure with strangely glistening eyes. In our hearts he kindled a flicker of faith in our survival. His bold pledges notwithstanding, we waited and listened for the ominous steps on the stairway.

On May 5 someone paused in front of our door and we stopped

breathing for a second. Then the bell rang. We knew who it would be. The only Jew permitted outside after 8 p.m. was the messenger of the community, carrying the summons for the deportees. The short, middle-aged man in a shabby suit held a worn briefcase in his hand. He opened it, fumbled in it and with an apologetic, crooked half-smile he preceded to hand us our verdict. We were to report in five days at the gathering place; from there we would be taken to the resettlement camp. From our family we were the first ones to be singled out for deportation but we all knew that it was only a matter of time before everybody would be expelled from Prague, converting it into a

Vera before deportation to Theresienstadt, 1941.

Judenrein city—a city without Jews. We had been readying ourselves for this moment for such a long time, and yet when it came, it hit us like a ton of bricks.

We had little time to pull ourselves together. We had to re-examine the long-prepared 50 kilograms of belongings. Then we had to roll the one blanket into a neat sausage-like roll, attach it to our luggage and, lastly, add some provisions. The next-to-last task was to prepare the signs indicating our transport numbers which had to be drawn on cardboard suspended on a rope hung around our necks. I do not have a formidable memory for numbers but those on the four signs which substituted for our names seem to be etched indelibly into my memory: my new identity was Au245, Eva's Au246, Mother's Au247 and Father's Au248. Although I wish I could erase the entire period from my mind, I still see the cardboard signs and, if I close my eyes, I can feel the rope around my neck.

Grandmother was not to go with us. Father arranged beforehand a transfer for her to the Jewish old folks' home of Prague where she (for a mint) was supposed to be allowed to live out her days. She was 82 years old, frail and quickly fading. Her normally sweet disposition was changed by our departure. She feared for our lives though we tried to tell her only the best rumors about the camp's existence. When we kissed her good-bye, she tried to be brave and smile but tears rolled down her pale cheeks. The thought crossed my mind that she might not last long: she seemed so weak, like an old doll made of parchment, brittle and breakable to the touch.

4

Our Struggle for Survival

The date of our deportation from Prague was mandated for May 12, 1942. This was also the birthday of my grandfather who did not live to suffer through this infamy for he passed away peacefully in 1938.

Prague was lovely on the day of our parting from the city we loved and called our home. As if decreed, Prague sent us off looking her best. Prague is fondly called "little mother Prague" by the Czechs; others call her "the city of hundred golden towers and spires." It's been claimed that Prague bears a close resemblance to Paris: the "City of Lights." As Prague grew and many architectural styles evolved, her final appearance became resplendent—a glorious blend of thoughtfulness and stylistic variety. Many books have been devoted to Prague's beauty, to her historical sites, and last but not least, to her Jewish quarters, the one-time "ghetto of Prague." Prague's Jewish cemetery is unique with many layers of graves superimposed on each other; there are many heaving stones, some toppled, others askew, many adorned, elaborate tombstones. It is a testimony to many centuries of Jewish presence which ended in the 20th-century tragedy.

Although we were about to leave, we did not want to concede that it might be forever, that we may never take in the sight of Prague again. We wanted to deal with our deportation as if it were a temporary inconvenience. The day of our deportation is seared in my memory; the weather was glorious and Prague had a near festive air. Flowers in the parks were in bloom exuding fine fragrances and the lawns were bedecked with lush green grass. Everything around us appeared in harmony. The only discord in this lovely vision was our forceful ejection. We were being expelled like lepers from our home, forced to embark on a journey into the unknown, to a place we knew little about. Only a few years ago our lives had been full of promise. Few worked harder or were more loyal and law-abiding citizens than my family. And now it all came to this ignominious end. Our hearts were breaking but we wanted to leave without tears, walking tall into the unknown future.

Shortly before we departed, I wanted to bring our last pet, a canary, to his new home at the Vrzaks. No sooner had I stepped out of the elevator than I was detained by our janitor, a mean old woman who wryly informed me that according to the reich's orders, all Jewish possessions must be left behind, not illegally removed. It was absurd to call the saving of pet bird smuggling. But I knew better than to argue; she had the authority to report me and get us into hot water. Disgusted, I handed her the cage and asked her to be good to the bird. Having done that, we locked up our apartment and set out with luggage and blankets, accompanied by our relatives, to the assembly place. We took our leave of them at some distance from the gate; it was risky for people to be seen accompanying someone to the site of the assembled transports. If an SS man noticed some signs of family parting, he could—if in the mood—include the escorts among the deportees. We were familiar with the appearance of the building and its annex; we visited there every year during the annual fairs—only then it did not seem threatening or ominous as on this May 12.

The moment we entered the large hall, our world changed in ways we could never have imagined. Initially it seemed as if there was noisy bedlam—constant shouting, commotion, blows and nervous tension. The orderlies shouted at us to sit on the floor immediately, according to the sequence of our numbers. We were assigned one mattress to a family; therefore, most of us had to sit on the bare floor. I was trying to make sense out of the confusion, the ear-shattering noise, and the screaming all around us. The officials responsible for organizing the deportation site, fearful of the supervising Germans, pushed people, at times brutally, attempting to bring about a semblance of order. Slowly I grasped what the agitation and turmoil was all about.

In the center of the hall there were several tables behind which sat officials of the Jewish community, closely supervised by armed SS men positioned right behind them. One family at a time would be ordered to step forward and return their food-ration cards. At the next desk, we had to return the remaining documents, namely the little booklets which every Czech citizen carried and which included a photograph to prove one's identity. Ours—like every other Jew's—was defaced by an imprint of a capital J (Jude for Jew). Now we would not need any other ID except the numbers suspended on our necks, our new names.

Quickly we were ordered to proceed to the next table where we had to give up anything that remained of our valuables—that is, if we still owned any. We were warned that failure to comply would elicit the harshest punishment. This was the part we knew the best: the Nazis' threats and punishments. Finally we reached the last table where the keys to our apartment were confiscated, and we were ordered to return to the spot assigned to us on the floor.

It was in this building that, for the first time, I experienced physical violence. It happened by chance but I never forgot the first brutal punch to my face. My lack of knowledge of conversational German provoked an SS man who likely interpreted my noncompliance of orders as defiance. According to the rules, when an SS officer passed through the hall, all Jews had to sit down. We were not allowed to stand or, God forbid, walk. On that particular occasion, I heard the bullhorns blaring, but, on the first day there, I had no idea what they were ordering us to do. My German was then only rudimentary because Father disliked the language, and so we were not conversant in it. SS officer Fiedler, properly announced, stared in disbelief at me, the young Jewess, walking straight towards him. I was not really defiant; I was just rushing to the latrines. I had delayed this need for as long as possible; I dreaded the filthy, crowded place and the total lack of privacy. I was not toughened up yet—that came much later. SS officer Fiedler did not waste much time looking at me; he motioned me to get nearer, and when I did, he smashed his fist into my face with such ferocity that I was sent flying. Somebody pulled me away from the irate SS man while the representative of the Jewish community accompanying him tried to calm him, explaining to him that some of the Czech Jews did not understand German. That likely soothed his temper for he left me alone, only I cannot forget this episode. My parents were shocked, and to calm them, I tried to make a joke of it all. The burning pain of my smashed face and the bleeding nose were not as painful as my bruised ego and the humiliation of being treated with such brutal force. At the time, I was not used to physical violence and I thought it was horrible; only later did I learn to cope with it, and worse. My poor father was disconsolate; he blamed himself for not providing us with German lessons and, to remedy the situation, he embarked on a crash course of conversational German. Eva and I were both fast learners, and later in Theresienstadt, we quickly mastered fluency in German. Needless to say none of us were sorry when we were ordered to pick up our luggage and march to the nearby railway tracks three days later. The SS, aided by the Czech police, screamed orders to move faster for we never seemed to be swift enough for our tormentors. No matter how much we hurried it was never fast enough. The waiting freight train was filled in no time and ready to go.

Strangely, much later I found out that the same "AU" transport included my close relatives the Klinenbergers: my cousin Oskar, his wife Ida (once a prominent singer at the Prague opera), and their only son Jiri. The short time we had for preparations for our departure was so inadequate; we could barely say hurried goodbyes to our closest living relatives. We had no inkling that we shared the transport with our cousins. The only people we had time to inform were our immediate neighbors. So it happened that we were in the same transport and never knew it. As the transport consisted of a thousand people forbidden to move in the assembly place, the only people you could interact with were those sitting on the bare floor next to you. The only time we were permitted to leave that area was to answer the call of nature to the abominable latrines; we voluntarily reduced those trips to a minimum because the facilities used for that purpose were revolting and filthy beyond description. The building was never intended to accommodate—even for a brief while—that number of people. The three days in the assembly hall were spent sitting on the floor, and if not called upon to report to one of the officials, we never moved from the assigned place. My close and dear cousin and his family went through the same experience at the same time and none of us knew it. I never saw them again, not in Theresienstadt or ever. Sadly, this story is typical of those tragic times.

The slow-moving train, loaded with frightened Jewish families, moved in a northeast direction. We all hoped that we might be resettled to this new camp. It was situated in the heart of Czech land, in itself a comfort to us. We were literally holding our breaths as we approached the camp's location. Failure of the train to come to a stop would mean that we would be deported either to Poland or the Ukraine, a fate we all feared. We stood in silent panic, praying fervently for the train to halt. In the packed box cars silence reigned; few uttered even a word. Our prayers were answered: the train came to a slow halt at Bohusovice, the closest station to Theresienstadt, which was only three kilometers away from the camp proper.

At once we heard shouted orders to get out, on the double, with our possessions. We formed columns on the railway platform and we were ordered to march in the direction of the camp. We must have been a sorry, dismal sight; hundreds of men, women and children of all ages, trying desperately to form an orderly column, just to prevent the blows which rained down on those who could not keep up and fell out of formation.

I was only 16 (my birthday was coming up in two days) but I felt like an adult, responsible for my parents. Interestingly, Eva and I adopted that duty almost by reflex, from the moment we realized that our elders had difficulty coping. Until then, we thought like many youngsters from a sheltered environment do, that our parents could resolve and guide us through any situation. Once we understood that the challenge they faced exceeded their strength, we automatically stepped into the breach. Somehow it was almost as if we had grown up overnight in the face of unprecedented perils. Then we still felt strong, energetic, and capable of protecting our parents. They were worn, tired and drained and it was up to Eva and me to fill the gap.

I watched Father try to move ahead at the clip ordered by the Germans. He was slightly stooped and had a hard time carrying his luggage. He seemed so frail that I felt that I should do something for him but all I managed was a little smile, which he tried to return, without much success. We were not allowed to talk; otherwise, I would have tried to cheer him up. Mother looked tired but not as resigned as Father did. Only Eva was in good spirits, and we exchanged a few furtive whispers every now and then. In that manner we arrived at the gates of the camp, where we were met by more gendarmes of the Czech police, armed SS men and snarling German Shepherds that strained at their leashes. I wondered why the Germans needed all their guns, dogs, the assistance of the Czech police—all the display of power. Were the members of the Herrenvolk, the Master Race, afraid of a few hundred tired and demoralized Jewish men, women and children? Later, I came to realize that the Nazis used these pressure tactics as a psychological tool to terrorize and intimidate us. The endless screaming, the orders to perform every single action expeditiously and the terrifying brutality were meant to overwhelm us.

Before I begin to relate the story of our incarceration I will say a few words about the place. Some general information about Theresienstadt and the inner workings of the camp may be helpful; it will cast light on the dynamics of life there. The town of Theresienstadt was founded by Emperor Joseph II in the year 1780. He wanted to erect a fortress to stave off invading northern hordes which periodically attacked the Austro-Hungarian Empire. He decided to name the new citadel in honor of his mother, Empress Maria Theresa. There is a wicked irony in all this. Emperor Joseph II was the one monarch who partially emancipated the Jews of the Austro-Hungarian Empire. Some 160 years later the Jewish minority was incarcerated in the same fortress that had been built by the friendly emperor.

He chose to build the fortress on a plain with a few small hills nearby. It is nestled at the confluence of the Ohre and Labe rivers, and one can admire, in the distance, the outline of the bluish Bohemian mountain range. Around it are rolling meadows and a peaceful countryside. Theresienstadt was equipped with high scarps and deep moats and trenches, which, filled with water, could protect the fortress from the invaders. Escarpments and trenches bordered the fort on all sides to form a many-pointed star. The citadel was surrounded by fortified octagon shaped walls, bifurcated casemates and underground passages.

A hundred years later, the fortress was deemed redundant and Theresienstadt was converted into a garrison town. Thus, Emperor Joseph II's vision underwent a transformation. The garrison of Theresienstadt was rebuilt, with straight streets intersecting at right angles. Theresienstadt boasted 11 barracks, situated in different parts of the town. The garrison could hold about 4,000 soldiers and roughly 3,500 civilians, mainly servicing and depending on the garrison for their livelihood. The civilian

Contemporary photograph of the Theresienstadt gate.

population lived in 200-plus drab-looking houses. In the center of the place was a rather large square with buildings for administration and an unimpressive church.

It was this town which the Nazis chose as a transit and holding camp for the Jews because it was isolated and could be easily guarded. This was the place to which most of the Jews of Czechoslovakia (now renamed the Protectorate of Bohemia and Moravia) were deported to. The Nazis had decided to deport Jews from the Protectorate as early as 1940. Initial orders to the Jewish community called for transports of thousands of Czech Jews to Poland; the Nazis could count on the anti–Semitism of the local population to do some of their dirty work. Because of logistics, the Germans decided to confine Czech Jews to a holding and transit camp before sending them to their deaths.

Theresienstadt was a mixture of a concentration camp and a ghetto, part of the Nazis' efficient network of mass murder. While the extermination camps in the east were intended as the last stage, bringing an end to those who had survived the ordeal until then, the other camps and ghettos served to round up Jews and facilitate the process of mass annihilation. Theresienstadt was a camp devised for the first stage of the operation— and then some. It was also responsible for detaining some famous Jews and their close relations. Among them were Franz Kafka's favorite sister, Ottla; Theodor Herzl's daughter, Trude; and two sisters of Sigmund Freud, to name just a few. The Nazis were concerned about potential backlash from the west; they feared that the disappearance of some illustrious Jews would trigger inquiries as to their whereabouts. This fear turned out to be totally unfounded; nobody questioned the Germans about the disappearance of Jewish elites of yesteryear. Nobody questioned why so many people vanished into thin air. It is difficult to believe their disappearance was not conspicuous! Last but not least, Theresienstadt would be used to deceive the Red Cross commission appointed to investigate the persistent rumors of mass killings of the Jews in the east.

Theresienstadt, then, was for most only a brief reprieve: it was a transit camp from which the inmates would be deported regularly to extermination camps. Because this was to be a temporary residence, no adaptations were planned for the old, abysmal barracks with primitive plumbing and inadequate hygienic facilities. These were now to serve thousands of Jews, exceeding many times over the number of soldiers and civilians the town was once designed to accommodate. Only a few additional huts were built for the steady stream of new deportees, arriving by the thousands, overwhelming every aspect of the infrastructure of the drab little town.

Men and women were separated; children were kept apart from their parents. Prohibitions, issued almost daily, restricted and regimented our lives every minute of the day. Men and women were officially forbidden to meet or to write to anyone unless granted permission by the Germans. Laws prohibited any communication with Gentiles who were still living in the town until the summer of 1942. Smoking was strictly prohibited and violators of this order were severely punished. Possession of tobacco, medicine and many other items was disallowed. Those who failed to observe these and many other ordinances were punished by 10 to 50 strokes administered with a cane. The punishment beatings had to be administered by inmates, supervised by the SS, who often took part in it. If the strokes of the inmate who had to deliver the blows were not deemed brutal enough, he received the same number of lashes as the condemned man. Even for a trivial infraction, the prisoner might be hanged, placed in the Small Fortress jail or perhaps deported to the east.

The men who had the power of life and death over us rarely mixed with the inmates, and if they came near us, it always spelled deep trouble. The first German commandant of the camp was SS Obersturmführer Colonel Dr. Siegfried Seidl, a typical German brute—his academic title notwithstanding. He resided in a nice building accompanied by his numerous administrative personnel. As long as all of their orders were executed smoothly, they were only too happy to enjoy their comfortable life in the command post, far from the Jews and even farther from the dreaded Eastern front, the site of major bloodletting.

The duty to convert Theresienstadt into a functioning concentration camp was thrust upon a group of men called the Council of the Elders. The first Council was comprised of several young men, all members of the Czech Zionist movement, all very capable and competent. Only they were charged with an impossible task.

Initially, to create the much-needed infrastructure of the camp seemed totally out of reach. There was a great need to establish kitchens and some workshops; the problem of water shortages had to be resolved as well as the inadequate supply of electricity. The issue of providing some basic health care was well-nigh insurmountable. Care would be conducted in appalling conditions by doctors and nurses lacking even the most primitive equipment. The German commander stressed time and again that the Jews were responsible for containing the spread of contagious diseases which could imperil the neighboring population.

One of the Council's major responsibilities was the coordination of the labor force. The several workshops had to be manned. There were many and each had a specific task. So, for instance, one was charged with the production of wooden bunks, coffins and small boxes for the remains of cremated inmates. There was a laundry, bakery, kitchen—all had to function at top efficiency under unimaginably primitive conditions. Hundreds of men and women toiled splitting mica; others manufactured boxes needed for the German war production. Still others were ordered to spray military uniforms with a white dye, providing for camouflage needed at the snow-covered Russian battlefront. Every object had to be hauled manually by men, women and even children. Work was compulsory, even for children, who were assigned menial tasks.

Those charged with the duty of regulating incoming and outgoing transports had to deal with nearly impossible demands. While those arriving on transports had to be absorbed into the camp, at least for a while, the departing ones had to leave on time, meeting the timetable stipulated by the SS commandant, who in turn got his orders from Berlin's Gestapo. The Council of the Elders received general directives concerning the numbers and categories of people to be deported, while the actual selection was done by this self-governing body of the camp. The type of people to be deported changed constantly, according to the Nazis' orders. For example, at times, age offered protection and then it became a reason for deportation as the old were seen as a hindrance to the efficiency of the work process. Occasionally, illness provided cover and then suddenly all those with TB or other debilitating conditions were removed. For 20 months the members of the first two transports (1,400 men) who built the camp were safe from deportation; later on, every one of them was deported. At times certain work categories were exempted, deemed indispensable, and later became expendable. The ghetto guards provide an example. The ghetto guards unit was dismantled and unceremoniously deported after the uprising at the Ghetto Warsaw (1943). Because a similar group of guards had joined the Warsaw rebellion, the Germans feared that the same might happen in Theresienstadt. Another order initially stipulated that families should be kept together in the transports but later it was reversed: husbands and wives were hauled away from the camp separately. Likewise, some distinguished personalities (be it in arts, sciences, industry, finance or politics) were allowed to remain for a time, only to be dispatched later on to the east.

The members of the Council of the Elders were granted permission to remain in the camp for as long the Council was functioning. They also could protect their nearest relatives. However, all their privileges could disappear once the Germans ordered one of the periodic demotions of the Council of the Elders. Then they would all be deported with the "SB" (Sonderbehandlung—special designation—death by gas, no selection granted). The awe-inspiring duty of the first Elder of the Jews was imposed on Jacob Edelstein, a Pole and an ardent Zionist who was a longtime resident of Prague; before the war, he was instrumental in helping Jews who wished to immigrate to Palestine. He was a friendly and decent man, intelligent and capable; however, the Herculean task thrust upon him was above any man's ability, even though he and his assistants gave it their best efforts. The functionality of Theresienstadt was at best marginal and, more often than not, the prevailing conditions sunk way below operational levels.

Besides the elders, there were others who were accorded privileged status. Near the top, right below the members of the Council, were those who administered and handled food, for any supplement to the official rations, no matter how trivial, often made the difference between life and death. The only Jews who enjoyed a nearly automatic stay of deportation were those who had fought in World War I and were invalids, decorated for service with distinction. Also for the time being, some Jews who hailed from Germany and were married to Gentiles were exempted from deportation to the east. Children sired in these unions were perceived as half-breeds, subject to different degrees of persecution through the Nuremberg Laws. For now, the "half-breeds" escaped the worst of the suffering. The Danish Jews fared quite well, as they were sheltered by a full and automatic exemption. Their king never abandoned them. All the others had to find loopholes to avoid deportation. These groups were the privileged inmates. For those who succeeded and temporarily remained behind, they were about to face new challenges.

Whether among the ranks of the privileged or not, no one knew if and when they would be called to depart from Theresienstadt but everyone dreaded the call. There were persistent reports about mass destruction by gas in the east. Even though most inmates pretended not to believe the hearsay, everyone had their silent suspicions and fears of impending death. The deportations, the steady tension, the instability and the nervous state of flux exerted enormous pressure on all the inmates who never knew what to expect. And while their plight never improved, it was my observation that the deportations intensified in autumn, with September being the worst month. Perhaps it had something to do with the obscene German sense of humor: the Jewish new year and Yom Kippur, the most sacred Jewish holidays, are often celebrated in September. Another example of the macabre mentality of the Germans was the gassing of the entire Czech family camp in Auschwitz on March 7, 1944, the birthday of President Masaryk, the one man all Czech Jews revered.

The only real hope for us to avoid deportation was our contact, Dr. Tarjan, the mysterious friend of Mr. Bleha. We pinned all our hopes on the feasibility of this plan. Before entering the camp, we decided that if it proved difficult to contact Dr. Tarjan then I should be the one to make the attempt. We believed that I would have a better chance because I was the youngest, of medium height only, and the least visible one. It might be easier for me to sneak in and out of the confinement unobserved. It would be a terrifying undertaking.

5

Trapped

Once inside the gates we were shoved into the courtyard of a military barrack (Die Schleuse) to be screened. The yard was barren except for a few rough-hewn tables. At one of them we had to register, at another we got our camp ration cards and at the next one they screened the content of our 50 kilograms of belongings. The men confiscated our toothpaste, edibles and whatever they thought desirable for the Germans or "unnecessary" for us. We were left with one pencil, soap and no food. We had brought with us some preserves and a hard salami, all of which had cost us a small fortune back in Prague. Now we watched helplessly as it vanished, confiscated in front of our eyes.

After that, we were ordered to march to another barrack, the Kavalier, the former stables of the military. We were jostled into a large barn and ordered to sit on the floor, scantily covered with dirty straw. We were ordered to remain silent. The guards were Jewish inmates and they distributed some tepid fluid called soup and a piece of bread which tasted like sawdust. We were very thirsty and we welcomed the soup that only partially alleviated our dehydration.

We had not finished the meal—our first and last of the day—when another man arrived, notifying all of us that we were granted a three-day stay in this camp. Following that, we would be combined with another transport arriving from Prague. After that amalgamation we would proceed to the east. That was the worst possible news and it threw us into deep despair. We agreed that I should immediately set out to find the only person who could possibly help us in this Godforsaken place, the mysterious Dr. Tarjan.

It was late afternoon; the barracks were guarded by Jewish camp police. We were forbidden to leave the places assigned to us lest we disappear in the midst of the Gentile population still residing in the town. I made some efforts to improve and straighten out my crumpled looks before embarking on a task of such importance in search of the one man who might rescue us.

62

It proved to be quite a challenge, to upgrade one's appearance without benefit of water, a comb or a mirror. But I was young and confident, trusting my skill to handle people. A young engaging girl will often try to gain the advantage over the men in her midst. Theresienstadt was no exception. The ghetto guards in the Kavalier barracks were young men who were kind and often willing to help a smiling girl. I engaged one in a conversation and convinced him to let me look around a bit. I told him that I was looking for a man who had an important position in the camp. I was pleased to notice that he was duly impressed when I mentioned the name of Dr. Tarjan. He obligingly informed me that the doctor was the physician-in-chief in the adjacent hospital which was run and used by the inmates. He must have believed that I was a scion of some important family with the right connections because I somehow knew Dr. Tarjan. Perhaps he hoped that some good would come his way if he helped me. He allowed me to scamper to the fence behind which the hospital was located, and he even told me where I could find the office of the man I was seeking. I needed to get there as fast as possible. I promised to return right away.

I raced across the courtyard and easily found the place the friendly guard described to me. I knocked on the door, and without waiting for a reply, stepped into a small room which had an alcove for a bed. There I met a muscular young man of medium height. I noticed that he had thinning hair, and it was distinctly red. He seemed surprised by my barging in, but he smiled and had a benevolent expression on his face. He asked me who I was and what I wanted from him. I mentioned the name of our mutual friend, and his smile abruptly vanished. He began to speak in a low-key voice, almost a whisper, and his tone was grave and urgent. He promptly memorized all information about our camp identities, promised to help and told me to run back as fast as I could. His easy smile never returned as he clearly indicated that we were discussing dangerous matters. He sent me off, stressing that if I was caught I should never mention his name. It would do no good to pull him into the abyss. We shared a dangerous connection that could imperil us and many others.

I raced back to my parents, panting, mindful of Tarjan's admonition. I tried to assuage their fears, reassuring them that help was on the way, and that Dr. Tarjan would honor his promise to Mr. Bleha. Both my parents remained skeptical. We did not understand the nature of the friendship of the two men who were supposed to be instrumental in our survival. But we knew that we had only three days to find out. Either we would be deported to Poland with the rest of the transport or we would be granted a stay.

The transport we were to be joined with, AU l, arrived the next day. The order called for amalgamation of both groups and preparations for departure a day or two later. New numbers were issued to the combined transport, and we listened anxiously for our numbers to be called. If we were assigned numbers, it would mean that we would be sent east and Dr. Tarjan had not been able to come to our rescue. In the noisy bedlam of the barracks, we thought we heard our numbers called. It came from two civilians who told us to follow them out of the stables. There they informed us that, as requested by Dr. Tarjan, we were exempt from deportation and could temporarily remain in the camp. We breathed a sigh of relief, filled with enormous gratitude, just to realize the very next minute that we were being separated from our father, who was led to the men's barracks. The three of us were directed to the women's quarters.

They also made the suggestion that I should be sent to the youth barrack which would have separated me from my mother and sister. I would have none of it. I did not want to be torn asunder from my family. I valiantly defended my age (16 years), which I had just attained within a day in Theresienstadt. I convinced them of my adulthood. Actually, age 16 marked the divide between a child and an adult.

We were marched to a military barrack named Hamburg which housed hundreds of women. We were directed into a corner room on the upper floor. The dingy, small space was crowded and smelled of a mixture of grime and sweat. The room was filled with three-tiered wooden bunks, each bunk holding several women. The room's Aelteste—the person in charge of the 50 or so jammed women—was a crude and aggressive woman in her late thirties. She was the one who distributed our bread rations, the occasional spoonful of sugar, the blob of margarine, the latter doled out at irregular intervals. She was evidently a very powerful person in whose good grace we hoped to remain. Bertha, our Aelteste, told us that two could sleep in the middle bunk and one had to climb on the top. Each level of these three-tier bunks was meant to hold two women but many more had to share the narrow, hard planks (the number changed depending on the degree of overcrowding). On one side of the bunk was a short ladder, enabling us to reach the upper bunk. For a moment we hesitated to join the women who already called these bunks their home, but then fatigue overwhelmed us. Eva volunteered to take the top bunk, for she knew that I suffered from vertigo at even the lowest heights. We made a perfunctory attempt to clean our bunks, but we were too tired and decided to give it a try the very next day.

The room was dimly lit by a naked bulb suspended above the bunk of the Aelteste. Soon, even this source was switched off and the room was plunged into darkness. Only the breathing, coughing, snoring and sporadic arguing disturbed our much-needed rest. The trouble was that anyone turning around disturbed the tightly squeezed others, and that provoked a storm of anger. Falling asleep, I sorrowfully remembered my comfortable bed in Prague. Mother whispered to me that tomorrow we would look for the money we had smuggled in, sewn into hems of our skirts and some in the shoulder pads. Before she kissed me good night, she sighed, mentioning Father and his predicament. Mother worried about him. She knew that she was his strength and that he would find it difficult to manage without her care and practical help. So our first night was spent in a fitful sleep interrupted by the presence of other women, constrictions of the narrow space and our anxious tension. The bites of the many bedbugs did not help.

The next day Dr. Tarjan looked us up. One of the benefits of his prominent position in the camp was his freedom of movement, awarded then only to members of the Council (they were holders of the much-desired Durchlasschein). Speaking at a fast clip, he told us that he had arranged for me to be assigned to work at the hospital, in his department, to afford him the needed pretext for the claim of our importance to the camp. He only added that my training in the Prague Jewish hospital was a God-sent blessing, because of the notorious shortage of trained nursing staff.

Dr. Tarjan managed to secure some good assignments for us. As originally planned, I was to work in the hospital. Eva got to work in a much-coveted unit of field workers (Landwirtschaft). The SS detachment in Theresienstadt used the plots on the ramparts and around it for growing vegetables and fruits for their very own use. The work was to be done by the inmates. Mother was to join the Ordnungsdienst, a unit responsible for cleaning of the barracks.

We began to settle into a routine. Eva worked in the fields around the camp and this carried advantages. First, she got out of the squalor into the fresh air and then she could, on occasion, gulp down a carrot, potato or cucumber. That was the easy part. All she had to do was make sure that the supervising SS man looked in another direction. The more difficult problem was posed by the need to stuff some vegetables into her clothes and smuggle them into the camp. But Eva, who had always been slim, was now

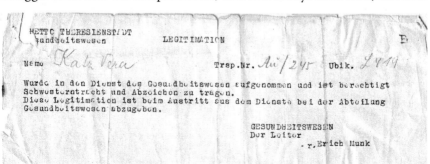

Vera's pass which allowed her freedom to move around the camp.

skinny, and what she wore hung loosely on her frame. Usually, she would bring in some leaves, a kind of spinach; it was called lebeda and it grew unattended in and around the camp. Mother would cook it on the corner stove. It tasted absolutely divine; we were no longer picky about our food. The only pitfall of Eva's assignment was the exposure to the rough winter cold as the same commando had to clear snow from the vicinity of the commandery. We had no warm clothing left after being fleeced of many of our belongings upon arrival.

We were so grateful to Dr. Tarjan. It proved once again the worn axiom "It matters more whom you know than what you know." In the camps it was a matter of life and death. My work in the hospital was of paramount importance. Dr. Tarjan reclaimed our stay in Theresienstadt as his personal privilege.

The men of the first two transports, AK1 and AK2—all 1,400—were bestowed the temporary privilege of staying in Theresienstadt because it was correctly assumed that their labor would be needed in the future. The Germans expected thousands of Jews to pass through the gates of this transit camp. Many more barracks and huts had to be assembled to house the thousands of inmates. Many were expected to pass through Theresienstadt on their way to the east. For this reason, the Council of the Elders wished to keep the nucleus of an experienced and able-bodied work force within the camp. They permitted these 1,400 to have immunity from deportation for themselves as well as their immediate families. Dr. Tarjan, a bachelor, chose to shelter us in lieu of his non-existent family. He was not only a generous man but also a wise one. He knew that luck and rules in concentration camps had ephemeral life expectancy, and the best insurances were some independent position within the camps hierarchy, which prevented an early expulsion. Tarjan also knew that he was only heartbeat between our stay and deportation.

Life was unpredictable in the camp and fortunes changed on a dime. It was his intent to secure my work position by stating it was of monumental importance to the smooth flow of the services in the camp's hospital. I was more than grateful for this opportunity. Firstly, I wanted to secure some permanency for us—we were so vulnerable with few connections or friends. While we arrived and long thereafter, the Council was comprised of men who were Zionists of long standing and friends from the youth movement. We did not know any of them, for back in Prague we belonged to the faction of assimilated Jews. Secondly, I wanted to be worthy of Tarjan's confidence, to prove to him that his trust in me was justified.

Dr. Tarjan headed the Ear-Nose-Throat Department. He had several assistants and a special operating room where many surgeries were performed daily. The ward was adjacent to the operating room. The most frequent invasive procedure was mastoidectomies. As no medication was available for conservative treatment, many ear infections progressed fast, leaving surgery as the only possible last-ditch attempt to save lives.

My duties began at 7:00 a.m. by preparing for the day's surgeries which usually lasted till the early afternoon. Then I had to clean the operating room and prepare for the next day's work. Any time remaining was spent tending to the many patients—many suffered agonizing pains. We had no analgesics to numb their excruciating agonies during the post-operative phase. The cries and moans often sounded as though emanating from a torture chamber and not a sick bay. The best we could do to comfort those in our care was to keep them clean and try to feed them with the camp's substandard soup. Matters were not helped by the fact that we suffered a dire shortage of trained personnel, and the lay people assigned to work were of marginal help. Many could not do much good because they were so revolted by the hospital routine and the patients' misery.

Dr. Tarjan would, on occasion, hint he was preparing conditions for me to meet Mr. Bleha. The risks were so enormous that the timing, the rendezvous place and disguises had to be worked out to perfection. Once Dr. Tarjan hinted he was involved in some clandestine operation with Mr. Bleha that made more frequent contact mandatory. The black-market transactions between the inmates and the Czech gendarmes, the SS men, and even the civilian population, were a brisk trade. Though it carried an extraordinary threat, it was exceptionally lucrative. Bleha and Tarjan were involved in the ongoing trade between the outside world and the interred Jews.

Our mentor, Dr. Tarjan, took it upon himself to teach us the complexities of camp life. First, he asked us to refrain from any initiatives until we familiarized ourselves with the maze of different happenings and undercurrents. Many dangers had to be avoided, and the minute chances of life improvement had to be discerned and snatched quickly. We learned that the management of the camp's infrastructure required a nucleus of skilled artisans and craftsmen. Some trades were more important than others. Right on the top were plumbers, carpenters and some foremen. It was Dr. Tarjan's scheme to find some contacts for us within these groups and so provide us with important connections and opportunities, for no one knew how long his position in the camp's hierarchy might remain intact.

While Eva and I handled our assignments relatively well, Mother found her duties difficult to perform. In our early days, she was assigned to the gate, where it was her responsibility to stand beside a Czech guard and count the number of women in each working column leaving or returning from work. As this assignment went to older women, the eight hours were divided into four two-hour stints. But at all times, until early July, when

Theresienstadt became an open camp and the Gentiles were evacuated, the Czech gendarme was assisted by an inmate who had to arrive at the same count of prisoners as the sentry did. The commandos of workers would usually leave in the morning and return at night so in between there was little pressure at the gates. Even though Mother's job seemed undemanding, it exacted its toll on her. Her energy level was quickly depleted, and the protracted standing was hard on her. To help out, I used to fill in, replacing her on the last shift from 8 to 10 p.m.

I would finish my shift in the hospital at seven o'clock and rush back to the Hamburg barracks where I joined the sentry at the gates at 8 p.m. The gendarmes got used to my substituting for Mother and did not raise objections. Some were nicer and better behaved than others, though all had been screened for camp duty and deemed qualified if they were staunch anti–Semites. Few of the guards were hostile to me; most ignored my presence and the occasional one would even smile or glance at me with a flirtatious twinkle in his eyes. But I, with the naiveté of my 16 years, did not want to notice and, when I was not carefully counting the returning formations, I looked demurely at the tips of my shoes.

One evening, there was a new sentry on duty. He was a middle-aged man. For me, at that time, anyone over 30 was middle-aged. He was tall and hefty with reddish hair and a crowbar moustache. For a while we stood silently side by side, though I could not help noticing lewdness in his glimpse. I did not feel threatened. I knew that no Gentile in his right mind would risk anything more daring than perhaps a word or two with a Jewess. They all were briefed and warned about undue contact with Jews. They dreaded the penalties imposed by the Nazis on those who infringed on this taboo. On that night we stood there for about an hour when he asked me if I was hungry. My truthful answer was that I was famished. He then suggested that he would not mind sharing his meat sandwich with me. He must have noticed my eagerness and my nearly drooling expression for he smiled amiably while he was leaving the gates for his rather late supper. It happened routinely that guards left their posts for a short break, usually around mealtime. They would trust the Jewess on duty to detain any late-arriving inmates for the final count and his approval before entry into the barracks. The evening duty was mostly quiet: few inmates returned past 8 p.m. and none left the premises.

I looked wistfully as the man who promised to share his supper with me was departing from the gates. I hoped he would keep his word and place the sandwich somewhere outside the guardhouse. He would be taking a grave risk by passing it to me in the open—perhaps someone would see him. In a camp, walls had ears and eyes, and hunger brought the worst out of some inmates. All these thoughts rushed through my mind while I waited for him to return and tell me where I could pick up the food. I made up my mind to take it to Mother who was rapidly losing weight and looked worn.

The life in camp was rough on all of us, but considerably harder for our parents who were already middle-aged and therefore had less resilience than Eva and I did. That was one more reason why I was so happy for the unexpected windfall of a delicacy such as a meat sandwich. The guard returned soon enough and whispered to me to go into the guardhouse and pick up the parcel he had left on the table. I rushed in, noticed the sandwich wrapped in newspapers, and I rejoiced upon seeing two layers of bread generously stuffed with meat. The entire guardhouse had an enticing fragrance, nearly making me salivate. The sandwich was soaked in fat. That was a gorgeous sight for me. The thought crossed my mind about the iniquity of it all: the Gentiles took for granted that nobody wanted to kill them, they could continue to live in their homes with their families and never go hungry. They did not have to risk their lives to alleviate their hunger. I snatched the sandwich and was about to leave when I heard heavy steps right behind me. My antennae on high alert, I sensed impending danger. I spun around and faced the guard whose face betrayed lechery. For a second he ogled me and then he lunged at me. I swerved, bending aside, but he caught me by the waist. His revolting paws fondled my breasts and buttocks. He was bending down, trying to force a kiss. He had the appearance of an ogre. His face was sweaty and poorly shaven, and he seemed out of breath, like a man who had just finished a long-distance race. I knew I did not stand a chance to fight him off. He was a hefty man, trembling with obscene lust. The only chance to get off the hook was to trick him. Instantly, I gripped both his hands and whispered to him urgently, "Look, someone just entered the gates, if they catch us, both of us will be killed. Is it worth it to die like this?" I frightened him all right. He let go of me and ran back to the gates at full speed. I did not wait for his return. I grabbed the sandwich and disappeared into the dark hallways of the barracks.

Back at my bunk, I gave the sandwich to Mother who looked at me askance. I assured her that the sentry on duty was a nice man, one who genuinely wanted to help. Mother gave me a sad smile. She probably did not believe a word but she did not want to embarrass me and force me to lie even more, so she did not probe for any details. She patted my hair but she had a pained look on her face. A short while later, while I was falling asleep, I felt a few warm tears on my forehead. There were only few instances when I saw my mother cry; for the better part of her life she kept her emotions well under control but she suffered watching us hustle for food, trying to survive. She had once doted on her daughters, believing them destined for lofty careers, and she was devastated by our fast spiral into misery.

Half asleep, I kissed her and reminded her that no sentry would dare to touch a Jewess—it would be suicidal. I felt that that comforted her to a point but even the humiliation of an incomplete sex act for the sake of food was difficult for her to bear. She had a hard time parting with her deeply ingrained middle-class values which were, in the turpitude of the camp's life, totally out of place.

Later on, I served a few more shifts with this man. He always shared his supper with me. He tried sometimes to steal a kiss but I no longer felt threatened for he knew only too well the mortal risk of Rassenschande, and I in turn never failed to remind him of that. Any physical contact between a Gentile and a Jew resulted in the death penalty. During those shifts, I reflected with gratitude on the double-edged sword of the Nuremberg racial laws.

We did not see Father for two long months because we could not get permission to leave the women's barracks and enter those which housed the men. Only those in charge of some important task were granted the special Durchlasschein (permits to leave the barracks) which allowed movement within the inner perimeter of the camp.

One day we were surprised by an unexpected call for volunteers to clean the men's barracks. The response was overwhelming. Women pushed and shoved one another to be chosen for the job. One and all wanted to see a husband, father, boyfriend or a relative. I was one of the lucky ones to be picked along with 15 other women. While I was overjoyed I did not realize that the privilege of seeing Dad would result in heartache.

At first I could not find him. We had to scrub and clean for a few hours and then we were allowed to spend time with our relatives. When I finally found him, I had a hard time recognizing him. The man I saw bore little resemblance to my dad. He was a broken man. He looked aged and he was almost emaciated. He was dirty, unshaven and his clothes gave off a foul odor. There was not a trace left of the spirited, brilliant man I used to call my father—a man who once had been such a successful professional, respected and loved by many. The well-read man who loved to travel, debate, lecture and much more had become an apathetic, listless person. His ruinous state was at least partially caused by his need for cigarettes, for in bygone days he had been a two-pack-a-day smoker. In camp, deprived of any access to cigarettes, he soothed his craving by exchanging his bread rations for a smoke. It was a sad ending for a man of his stature.

On that day I cleaned his place and clothes as well I could and I told him about the help we got from Dr. Tarjan. That cheered him up a bit. I waited until he finished the piece of bread I had brought him. I also extracted from him a promise that he would stop the ruinous habit of bartering his food rations for cigarettes. I did not really believe that he could give up his dependency on nicotine but I pretended to have faith in him and every word he uttered. When I had to leave, I kissed him and he gave me a sad smile that felt worse than any argument over his need to stop the smoking addiction. He knew how hurtful it was for me to see him in such distressing shape. Mother waited anxiously for my report on Father. I uttered a few white lies and embellished the facts but I believe that my looks gave the truth away. In any event, Mother understood Father's disposition.

There are many ways men died in Theresienstadt. Some, the lucky ones, got sick and passed on quickly. The bodies and minds of the less fortunate ones lingered for a while; then there were those, like my dad, whose bodies slowly faded until they were only shadows of their former selves but their minds remained lucid for a long time. Though my father's world was crushed at the Munich conference table back in 1938 where all he believed in was trampled upon, he lived on. And while he did so he never adjusted to the new realities that ensued. All that he lived for and upheld was crushed, everything around him slipped into darkness, brutality and violence. He could no longer understand the world around him. He could not adapt to Nazi rule. His faith was demolished, his spirit could not recover and his mind could not find solace, but his emaciated body still dragged itself around the camp.

I met Mr. Bleha only once during the early stages of our imprisonment. We would hear from him on occasion through Dr. Tarjan who would bring us some supplement for our camp's rations but one day Dr. Tarjan arranged for me to meet him because he wanted to wean us of any dependence on him and facilitate direct clandestine contact. The carefully arranged meeting was extremely hazardous, and its success hinged on swiftness and absolute discretion. Dr. Tarjan told me where the secret meeting spot was and instructed me to wait there. It took only a short while in all likelihood, but overwrought as I was, it seemed like an eternity. I did not dare to breathe; I was frozen by anxiety. Afterwards, I discovered that I had nothing to fear. The German heroes never ventured into the underground corridors, to the dim, secluded passages under the former fortress. The Supermen, armed to their teeth, were more comfortable in open daylight, preferably in groups. They shunned any potentially dangerous place.

Suddenly, Mr. Bleha stood in front of me. He scared me to death, and I had to suppress a scream. He reassured me with a warm smile, whispered a few comforting words, handed me a parcel of food, sent his love to Father and promised another meeting in a short while.

I grabbed the parcel and ran through the dark passages at record speed for my 16 years. I surfaced in the camp, breathing a sigh of relief. Had we been caught both of us would have been shot. Back in the barracks, we opened the parcel. It was a rare moment of joy. The package consisted of goodies we had not seen in a long time: marmalade, lard, toothpaste and cookies. These delicacies boosted our morale. Fearing theft, we opened the parcel in secrecy. All of us handled contraband and it was a part of our survival technique. Most of the food went to our father.

The next time it was Mother who joined the cleaning unit assigned to the men's quarters. She was more upbeat upon her return. She felt that Father was slightly better adjusted and that his morale was helped by Mr. Bleha's steadfast resolve to see us through these evil times. Just as events began to look up for us, another favorable rumor swept the camp. The Gentile population would be evacuated from the town and the inmates would be allowed to move into their dwellings, thus improving the appalling congestion in the barracks. The Gentiles were to be evacuated in July 1942. Some 200 drab houses would become available for the burgeoning numbers of the daily arriving inmates. For once the German fear of potentially highly infectious epidemics was beneficial to the inmates.

All things being relative, the houses seemed beautiful to us; anything would be better than the abominable barracks. In addition, Theresienstadt's streets were renamed. They became identified with letters and numbers. L stood for Long and Q for transverse. Our family, however, felt somewhat uneasy. We were concerned about Mr. Bleha's evacuation from the town. But we comforted each other with the fact that Mr. Bleha had lived for a long time in the area and would certainly find a way to reach us from his new place. We did not suspect then that we would never see him again. For a long time, we nursed hopes that he would return.

Sometime in mid–June I became ill. I woke up with a sore throat, rash and high fever. The barrack's physician was summoned by the Aelteste; I was diagnosed with scarlet fever, an infectious disease rampant in the camp. The diagnosis resulted in compulsory hospitalization in the isolation ward for six weeks. I was not really ill for that long but it was the rigid German rule, prompted by concern for the surrounding German population which made the six weeks of segregation mandatory for any potential carrier of a contagious disease.

The hospital of Theresienstadt was called Hohenelbe-Vrchlabi. It was originally a military hospital that serviced the garrison and the civilian population of the town. It retained its function following the conversion of the town into a concentration camp. The hospital's design would correspond to any small-town facility; it still maintained its various departments (surgery, infectious disease, internal medicine, otolaryngology, ophthalmology, gynecology, and urology) with room for a pharmacy and a laboratory for good measure. Under current conditions, however, no medications or other supplies were replenished. The Germans allowed into the camp only those drugs that were confiscated from Jewish homes or taken from the luggage of newly arrived inmates. As a result, there were very few medicines in the camp. On account of the reigning conditions, the hospital became a farce; there was little we could do for the suffering inmates.

Some of the most illustrious physicians of Europe manned departments that had nothing to offer to their patients. Ironically and ridiculously, many clinicians tried to emulate protocols practiced in reputable clinics where they worked before the deportation. We had next to nothing to offer to those under our care and in reality we were an understaffed palliative station. Not only were we desperately short of medicine, we also had to make do with equipment that was broken, rusty and unusable.

Psychiatric patients had to be locked up in the Kavalier barrack (the one-time stables of the cavalry) where they awaited the next eastbound transport for expeditious death by gas. No emotionally unstable patient or pregnant woman was granted even the shortest stay in Theresienstadt. The hospital was a symbol of the insanity of those times.

I worked in the operating room shared by ophthalmology and otolaryngology, headed by Dr. Tarjan. I was accustomed to problems and shortages from the days of my training in the Jewish hospital in Prague, but little prepared me for the total absence of all that was needed in the camp's medical facilities. Sometimes we had a little ether or chloroform to put the patient under during lengthy surgeries; at times we had none. Gauze was in short supply, and we had to use paper which somehow stuck to the incision. As mentioned, the most frequent surgery was a mastoidectomy, daily performed on several patients, provided we had some anesthetic. Many inmates suffered from middle-ear infection, aggravated by malnutrition and a lack of basic hygiene. With no medication to treat the inflammation, the only remaining option was surgery. The reasoning was that if not dealt with surgically, the patient would succumb to meningitis. But the reasoning was questionable, for the mortality following this drastic surgery was astronomical. The Germans thrived on efficiency and meticulous record-keeping, and the high frequency of death suited their needs perfectly.

The Jewish physicians gladly complied, hoping that as long as the commandant was pleased with the statistics, they might be permitted to remain in the camp. Both parties, albeit for different reasons, cooperated. Unfortunately, many young and middle-aged inmates died either during or immediately following the procedure. The same grim conditions prevailed in the department of general surgery where patients with countless stomach aches were rightly or wrongly diagnosed as appendicitis; these operations were conducted in steadily deteriorating conditions. The surgical wounds would not heal; many became infected, spilling pus and, in many cases, bringing about a protracted and painful death. The entire surgical floor was filled with the stench of pus, blood, dirt and excrement.

The department of urology was headed by Dr. Braun, a renowned urologist who had once worked at Prague's best clinic. He regrettably had a wicked temper and a vulgar mouth, and the patients were petrified by his outbursts. To be fair, he had ample reasons for his irritation. It was extremely difficult if not impossible to catheterize men with old, brittle and leaking catheters: the rubber on them was all but boiled away by the many repeated attempts to sterilize them. Dr. Braun frequently threw a useless catheter on the floor, which lead to yet another boiling for the illusory sterilization. These scenes occurred daily, so that the staff became impervious to his outbursts.

In Europe of the early 20th century, the authority of a department chief was uncontested and his behavior was restrained only by the ruling conventions. Only under normal circumstances would Dr. Braun have maintained some semblance of civility and these weren't anything approaching normal circumstances. An overpowering stench of urine saturated the ward. It was impossible to maintain hygiene; the mattresses were soaked in urine and were only occasionally dried but never cleaned. We had but a few sheets, rarely warm water or towels—all of which would have been imperative for basic care.

While I was confined to the isolation ward with scarlet fever, my aunt Miriam and her daughter Milada arrived in Theresienstadt. Their arrival echoed our own first days but they suffered a more tragic outcome. They were immediately sequestered and registered for an eastbound transport with only a few days' delay in Theresienstadt. In the isolation ward, I knew little of what was happening on the outside. However, my cousin managed to find a little window with rails, used unofficially by the patients for communicating with the outside world. We exchanged notes, trying to find a solution to the predicament of their impending deportation. I thought of Dr. Tarjan, and I asked my cousin to contact him. Regretfully, this time he could not help. The Council of the Elders granted each member a limited number of people to protect. Tarjan's Schutzliste was filled to capacity. There was little time left and we failed to delay their deportation. A few weeks later, my other aunt, Olga, the older sister of my father, her husband and their daughter, Rose, suffered the same fate. This tragedy occurred in quick succession, even before I was discharged from the isolation ward. I was saddened by our inability to secure their stay but in camp everyone was on their own. We were aboard a quickly sinking ship with few lifeboats.

During the summer of 1942, the Jews of the Protectorate and Austria were often sent to a death camp named Maly Trostinec in a district of Minsk in Byelorussia. Most of my relatives on my father's side perished there. My cousin, his wife and child vanished in this extermination camp, and there, but for the grace of God, and the help of Mr. Bleha and Dr. Tarjan, we too would have died. The date of our execution would have been May 17, 1942.

I did meet one man who survived the death camp of Maly Trostinec. He furnished me with information about this grievous place. Most were murdered upon arrival in mobile vans which had the exhaust pipes rerouted back into the cabins so that the Jews inside would be poisoned with carbon monoxide. Mr. M. managed to save his life because he was a locksmith. In this capacity he got to know some rapacious Lithuanian SS guards who he managed to bribe. For a small fortune in diamonds they sold him a gun. He fled, joined the roving bands of partisans and lived to bear witness to the tragedy of Maly Trostinec. When the fortunes of war took a turn and the Soviet armies began to drive the Germans westward, the withdrawing SS hordes pushed the few hundred Jews who were still in the camp into a barn, set it ablaze and then watched it burn. There were no survivors. If not for his witness, the 250,000 Viennese and Czech Jews would have perished anonymously.

How lucky for us that we knew so little of the fate of our loved ones. We even managed to dismiss the persistent rumors of mass annihilation to which we were already sentenced, albeit in absentia. In January 1942 in Wannsee, a Berlin suburb, a conference was convened that sealed the fate of European Jewry.

While I was confined to the isolation ward, I met a young man, another patient suffering with scarlet fever. He was a physician, a graduate of the German university of Prague. He had completed his studies in 1938, in the nick of time, just before the expulsion of all Jews from all learning centers. During our shared recovery he told me about his childhood, his mother and his fatherless adolescence. I was impressed by him. He looked and sounded every bit a man of the world to my 16-year-old self. I liked his looks, too. He was of medium height and had an athletic build; his handsome face flashed a ready smile. He had thick, black wavy hair, neatly combed, and he was always well groomed. My childhood boyfriend, Bobby Weisskopf, and our puppy love seemed long gone: Bobby was deported to Poland in the fall of 1941. My new friend was nice and mature. Our obvious liking for each other evolved from an innocent flirtation into a romance, Theresienstadt-style.

Once we were discharged from the isolation ward, we spent some wonderful moments together, the kind that only young love can create, even in such a Godforsaken place as Theresienstadt. Both his mother and mine approved of our relationship, hoping that in the future we would create a happy family. Mother, always faithful to her values, wanted everything to remain prim and proper and, in Max's presence, she would hint gently at the consequences of premature indulgence for couples before they tied the knot. She did not need to worry. Max's middle-class values were also deeply ingrained and he planned to build our future on a solid foundation. Though Max and I kissed, petted and necked during our rendezvous, we never crossed the line. He worried about a potential pregnancy which would have made an abortion mandatory as well as have a negative effect on our marital future. I loved him but at times I resented his iron self-control because, for no particular reason, I began to lose hope that we had any future. I did not think we would ever marry or live to see the end of the war.

Concerning relationships between the sexes in the camp, it would be preposterous to pretend that young men and women are not attracted to one another even when thrown together in the worst of circumstances. Perhaps the opposite was true. The imminent danger intensified every feeling and did not tolerate delayed gratification. How many of us really believed that we would live to see a tomorrow? Any sexual contact was most emphatically forbidden and warnings were issued that anyone caught would be severely punished. But the only watchdogs of the SS in the camp, the Jewish ghetto guards, looked conspicuously away from "crimes" they too were guilty of.

The threat of severe penalties was ubiquitous but we learned to disregard these continual exhortations. We reasoned that almost all we attempted to do to survive was strictly forbidden. Only death was approved of but we had little predilection to comply with that. Within the German compilation of our crimes, pregnancy was one of the gravest. Since the Nazis were bent on eradicating Jewish life, they were obviously intolerant of procreation. Any pregnant woman, if her condition was reported, was dispatched to be gassed. Therefore, sexual activity endangered the life of women for there were no contraceptives available. The camp's physicians decided to save as many pregnant women as they could by performing therapeutic abortions. These procedures would be reported in the daily census as cures for endometritis.

But all that had a hitch, Theresienstadt-style. Women stopped menstruating during their time in the camp. Gossip had it that the Nazis added some chemicals to our food that caused the stoppage of ovulation. Another hypothesis had it that our starvation diet was at the root of the interruption of the menstrual cycle. Nonetheless, some women conceived in the camp. Others were in quite advanced stages of gestation when they first arrived, and for the most part they too subjected themselves to the surgery; otherwise they would be sent to gas chambers either before or after delivery. I think the Germans knew all along. Certainly, they had to wonder about the many women who suffered from endometritis, necessitating admission to the hospital, where they miraculously recovered within 24 hours.

There must have been a tacit approval by the SS for the many abortions performed in Theresienstadt.

The many risks and the lack of privacy did not deter passionate couples. With the exception of the few privileged members of the Council of the Elders who had little rooms for themselves, few found secluded spots. Anybody passing through the long corridors of the barracks was used to seeing couples hidden behind various pillars, in corners, in every nook and cranny, in various states of sexual arousal. It was so much a part of our lives that no one paid any attention. Sex was also a bartering chip. It could make the day easier; a pretty girl could get extra rations and perhaps even stave off her deportation temporarily if she found a lover who had clout and power. As a result, the most attractive women competed mercilessly, vying for the favors of the handful of powerful men. Next to the members of the Council on the hierarchy of desirable protectors were the cooks and bakers for they had access to food. Many of these men had their pick of women because they had the power to avert starvation. The greatest assets of a man were twofold: to delay deportation and reduce starvation. Little else mattered. It was striking to see many men with mediocre looks who in normal times held little allure for the opposite sex selecting girlfriends from among the most attractive women. The very same women would not have considered some marginally educated man as her bedfellow even if he was good looking, but in the fight for survival, the standards of the past were irrelevant.

The men who wielded power knew that they had not undergone a sudden metamorphosis and become seductive Casanovas. They only used their power to get what in normal times would have been unattainable; they made the most of their short-term opportunities. Although I could see early on the benefits a pretty girl could reap in an environment of Gotterdammerung, I also realized that I was no match for these beautiful girls who were older and more aggressive than I was. Besides, I believed that we could survive protected by Mr. Bleha and his proxy Dr. Tarjan.

At the beginning, of course, all this was an eye-opener, and, at times, a dilemma. Our middle-class values, reinforced by my naiveté, were that sex was a part of marital intimacy and that premarital sex trivializes that union. This view did not facilitate adaptation to the new realities. Actually, sex is just one example of how our values clashed with those of the cesspool we had entered. We had to modify our language to camp life. We never stole, we "organized." Perhaps our background prevented us from using the socially unacceptable term. Obviously, all of us had to transform, and the sooner we did, the better our chances for survival were. There was little time to get over the initial shock. Those who were unable to fit in went under, and at a fast rate.

Right after I was discharged from the isolation ward, I had to report for work. I found there was a new boss of the department of ophthalmology. He was Docent Richard Stein, a world-renowned eye surgeon. Dr. Stein, who patterned himself according to the German model of a physician-in-chief, handled his staff as a general would treat enlisted men but he did run the department efficiently. He cared for his staff and he was even more concerned for his patients. No one could argue with his medical expertise which had nearly miraculous results. Even the SS men depended on his skills. When Dr. Stein treated one of the SS officers he was plied with cigarettes as a reward for surgeries performed. These were the "happy" days. Having something to smoke made him bearable but in regular times of dearth of cigarettes he struggled with his addiction to nicotine. His mood swings were legendary. Docent Stein had a short fuse and the only one who could calm him was his wife who was his most able assistant. She knew how to assuage his cold-turkey withdrawal from nicotine. She took it upon herself to be at his side, making his life, and also our lives, much easier.

Our days and nights in Theresienstadt offered little diversity. Mostly, days and nights merged into a long spell of wretchedness and desolation. Only the numbers varied: numbers of newly arrived inmates, those who were deported eastward, those who were admitted to the hospital, and one which always seemed to climb up—those who died.

There was one night, however, that does stand out. On one of my graveyard shifts, Docent Stein entered the ward. This did not surprise me for he visited often—at all hours—to check on his patients who meant the world to him. Without a doubt, they were his main concern. The only surprising sight was the fact that on that night he carried a small parcel in his arms. Though dead tired I became curious. What was he bringing to the department at two o'clock in the morning? He motioned me to follow him to an adjacent little room, where I watched him expose the tiny package, wrapped in a sheet. I could hardly believe my eyes. I saw a newborn baby boy, pink and sound asleep, lying on the piece of cloth. The baby was breathing regularly, his tiny body still soiled by the whitish substance from his mother's womb. I never saw a newborn in Theresienstadt. Now, during this unusual night, I looked at a thriving baby amidst this squalor and death. Docent Stein must have noticed my obvious delight, and clearly displeased, he gestured me to get nearer. He whispered in a compelling voice, "This baby was born tonight. The mother managed to conceal her condition when she arrived here a few days ago. But if the truth were to become known, she would be murdered." He took a deep breath and quickly continued, "The mother is a friend of mine, and I wish to save her life. She could be saved," he insisted, "if only the baby would not drag her into the abyss." He said flatly that we had to help her to get rid of the child, for she could not muster the courage to do it herself. He had asked her to suffocate the baby but she had been too weak and emotional to do it.

Docent Stein was a man of short stature, and therefore we looked directly into each other's eyes. I discerned his impassioned request for understanding. I knew that he could hardly articulate his feelings. He was not accustomed to asking or begging; he customarily issued orders. While he made his silent plea for help, he pulled a syringe filled with some whitish fluid out of his pocket. In an almost inaudible whisper, he implored me to inject the contents into the baby, to resolve this painful dilemma. Now it was my turn to respond and I became angry, indeed furious. I replied, also in a whisper, "Why don't you do it? Why involve me when I don't even know the mother of this tragic newborn? I am not driven by compassion for a woman I don't know. I don't want to have a part in this tragedy." His reply startled me; he told me that he could not do it for he was bound by the Hippocratic Oath to save life, not destroy it.

For a moment I thought he had taken leave of his senses. The life of this newborn, as well as his mother, was beyond anyone's deliverance. But Docent Stein was not insane; his problem was that he could not shirk the solemn oath he had taken in other times and in another world. Again he turned to me and almost implored me to do it as a personal favor. Although I was not bound by any oath, I found it impossible to just calmly take the syringe, empty the contents into the baby and walk away. We were both unnerved by the deliberate act of extinguishing a life, even the life of a baby who was doomed to die, even if it was to try to save the life of his mother.

We exchanged a pained and embarrassed glance. Then, the boy began to whine, making Docent Stein's hair stand on end. Coldly and tensely, he snapped that we would do it together. Before I could say anything, he grabbed my hand, pushed the syringe into it and, with his hand wrapped around mine, he forced the needle into the thigh of the baby. It hardly took a second but the memory of that moment has followed me my entire life. The baby shrieked, and Docent Stein covered his mouth with palm of his hand. It took but moments for the baby to turn silent. He breathed in only a few more times and then he lay there motionless. His little chest no longer heaved and he laid there lifeless, his pink color quickly fading. Docent Stein regained his composure and poise, covered the little one with the cloth and said abruptly, "Make sure that the crematory attendants collect it first thing in the morning."

They would not question its identity. This little baby could not be entered into the camp's census like everyone else who died for it would incriminate its mother, and even though the baby was dead, she would be punished by deportation. Officially, then, this little boy never existed but he did live with me, mainly in my sleepless nights, long after our liberation. I do not know if the mother survived. I never even knew her name nor did I want to. The last person I wanted to meet was the unfortunate woman who knew that her baby had to die to give her a chance to live. Docent Stein not only violated his Hippocratic Oath—something he claimed he could not do—but he had also made me his accomplice in his perhaps noble attempt to save the woman's life.

Each day in Theresienstadt presented a myriad of challenges and hardships. Typically, an inmate got up bone-tired after a fitful sleep caused by the bites of the swarms of fleas and bedbugs who feasted on our bodies. It did not help that the three-tier bunks were always overcrowded, exceeding their capacity several times over. Many fights resulted while one woman would turn around and in doing so wake up her bunk buddies. They would blame each other, resenting the interruption. Only the fear of a potential intervention by the Aelteste limited the noise and fierceness of these altercations. No amount of effort spent cleaning the barracks helped to rid us of the insect infestation. Even the occasional gassing of an entire block did not help for the returning prisoners brought back the eggs of the vermin on their clothes. Still, those of us who had a bunk were the lucky ones.

Many inmates were thrown into the attics and bare rooms where, if they were fortunate, they found a stack of dirty straw. Others had to contend with sleeping on the bare ground. The night offered the occasional bliss of unconsciousness and a reprieve from distress and agony.

Waking up was the worst time of day in camp for me. The moment I opened my eyes I became aware of the surroundings: the desolate barrack hall, the foul body odors of the other women prisoners, and the whole gamut of misery of our lives. I used to close my eyes again, hoping that all of that grimness would somehow vanish. I began to loathe opening my eyes for another day of torment, hunger, loose bowels and oozing sores that afflicted my body. From the moment of getting up in the morning, you needed an aggressive drive to push ruthlessly for the basic necessities. Long after I had left the camp, my first instinct upon waking up was to shut my eyes again, to repress the anguish the new day might bring.

At dawn, we all dashed to the few rusty water faucets, in a futile effort to cleanse ourselves. Most of us suffered from chronic diarrhea that, if untreated, was almost impossible to clear up. Our mornings were not enhanced by the many bedbugs and fleas we squashed at night; it was hard to feel ready for the day. Even though I did the wash in the evening, losing out on some rest when the sinks were less crowded, the filth of the night made another attempt mandatory. So the day began with the fight for access to the cold-water faucets. Underneath these taps were long gray basins into which the precious water dripped but we had no plugs to prevent it from draining out. Perhaps these facilities were once suitable for the young soldiers who were housed here previously but they were totally inadequate for the thousands of us.

All our bodily needs had to be dealt with on the double because the next moment we had to queue up for coffee. It was basically tasteless water but at least it was warm. Hardly anyone had anything to eat. It was dangerous, if not downright impossible, to keep anything edible overnight. All would be stolen. Some who dared to sleep on a chunk of bread more often than not did not find it in the morning.

The official diet consisted of three meals, starting with an unsweetened substitute of black coffee in the morning. Lunch was a watery soup—euphemistically called lentil soup by the Germans—that occasionally contained some potato peels or small pieces of turnip. Supper was a thin piece of bread and the watery soup. If the cook distributing the soup was a friend, he ladled it out from the bottom where there might be slivers of turnip or potato peels, while a stranger would skim the soup from the top which was always clear. Once a week a piece of cooked dough was distributed that they called a dumpling. We were issued bread rations every third day amounting to one thin slice a day, sometimes less. For every meal the inmates had to queue up in long lines.

Actually, in the later stages of the camp's existence our diet improved somewhat, augmented by a sporadic spoonful of sugar or jam. Later we occasionally received a few pieces of horse meat stew called "goulash," and although it took some imagination to compare it to the dish by the same name, to us it tasted divine. With time the soups became less watery but the diet was still grossly inadequate, and inmates continued to suffer from acute hunger.

It did not take long for us to realize that if we could not supplement our rations, we would have a very short life expectancy. The inadequate amount of food was deliberately designed to shorten the lives of the inmates. Worse yet, the inmates' rations were further reduced by those who handled them along the way. Those who transported, cooked or handled the food ate at the expense of other inmates. They even managed to smuggle some food to their own loved ones. Every step of the way those who touched the lifeline used the opportunity to pinch as much as they could to provide for their starving families.

Fortunately, Eva's work was connected with the food supply. In addition, my advantage of working in the hospital was that, at lunch, the amount of soup ladled out corresponded to the number of patients of the day before, but more often than not many died overnight. Many of our patients were too far gone to claim their rations, and even with the arrival of new patients, we nearly always had some leftover soup which we divided equitably between the staff. In general, hospital staff was not entitled to extra rations: only those who worked for the German war production received supplemental food. It was this extra soup I was usually allotted in the hospital that allowed me to offer my bread rations to my ailing family or barter it for something extra to supplement our diet.

Another huge problem was created by our inability to buy new clothing. With time, what we brought from home became threadbare and torn. Most of our best clothes went to the Winterhilfe (winter help) organization in Germany. Lesser items were stored in the Kleiderkammer, a warehouse for clothing, shoes and blankets.

Officially, we could neither buy anything nor get any allotment of garments. The only way to replace items was through contact with those who worked in the warehouse where clothing was stored or to barter for it. With some ingenuity, inmates who worked in the warehouse stuffed items into their undergarments to smuggle back into the camp. There they would barter it for food. The highest value was placed on warm sweaters and coats, boots and shoes because, without proper protection, the bitter winter frost caused frostbite, and, later, gangrene often caused loss of limbs. It helped a great deal if one had a friend who worked in the Kleiderkammer or had some bread or cigarettes as bartering chips.

The chance to live another day demanded a strong will, contact with other inmates and a persistent determination to fight; daily we had to nurture the resolve to live. More importantly, one had to have a great deal of luck—not to be in the wrong spot at the wrong time; not to succumb to the chronic diarrhea which we called the terezinka or another illness; not to be deported east; never to withdraw into one's shell. It was usually the young and strong who managed to withstand pressure of such a magnitude. Luck, however, was the most important aspect of survival.

Death was omnipresent in Theresienstadt. Inmates could only pray that death would be merciful and quick, sparing them the agony and humiliation endured by the Musselmen. In the early stages of camp life in Theresienstadt we hardly knew the tragic figure of the Musselman. However, towards the end, they became a common sight. These were the "Siechen," a German term describing an old, worn, run-down, death-marked individual. These were shrunken, atrophied men and woman of indeterminate age, seemingly older than Methuselah. I do not know why we used the moniker Musselman for the shadowy death-like individuals who began to appear in the later stages of our camp's existence; perhaps because they were always wrapped in some rags. They were unique apparitions, specific to German concentration camps. There was no similarity between a normal human being and a Musselman. They lost all gender distinctions; they shuffled through the camp on their monstrously swollen legs, their soiled bodies wrapped in the remnant of some blanket, emaciated with expressionless eyes which were sunk deep in their sockets. They did not talk or think—they were too far gone to do either. Though obviously starving, they no longer had any strength to put up a fight for a morsel of food. They were oblivious to the world around them. Their only companions were the ubiquitous lice. These apparitions were the ultimate insult to the Almighty, that is, if He created humans in His own image.

There was not a shred of human dignity left to the Musselmen, who dragged their pained bodies through the camp, not caring that they were covered by dirt, that the sores which covered their emaciated bodies oozed puss, that their shaven heads wobbled on their thin necks. Their tormented bodies reeked and to make matters worse none of this seemed to bother them. They no longer belonged among the living but they were still not called into the Beyond. We all dreaded this state of absolute wretchedness, and we all hoped that death, if unavoidable, would take us before we suffered the same fate. It is for the many Musselmen that, I believe, the Nazis can never be forgiven, for they did not simply kill, they reduced people to depths until then unknown, and hopefully never to be seen again.

6

The Fatal Blow

Theresienstadt was bursting at the seams in the fall months of 1942. The daily harvest of death rose to such heights that the Germans realized the impossibility of burying the corpses in the mass graves. The mammoth congestion was caused by numerous transports of Austrian and German Jews, mainly of an advanced age. The situation became so appalling that in September alone, nearly 4,000 people perished, mainly because of hunger and the appalling and unsanitary conditions. To resolve the problem and clear up the backlog they ordered the erection of a crematorium. It was furnished with four furnaces that worked around the clock.

The story of the old German Jews is particularly revolting—typical of Nazi cynicism and malevolence. The representatives of the once respected and affluent Jewish community of Germany were advised by the Gestapo that there was a chance for the elderly to pay for a safe haven in a spa-like town organized and managed by Jewish administrators. There, those who could come up with the funds would have a chance to live out their days in comfortable conditions. Admittedly the fee was steep but it assured pleasant twilight years. Many sadly believed and rushed to scrape together the outlandish sum.

Some came up with the pile of money, pooling their resources, and were assured they would get their money's worth. They offered quite a sight, elegantly dressed in their expensive, old-fashioned, sartorial suits, wearing hats, carrying umbrellas and walking sticks. The ladies had on fine silk outfits, laced collars and matching accessories. The train that brought them in consisted of Pullman cars, and the passengers carried elegant cases and handbags. As they disembarked, we watched the show in total disbelief. We were amazed by their naiveté; they had no idea of what was in store for them. They requested rooms with a view of the lake, for which they had pre-paid in Berlin or some other specification with respect to their accommodations. The SS guards guffawed, much amused by their demands, and I have to admit that, at the time, we too thought that it was hilarious.

The Germans did not find it comical for a long time; soon they ordered all the old German Jews to be thrown into the attics or cellars of the drab houses that used to belong to the Gentiles. There in the indescribable filth, unable to fend for themselves, they died by the hundreds. The attics turned into a nightmare; the stench of decaying corpses permeated the camp. Those who were still alive lay in their own filth; most of them succumbed to the perennial terezinka (dysentery). We were not able to bury the piles of dead bodies fast enough.

The Germans were pleased with their ingenuity. How well they had squeezed the last hidden money from the old Jews by promising quiet and peaceful declining years! We became accustomed to their wretched apparitions as some of them staggered through the camp, uncomprehending and helpless. I am ashamed to say that we became used to their plight and suffering.

On one late September day, I ran into a cousin of my father, Dr. Karel Lustig, a laryngologist from Prague who had recently been interned in the camp and who was assigned to the same ward where I worked. We did not enjoy the warmest relationship because of the friction between him and Dr. Tarjan. He could not understand the nature of our relationship with and our dependence on Dr. Tarjan, whom he perceived as his personal nemesis. To my surprise, I saw that he signaled me to come nearer and I could not help but notice the expression of urgency in his face. He shared with me that the residents of Prague's old age home had arrived in the camp, which probably included my grandmother. The transport of those old and sick people was expected to continue east for extermination by gassing in mobile vans. While inspecting the sorry human cargo in Bohusovice, it was evident that most had passed away and the others would do so within days. The train was permitted to unload the people in Theresienstadt.

Dumbfounded, I ran to the Kavalier barrack where I had to search for a long time through a large number of bodies, scattered helter-skelter, most moribund in various stages of expiry. Finally I found my grandma. She was nearly at the bottom of a high pile, lying on a bare floor. She was still breathing but was mercifully deeply unconscious; her always slim body was emaciated, dehydrated and badly soiled. I would not have recognized her had she not been labeled, with her name written on her bare chest. Around her was scattered some soiled straw but "Omama" (that's what we called her in better days) laid prostrate on the hard ground.

Only one nurse was assigned to attend this tragic multitude of dying people. She pointed to a corner where I found some less revolting straw and I placed my grandmother there. At first, I tried to clean her, but this proved to be an arduous task. She had probably not been looked after for a long time, certainly not since the deportation from the old age home. Dirt was caked on her body and her hair was matted and tangled but fortunately she was oblivious to her pathetic and humiliating condition. I worked for a long time attempting to make her look somewhat respectable. I had to cajole the matron in charge of the barrack to let me have to water and rags to dry her body. Finally, when I thought that she looked less sickening, I went hesitantly to the Sudeten barracks to tell my father about the ignominy committed on Grandma. I feared his reaction; he seemed to have little reserve for further misfortunes. He loved his mother dearly and had spent a great deal of time, effort and money to secure her last years, all to no avail. I feared that the pain of seeing her in such a ruinous condition might further fracture his already weakened resistance.

To my surprise, he did not appear shocked. He only mentioned that he expected that to happen. He feared that Prague's old age home might meet the same fate as did similar institutions in Germany. As we walked towards the Kavalier barrack where Grandma was dying, Father was downcast. We both remained with Omama, sitting on the floor, until her peaceful death. My father held one of her hands and I gently stroked the other. She stopped breathing almost imperceptibly, leaving us in the most odious place and time in history. Death treated her gently and appropriately for she was a sweet and kind soul. Death allowed her to pass on without a struggle; it seemed a tranquil transition. Father closed her eyes gently, kissed her softly on her cheeks and said that it was a special gift of God to be released from this hell. When I kissed her cheeks, I closed my eyes, trying to recall her appearance in bygone days when I used to caress her. Back in the good old days she was always neatly groomed and scented with her favorite eau de cologne.

The next morning, September 30, we followed a hearse carrying the dead of the previous day to the fence of the camp. We had to remain behind while the sorry load proceeded to the nearby cemetery for a burial in mass graves. Grandmother is the only member of our family whose resting place is in the mass graves of Theresienstadt. The rest of my loved ones were cremated because the Germans had run out of space to bury the thousands who perished.

In course of the fall and winter of 1942, the frequency of the arriving and departing transports rose at an alarming rate. In spite of our privileged status exempting us from deportation, the somber mood affected us all. Most people around us were deported. Nobody knew when their turn would come, and we all dreaded the call for the journey to the killing camps in Poland.

To make matters worse, Mr. Bleha had all but vanished. Our anxieties were now aggravated by fear for his personal safety. We also sorely missed the little parcels with food he brought us which augmented our meager rations. Not even Dr. Tarjan had the slightest inkling as to the reason for his disappearance. Perhaps the mass arrests intimidated him, perhaps he had been denounced by someone for meeting secretly with Jews. Or was he moved far from the camp during the evacuation of the Gentiles in the summer of 1942? Was there a simple explanation or had he stumbled into harm's way? We missed him and worried about him for he was one of the few decent men who remained faithful to their Jewish friends and retained his past loyalties, even though he was aware of the perils that it entailed.

My friendship with Max continued, and it blossomed into a beautiful relationship. Max was a generous young man who tried to cheer me up by bringing me little gifts such as a small metal pendant profiling the skyline of Theresienstadt. On another occasion, it would be my initials cut from leather or some other trinket, all of which I keep to this day, knowing that he must have denied himself many bread rations to buy me these presents.

When we arrived in Theresienstadt, we were a lonely family. As mentioned, we were assimilated Jews and the camp's leadership was comprised of members of the Zionist movement. Friends and connections were essential for survival; a loner did not have a prayer there. In our early days in the camp I set out deliberately to make friends because our isolation was not conducive to survival. I befriended a number of people, some in positions of influence, and some holding the much-envied jobs in the kitchens or bakeries. Soon I felt as if we no longer were the loners, for now we had some friends we could turn to for advice or simply talk to a kindred soul. But it was always an unstable, changing scene, for people were deported, new transports arrived, everything was in a continuous state of flux. In spite of that, most of us made efforts to bring some stability into the daily routine of our existence. Even though we lived day to day we found ways to continue as best we could, to recreate a semblance of our past. To this end, courses were devised to teach children, lectures were given, some musical evenings were offered, recitals, concerts, and even operas were studied and performed. The inmates offered their talents and skills to improve the quality of life in the camp. Ours was a valiant effort not to allow the Germans to dehumanize us, strip us of our dignity and self-worth.

I too tried to pull my weight but was hindered by my long working hours and by my wish to share time with my parents who waited anxiously for their girls. I contributed by my assignment in the hospital where we needed superhuman efforts to nurse our gravely ill patients. I tried to take care of my parents too but it was clear the camp was taking its toll on us all.

During the first year of our imprisonment, my mom already showed alarming signs of deterioration. She suffered with frequent bouts of influenza, and I noticed that she was losing weight faster than most of us. I suspected that she passed some of her rations to Dad and I was determined to share as many meals with her as I could, to ensure that she did not short-change herself.

The greatest help came from Eva, who became very competent in organizing some produce while at work outside the camp, and we also received a few small food parcels. It remained a mystery who sent them but we hoped that it was perhaps someone delegated by Mr. Bleha. On occasion Dr. Tarjan would bring us some bread, and according to the camp rules, we never questioned the source. These were some of our better months in Theresienstadt. However, the situation took a turn for the worse at the beginning of 1943.

Eva became ill. Initially, she did not let on, refusing to admit any discomfort, trying to prevent Mother from worrying. But one morning she could not climb down the ladder from her upper third-tier bunk. Both her knees were badly swollen and she ran a high fever. Upon our urgent request, the Aelteste arranged for a visit by the barrack's physician. When he finally came, he did not have much to offer. Dr. Guttwillig did not climb up to see Eva; he just listened to her complaints and authorized her sick certificate, excusing her absence from work for the next three days. His medical advice was to apply warm compresses on her painful and grossly puffed-up joints. He had nothing else to give her, besides a few friendly, compassionate words. Even the applications of pads were not simple, for it was difficult to get access to warm water.

The next few days did not bring about any improvement. Just the opposite happened, more joints swelled up, became painful and inflamed. Filled with apprehension, I turned to Max, reporting to him that Eva's sore throat and high fever ran unabated. He came, almost running, climbed up and began to check Eva over. She was very apologetic, minimizing her problems, even suggesting that it was me who panicked and that she would be better in no time. It did not seem that Max agreed with her, for his face showed concern. Out of earshot of Mom, he told me that he was worried. He suspected that Eva suffered from rheumatic heart disease, a complication of strep throat, and that her condition gravely affected her joints and, worse yet, her heart. Had lightning struck me I would not have been more shocked. Max promised to do everything he possibly could and began to organize and plan a course of treatment for Eva.

The only trouble was that the required medication was hard to come by. Max managed to organize some aspirin and digoxin and conferred with the barrack physician how best to treat Eva. Max not only arranged Eva's transfer to the sick bay but also established some kind of a medical protocol. This proved to be a tall order, for the supply of drugs was erratic, and Max could not sustain a smooth flow of all he needed.

The patients in the sick bay had a bunk with a straw mattress which, although filthy, still provided some degree of comfort. As it was she still could not climb the ladder to her upper-level bunk. Mother began to organize a better diet for Eva, spending our last hidden money for what she could get in the way of nutritious food. Soon all our money was spent, and Mother indefatigably bartered, cajoled and even begged to get what she needed for her ailing child. One day she would organize an apple, and although green and not yet ripe, she cooked it, added some sugar and brought it to the sick bay. Or she would get hold of a cookie baked in the bakery which supplied the SS officers, and she would triumphantly rush with it to Eva.

Eva, however, was not responding; she did not look well. Max tried to comfort us, reassuring us that the slow progress was caused by the delay between the onset of the illness sometime in mid–February and the transfer to the sick bay in early March and that we would now see an improvement in her condition. But he never sounded very convincing to me. My parents and I kept exchanging our bread rations for different foods for Eva. We starved, worried, prayed, hoped and, at times, despaired. The physicians summoned by Max stood around her bed and appeared grave and solemn. They worried about the onset of complications of myocarditis, endocarditis and pericarditis. Throughout all this time, Eva grew skinnier and grayish pale, almost translucent. Mother sat by her side every minute. Both of my parents seemed to fade away; Eva's ordeal was more that they could bear.

Sometime in mid–April another complication worsened her already critical condition. She slipped into severe heart failure, a serious condition at the best of times. In Theresienstadt it was nearly a death sentence for there were no drugs to treat the accumulation of fluids. Eva became grotesquely swollen; her entire appearance became distorted. Her condition deteriorated further because of a massive infection in her right thigh. It was not only extremely painful but under prevailing conditions it was untreatable. Throughout her illness Eva had been running a high fever, but now she was truly burning up. Her lovely features almost vanished; only her large, dark shiny eyes were glowing, expressing endless sadness. On one occasion, when Mother was not at her bedside, Eva motioned me to come closer; she no longer had the strength to talk at an audible volume. She whispered haltingly that she knew that she was beyond help; she just wanted to remind me that it would become my sole responsibility to take care of our parents. With considerable difficulty, she asked me not to contradict her. She knew her time was short; she only wanted a promise from me to try to make up the loss our parents were about to sustain. I promised that and more. I would have pledged anything to give her some comfort. Inside I cringed with pain, hoping against hope that she was wrong.

A few days later, we all realized that she was not going to make it but we would not admit it, not even to ourselves. Filled with despair, we still tried doggedly to reverse the course of her illness. We strove to strengthen her by bringing her food; she no longer was able to digest or at times even swallow. We wanted her to fight the impossible odds, but she had no strength left and was fading in front of our eyes. Anyone who has lived through a similar tragedy can appreciate our heartbreak.

On the 20th of April, the physician of the ward made a last-ditch effort to help. He decided to open the throbbing infected thigh, hoping to allow discharge of the infection and to ease her ailing heart. They could not offer any anesthesia but I don't think that Eva was really fully conscious any longer. Following the surgical intervention we were allowed back into the crowded room, where the many cots were tightly packed side by side. Therefore, we had little room to stand. It was difficult to squeeze in. Mother was there every available second; she would not give up even a moment with her dying child. I replaced her at work as often as I could for I wanted to prevent the anger of her supervisor who could have had her deported for neglecting her assigned duties.

After the surgery, Eva seemed a little less restless. Perhaps the pain lessened or maybe she just was exhausted from all the torment. However, she did not respond to any stimuli. The wound yielded a huge amount of pus, leaking through and around the thick rubber drain inserted to prevent closure of the incision. The small room filled with the foul smell exuding from the bloody discharge. All the other women, gravely ill, squeezed into this airless room, were in a great deal of pain caused by their own near-death conditions but most complained bitterly about the added distressing stench, a few cursing us in rough language. Mother and I kept on cleaning, washing and changing the small pieces of rags, the only material we had to wipe off the malodorous discharge. We tried to wash and clean the gash in her thigh but there was an endless quantity spilling out of the emaciated and tortured body of my poor sister. Little changed over the next three days. Time ceased to have meaning while we took turns at Eva's bedside. But Eva grew weaker and became more removed from us. On Thursday, April 22, 1943, she took on the unmistakable look of impending death. Eva closed her eyes. Her breathing was labored and shallow; at times, it appeared to have stopped entirely.

I did not go to work. I sat there, next to Mother at the foot of Eva's narrow bunk. Father would periodically peek in, his eyes bloodshot. He would scan Eva's face fearfully. Mother was holding Eva's hand and the three of us sank into a deep, despondent gloom.

At times, the intervals between her gasps became longer, and I feared that she had died already. Then a moment later, she would take another breath, and for a moment I was grateful that she was still with us.

So we sat, almost in silence, hopelessly heartbroken and dispirited, until the time came when Father had to leave. Men were not permitted to stay in women's barracks after 8 p.m., no matter what the reason. Before Dad withdrew, he approached Eva's bed one more time. He knew she would not pull through the night. He bent down, kissed her sunken cheeks gingerly. He softly stroked her black, wavy hair and whispered a few endearing words of affection into her ear. Then he stumbled out of the room with his eyes filled with tears. During the entire ordeal of her illness none of us wept or gave in to self-pity but now the struggle was all but over.

The night wore on; Mother and I sat together, keeping our vigil. I did not have a deeply religious upbringing but that night I prayed fervently, sending silent prayers to the Almighty, begging, promising anything, offering my life in exchange for one more chance for Eva. Never have I prayed so passionately. I was still young and I believed that I could sway the odds if I only prayed hard for a miracle. No supernatural rescue was ordained for our Eva. Shortly after midnight the intervals between her gasps became even longer.

Mother took her into her arms, cradling her softly, stroking her hair and at times kissing her. There, embraced by her mother, she died around one o'clock in the morning. It was Friday, April 23, the day the Christian world marked the day of Christ's crucifixion. Suddenly, the sinister superstition of the old concierge in Prague came back to me: children born on Christ's birthday live a short life and die young and in pain. Eva was 18 years and four months old.

When the last pained breath was exhaled, Eva laid motionless. My mother sat as if struck by lightning. She was immobilized, despondent beyond tears. She kept on holding the lifeless body of her child for a long, long time. I do not know what thoughts went through her mind, if she reflected on our past or if she imagined the bright future all imagined for Eva. Now with her firstborn daughter dead, we knew that nothing would ever be the same. Or perhaps she just grieved the one loss no parent should be cursed to endure: the death of a child preceding the parent into the beyond. I did not dare talk to Mother. I wanted to ask her to let me wash Eva's tortured body, to put her to rest clean, her gorgeous hair combed the way she liked to wear it, but I could not summon the courage to disturb the last private moments Mom would spend with her.

My own heartbreak was deep and unimaginably painful. I nursed my pain and bitter grief of this abysmal injustice and the incredible pain of an irreplaceable loss. Eva was more than a sister to me; she was my companion and my confidant, my strength and my best friend.

The next day we buried her. We joined the procession of mourners behind the hearse loaded high with coffins, one of which was Eva's. At the fence of the camp, the throng came to a halt; from here on we could not follow. The bodies were transported to the crematorium. We stood at the fence, watching the rapidly vanishing cargo of death. We were overwhelmed with pain and despair. I knew that my parents had sustained a blow from which they could not recover. A big part of us had died with Eva.

A few weeks later, George Synek, my cousin and a fourth-year medical student who was assigned to assist in the morgue, gave me the final painful summary. While the task of the crew was mainly to pull out gold from the mouth of the deceased and check all cavities for valuables, the pathologist had permission to autopsy some of the bodies. George was enraged and filled with grief for the loss of his cousin, but he wanted to know if more could have been done. His report informed us that Eva's heart was destroyed by the complications of rheumatic heart disease, and had she survived, she would have been severely handicapped by her massively damaged heart valves. Oh, God only knows how I wished she were with us, and if it could not be in good health then I would have nursed her, taken care of her, no matter how crippled she might be; her presence would have been all that mattered. But it was not to be.

We could not adjust to life without Eva. We tried but it was an uphill battle. We missed her from dawn to dusk, and although we made valiant efforts to grieve privately, our cloaked heartache was obvious. It seemed that much of our cohesive strength left with her. She had brought much joy and optimism into our small family; she was cheerful, brave, diligent and resourceful. She was also intelligent, helpful and selfless. My parents were bereft, beyond consolation. Eva had made me promise to fill the gap, and I had to pull up and help my parents, although I did not feel equal to the task. It felt as though a drop of water should fill an ocean. Even though the months of her illness eroded our strength and took an enormous toll on our health, we still nursed a flicker of hope that she would recover. Her death left us devastated; we were no longer whole. There was a tear in the fabric of our family that could not be repaired.

My always cheerful and optimistic mother was changed. She stopped smiling; her eyes always seemed glistening, filled with unshed tears. She was beyond consolation for a long time. My father, who had lost most of his vitality even before this tragedy, was withdrawn and much too crushed to have faith in some nebulous future. As if all that was not enough, another tragedy was coming my way.

One morning during a surgery, I received an urgent message to come immediately to the barracks where Max lodged with a few other physicians. I raced there and found Max ill and in severe pain. He was feverish and in obvious distress. His colleagues checked him over and, by the time I arrived, they had made a tentative diagnosis of renal abscess.

He was carried over to the main hospital, where he became a patient of Dr. Braun. Somewhere his friends raised enough cigarettes to barter for the drug sulfanilamide prontosil. Unfortunately, they did not come up with a sufficient quantity for the treatment to be effective. Prontosil had the side effect of discoloring the complexion of the patient. The drug changed his skin to a yellowish-orange color. His looks changed to a distorted caricature of his normal self. Within a day or two he became a shadow. Half-heartedly, Dr. Braun suggested surgery as the only option, but one with little prospect of success. Max, who understood the medical problem, hesitated to subject himself to this last-ditch chance for recovery. The infection was spreading quickly from one kidney to the other. We also ran out of drugs and, once more, we watched helplessly as Max faded fast. Max's mother and I looked on in disbelief: this young man seemed in the best of health only a few days ago. While I sat at his bedside, I realized that there was hardly any chance to save his life. I made an effort to put on a brave front, mainly for the sake of his mother. She gazed at me, hoping to hear that her only child could be saved. Paradoxically, as Max declined, she got a better hold of herself, but I began to lose my fight against the endless sorrow that threatened to engulf us. The potential loss of Max, the man I loved dearly, filled me with despondency and anguish. Only a few short months had passed since Eva's death, and the imminent death of Max plunged me even deeper into the abyss. Max no longer resembled the man I knew. His looks, laughter, optimism, energy, love of life, all his glorious plans for our future, his medical career, all was gone. Everything lay in ruins.

A few days down the road, surgery was no longer considered an option. Max sank into a deep coma. Two days later, Max passed away, never having regained consciousness, never feeling the last kiss with which I took my leave from him. Broken-hearted, his mother and I walked behind the hearse, again piled high with those who had passed away on the same day as Max. I supported Max's mother, who staggered, half blinded by tears. She spoke to her lifeless son as if he could hear her. She whispered about her love for him, that he was all she cared about, loved and cherished in this world. I supported her with both my arms and wiped away our tears. I could not believe I was burying my first love, laying to rest our dreams for a shared future.

While our family sustained one disastrous blow after another, the camp underwent a few major shake-ups. The most important perhaps was the appointment of Professor Paul Epstein as the new Elder of the Jews. This piece of information shook us up badly, but in its wake came Dr. Tarjan's reassurance that Edelstein remained in the Council as Epstein's first deputy. Our lifeline, the Schutzliste, remained in place. All of that transpired while our entire attention was diverted by the unfolding drama of Eva's demise.

In our state of grief, we hardly noticed that the deportations had ceased and for the next seven months the ultimate threat was lifted, making the camp a somewhat more normal place. At that time, there were about 45,000 people crammed into the small town; even though it was cramped, the fact that the deportations were called off provided an almost idyllic break. Within these seven months, the Germans even transferred some war industry to Theresienstadt, opening a crate production. To this end, a large circus tent was erected in the central square and about 1,000 inmates were ordered to work.

The next sign of stability was the establishment of the camp's bank, hypothetically charged with the duty of handling the new currency which was specific to Theresienstadt. A strange collection of bank notes was issued in various denominations from 1, 2, 5, 10, 20, 50, up to 100 crowns. None had any value, and nothing could have been bought with it, but the institution had a calming effect on us, for it had a ring of familiarity, a feature of the past, only we had to overlook the eyesore on each bill, the face of Moses, disfigured with a long, hooked nose, adorned with a long beard and a luxuriant mustache, holding up the biblical tablets.

It was around that time that we experienced another heartening occurrence. A transport arrived from Westerbork, a Dutch transit camp, and it contained some well-known, famous Jews of Holland. We perceived their arrival as a good omen for certainly they were not destined for an immediate execution. Temporarily, we experienced some relaxation of our fears. That must have been the only time that we felt a sense of diminished danger. This period also marked the initiation of the train connection to Theresienstadt proper. Newly arriving transports no longer had to trudge the nearly three-kilometer distance, dragging themselves and their few belongings on foot to the gates of the camp.

All these improvements were almost lost on me. I was mourning the loss of Eva and Max. I felt defeated, filled with dreariness. Yet I had to pull up, for I had to provide and care for my parents who were devastated by Eva's passing. Therefore, I made a deliberate decision to meet people and attend some of the activities after work, but it was to no avail. I hardly enjoyed any of it because my pain went with me everywhere. The only time I was not hurting was at work, and I began to be grateful for the insane pace and demands of my assignment.

7

The Loss of Dr. Tarjan

Halfway through the summer of 1943, we heard rumors that the camp commander, Dr. Seidl, would be sacked. The news of Seidl's demotion would have moved few to tears; our only concern was who might become his replacement. Apparently someone much worse and gruesome was about to arrive. As always, the hearsay was correct. The appointment of Anton Burger spelled bad news indeed. He was known from his days in Brno for his brutality and sadistic savagery.

No sooner had Burger assumed his position than he issued an order for the dissolution of the Jewish guards of the camp, the Ghetto Wache, followed by the order they would be deported east in the next available transport. On the heels of these changes, the camp was hit by another shock in August of 1943.

Several months prior, outside the walls of the camp in a place called Kreta, a commando of young inmates was ordered to speedily build some barracks under the supervision of the SS. Then, on August 24, all inmates were ordered to remain inside their working places or their barracks (Kaserne Sperre). Every activity was banned, even peering out of windows. The slightest violation invited serious punishment. We all held our breaths, wondering what was in store for us. Most of us peeked out intermittently, filled with foreboding. Then they appeared, the trudging procession of youngsters who for some reason merited a very different treatment than the rest of their peers.

Some weeks ago word of mouth had it that the Nazis were seeking volunteer nurses for a special project. Those picked would ultimately accompany some VIPs to Switzerland. I mentioned it in passing to Mother and she became excited and insisted that I submit my name. I looked at her, not trusting my ears. She, who had always insisted on family unity, who wouldn't even register Eva and me for the kindertransport out of the country, would now want me to leave them? How could she trust the word of the Nazis? Then I began to grasp her point. Her faith in our survival had likely eroded, she had serious doubts that she and my father could persevere to the last, and it was her wish to save me, to give me a chance at life. Since Eva's death, she did a lot of soul searching, and the infinitesimal chance of Eva's life being saved by marrying the friendly Gentile boy likely bothered her. In the early stages of the Nazi persecution she came to believe that if we stayed together we could help each other and we would do better than each on their own. Remorse had eroded her shaky equilibrium and now she wanted to do what was right by me. I kissed her and told her to forget it. I would not budge without her and Dad.

On that August day I did not connect the order of Kaserne Sperre, enforced curfew, with the past canvassing of volunteers for some covert mission. I heard that quite a few nurses had jumped at the offer and also a few physicians were drafted. I wondered why anyone would place his trust in the Nazis and their promise of relocation into a neutral Switzerland. Little seemed less likely.

On the day of our forcible confinement I was not only curious but also impatient. What was afoot now? Periodically, I glimpsed out and then I saw them, a column of hundreds of children between the ages of four and 12 marching in the pouring rain, clad in soaked rags and guarded by a heavily-armed SS contingent. They were skinny, pathetic, holding hands; the younger ones were propped up by the older children. Who were these special kids who resembled emaciated, bedraggled ghosts, trailing on the road to the disinfecting and shower station?

Shortly before their arrival, a few physicians and some nurses were sent to Kreta, and the camp warehouse was also ordered to send the best available supplies and food to the new barracks. The nurses ordered to the shower station watched the petrified youngsters as they refused to undress, holding hands with each other. They clung to their filthy clothes which covered their tiny bodies full of oozing sores, enveloped in lice. Near the shower gates, they broke out in piercing cries, refusing to enter, screaming time and again one word only: "gas." Eventually, the staff pushed them into the showers and later led them away to their special, separate quarters.

The children remained isolated in the Kreta barracks for six weeks. They were better fed, well attended and gradually recovered, gaining not only weight but also some confidence in those who cared for them. The nurses and physicians in charge of the children were forced to live outside the camp and were strictly forbidden any contact with us. But Theresienstadt's walls were permeable: nothing remained secret and all orders were transgressed, so we too became privy to their tale.

The newly arrived kids were from Bialystok, a Polish ghetto. The Jews imprisoned there staged an uprising sometime in early August. The rebellion was brutally put down, the ghetto was torched and the handful of survivors were sent to extermination camps. Roughly 2,000 children were torn from their parents and sent to Auschwitz. The rest arrived in Theresienstadt. They received exemplary care. No one was harmed with the exception of those suspected of having a contagious disease and they were killed by order of the SS. Rumor had it that plans were in place for the Bialystok children to be exchanged for German POWs. The swap was sponsored and mediated by the Red Cross. Then, in early October 1943, in the early hours of the morning, the orphans of Bialystok departed. Along with them went the 53 attendants, physicians and nurses who were supposed to accompany them to the free world.

We were happy for them, hoping that the exchange of the kids for German POWs would pass without a hitch. Sometime later, hearsay reached Theresienstadt. All the orphans from Bialystok were murdered in the gas chambers of Auschwitz-Birkenau.

What went wrong? Why did the exchange not materialize? Why did the entire transport die in the gas chambers of Auschwitz? Even after the orphans of Bialystok were gone, their screams of the word "gas" when they first arrived rang in our ears for a long time. It brought a new awareness of our impending fate. We all heard and feared, but mostly we chose to deny, the persistent reports about the mobile vans gassing Jews upon their arrival in some camps. We preferred to live in the denial of such a calamity—the magnitude of which boggled the mind. The wholesale murder perpetrated by a nation deemed civilized in the 20th century? We knew little then of the Wannsee Conference of January 1942 that laid the groundwork for total annihilation of the Jews.

Under the new command of Anton Burger, the deportations from Theresienstadt resumed. Thousands were sent to Auschwitz. In early October 1943, a new transport arrived. Surprisingly, the new inmates were not shabby, hungry or frightened Jews. The transport was made up of well-fed and equally well-dressed people without any trace of past suffering. They did not even wear the ubiquitous Star of David on their clothes. Who were they? Were they Jews or some other nationality that displeased the demented dictator in Berlin?

The answer was not at hand for the newly arrived were led to a special quarter of Theresienstadt, until then inaccessible to Jews. But nothing remained hidden or concealed to the curious inmates, and we found out a day or so later. They were Jews all right, but Danish Jews who enjoyed the shelter and protection of their king, Christian X.

Those who arrived were but a fraction of the small Jewish community of Denmark. The majority of Danish Jews, some seven thousand or so, were spirited out of the country and into neutral Sweden. On the night preceding their deportation by the Nazis, the Danes organized an improvised flotilla which ferried the Jews into Sweden in anything that floated on water. A few could not be found and were apprehended by the Nazis the next day. But the noble king of the Danes had insisted on a German pledge that his Jewish minority would be allowed a permanent stay in Theresienstadt. They were to receive better shelter than the rest of us and the Danish Red Cross was authorized to supply them with food parcels on a bimonthly basis. These packages contained butter, jams, cookies and other delicacies, the kinds of treats we had not seen in years. To us, they became an instant aristocracy, living as close to paradise as you could get in Theresienstadt. The Danes were a class unto themselves, spared pain, fear, beatings and hunger. The only indignity imposed on them was the theft of their possessions after they wrote the compulsory cards about their safe arrival in "beautiful Theresienstadt." We all thought and marveled about the extraordinary qualities of the Danish monarch and his subjects. Though his country had been defeated in the war and occupied by the Nazis, the king faced up to their military conquerors and extracted the Nazis' promise to protect the weakest among them—the Jews. To this day, the word "Dane" means noble, brave and gallant to those of us who survived Theresienstadt.

No other Jews ever received similar treatment. However, initially, the Dutch coming from Westerbork were treated slightly better than the rank and file. But it all ended there for the Dutch Jews after they had filled out the compulsory cards; they were subjected to the same treatment as everybody else.

Most German concentration camps exhibited a predilection for the bizarre and insane. For example, in accordance with the German motto "Kraft durch Freude" (strength through joy), starving prisoners marched to the pleasing tunes and songs of the camp's orchestra. The same orchestra would welcome the returning work units 12 hours later. The engaging sounds of waltzes, harmonious arias and marches were in sharp discord with the exhausted men and women who carried the dead and dying and supported those who could no longer walk on their own. The rigid rules, a shining example of German perfectionism, dictated that everyone had to be brought back and included in the evening roll call, for the numbers had to concur with yesterday's census. But Theresienstadt even outdid the rest when it came to culture and caring as a means of survival.

In Theresienstadt, the inmates were supposed to live as trustingly and submissively as possible. To this end, the Germans permitted and openly fostered the Freizeitgestaltung (cultural and recreational activities). They thought that some semblance of normality might foster the belief we could see another day; this would lessen the chances of inmates staging a major revolt.

Even today I can understand why we had to make the attempts, if in vain, to keep and maintain the camp's functionality. We had to live there, but with hindsight, I believe that we should have faced up to the bitter reality. Some of us knew the distressing final purpose of our internment and the rest suspected it. I believe that we all guessed that ultimately the Germans would succeed in putting us to death. Little else could have resulted from their hatred. But we wanted to live, almost at all costs, and, therefore, we convinced ourselves that we had a chance and we nursed our self-deception with great diligence.

The Elder of the Jews and his Council were well aware of the mass annihilation in progress. They reached a decision, faithful to the then prevailing Zionist philosophy, to facilitate the survival of the strong few, a tiny nucleus of youngsters. It would be their duty to rebuild the decimated Jewry in its homeland, Palestine. The Yishuv was in full accordance with this plan; only a handful—if that many—could be salvaged from mass destruction perpetrated by the Nazis.

Jakob Edelstein, an ardent Zionist and believer of this plan, ordered that the rations of the youngsters be increased at the expense of the aged and weak inmates early on. He reasoned, and perhaps rightly so, that inmates 40 years or older were doomed anyway. He wished to support the chance of the young resilient individuals, thus promoting the survival of the nation. Once this philosophy was adopted, many decisions flowed from it.

The best buildings in Theresienstadt were reserved for the children's homes. These were two yellow buildings that were once officers' quarters. Youth, qualified as children under the age of 16, were ordered upon their arrival to be separated from their parents. The homes that sheltered them were equipped with the best the camp could muster. There were actually two homes, one for girls and one for boys, right in the center of the camp. The German-speaking children from Germany and Austria had their separate quarters. The youngsters received better bunks, blankets and care, but above all, their food rations were much superior to the ones of an adult inmate.

Caring for the youngest among us extended well beyond physical care; guidance and education were also provided, assuring the young inmates had at least some exposure to knowledge. Though the Nazis issued a strict order banning all teaching of Jewish youth, the children were taught a great deal in secret.

In retrospect it seems almost absurd that curricula were prepared with much care to include disciplines taught at various levels of the young children-prisoners. On occasion, erring on the side of safety, the lessons would be offered in rather unusual places like a broom closet or storage space. The instructors had to be on guard, for if an SS guard were to barge in the youth quarters, all hell would break loose. In the shadows of death and deportation, the youngsters studied, drew pictures, were taught songs and even prepared a performance of a children's opera, "Brundibar." The opera was chosen for its content; it boosted the morale and courage of the youngsters. The heroes of the opera were two children who had to fight a wicked organ grinder, Brundibar, who tried to thwart their efforts to provide for their ailing mother. At the end of the tale Brundibar was defeated, Good triumphed over Evil, reinforcing the daily hope for a better and just future in times to come. The many drawings of the children of Theresienstadt are today displayed in Jewish Museum of Prague, testifying to the indomitable spirit of the imprisoned youngsters and their dedicated teachers.

The battle of the will and spirit was not confined to the children alone. In Theresienstadt, gifted musicians created all types of compositions. From serious music to cabaret songs, they produced the full scope of musical creativity. Others entertained and educated through discussions about art and musicology. Different groups debated philosophy, politics, history, economics and many other subjects. People rushed to these activities right after work, as if life depended on them, and in a way perhaps it did. This was the only way available to forget the misery of the camp, fostering "mind over matter."

The Germans watched all this activity with amusement, unperturbed in their comfortable abode in the commandery, and pretended to ignore it. It was very much in their own interest to keep us diverted from despondent thoughts or acts until it was time to send us to the gas chambers. They could not be bothered to risk an uprising lest rebellious inmates might take some Germans with them to the Netherworld. The key was to keep us docile and submissive to the very end.

In early November 1943, there were rumors of a shuffle and some dismissals within the Council of the Elders. Apparently the intended victim was Jakob Edelstein, the first deputy to the incumbent Elder, Professor Paul Epstein. As was customary, many other heads would roll. We held our breath. We were concerned all along about the position of Edelstein. After Burger replaced Dr. Seidl as the camp's commandant, he displayed unconcealed contempt and hatred towards Edelstein. Perhaps it was Edelstein's personality that repelled Burger who always demonstrated the characteristics of an SS officer—brutal, rigid, primitive and uncultured. Edelstein was just nearly the opposite: a friendly, intelligent, competent man equipped with almost all the attributes Burger loathed and lacked. In addition, Edelstein hailed from Poland and, while German Jews were not considered human by the Nazis, Polish Jews rated even lower, right below scum. Whereas Epstein's use of the German language had a cultured Berlin sound, Edelstein, though in command of perfect German, had a soft Slavic accent, which supposedly was unbearable to Burger.

As first deputy of the Elders, Edelstein's duty was to receive German orders and forward them to the Elder. He in turn informed the respective departments responsible for the tasks ordered by the commandery. Burger accused Edelstein of providing cover for Jews escaping from the camp and of running a sloppy administration. Burger could have had him killed or sent away, but he chose to play it by the book. Edelstein was made responsible for the discrepancies in the numbers of the daily census. Burger knew only too well that it was out of the realm of any man to provide an accurate count of inmates every single day. The numbers changed steadily, due to death, arrivals and deportations, all of which allowed only for an approximate count. But Edelstein was accused of sabotage and covering up for several escapees from the camp. He was arrested, jailed at the commandery and deported to Auschwitz in 1943. His wife and son were sent to Auschwitz later and they would all be executed in 1944.

The bitter irony was that before the outbreak of the war Edelstein had made several trips to Palestine. In his capacity of a functionary of the Zionist organization, he did not have to return. But he wanted to help the beleaguered Jews of Prague and had forfeited his chance to remain in Palestine. He worked indefatigably for the Jews of the Protectorate and, during his service as the Elder of the Jews and later as the first deputy to Epstein, he remained decent and compassionate in spite of the enormous pressures exacted by his duties.

While Edelstein languished in jail in the commandery, Burger decided to establish the accurate census of inmates held in the camp. Burger, who was paranoid, decided to order a body count of all inmates, assembled in an open space. Early one morning, in November 1943, all inmates were ordered to march towards a nearby large field, actually a "Bohusovic hollow basin." At that time we were about 45,000 in number. We had no idea what was in store for us. Some claimed that we would be executed, and certainly, the massive presence of Czech guards, with cocked machine guns, did not boost our confidence. A plane circled overhead; the prevailing mood was ominous. We were ordered to form columns of five, standing in tight rows; talking or moving was strictly forbidden. We stood in that valley all day long while the counts were repeated over and over again without yielding a proper tally. Three independent groups, the Germans, the Czech guards, and the members of the Council of the Elders, tried to come up with the same results. The Germans made it clear that the task would be considered concluded only when all three parties arrived at the identical sum total.

That particular November morning was cold and rainy; icy winds lifted decayed leaves in a mad whirlwind, turning the valley into a surreal scene. We shivered, for our threadbare clothes did not offer much protection against the inclement weather, and we were overcome with anxiety, contemplating our uncertain future. We did not get anything to eat or drink all day long. Soon sunset was replaced by twilight, and people began to faint, keeling over onto the wet grass, where they stayed unassisted because we were ordered to remain at a standstill.

I stood next to Mother, who, though unwell, retained a relatively good composure. We exchanged silent glances, scouring the vicinity for any sign of Dad, but we could not make out individuals amidst the mass of people jammed into the basin. We were drenched, tired and despondent, for with every passing minute, we grew to believe that we would be shot. The counting went on and on. Every time they reached a total, it was different from the previous one; no counts tallied. The Germans were angry, screaming for yet another count, beginning all over again. While the darkness deepened, panic began to overcome us as rumors spread that our death was imminent. I remember the only thought of mine: Lord, please, if we have to die, let it be over and done with quickly. I glimpsed at my mother, who stood next to me and who became unsteady on her feet, wavering on occasion. In the twilight, I could support her secretly as the Germans could not see all that well.

I became alarmed that she might faint—or worse. Finally, around midnight, the Germans gave up and issued orders to march back to the camp. The field remained littered with scores of dead and unconscious bodies. We had to carry all of them back; they were an integral part of the camp's census. We were dirty with excrement for we could only relieve ourselves where we stood during this ordeal. Because none of the counts on that day agreed, the census was repeated later in the barracks.

Several days later, the camp was awash with news that Epstein had appointed a new Council. That was the worst scenario for us because of the domino effect. When the Council was toppled, all those who were appointed by it went down with the one-time leadership. We worried that the ripple effect might include Dr. Tarjan, for all who surrounded Edelstein became marked people.

Then, I knew very little of Paul Epstein, a former professor of philosophy at the University of Berlin. He had a deserved reputation as a man of cold, impressive intellect, reasoning and erudition. Later, I got more insight into his complex personality. A friend of mine, Helen, a woman of unusual beauty and charm, became his mistress. Helen's bunk was near mine for a while, but later on she moved to a small room in one of the houses of the camp that provided her with some privacy. Though she loved Epstein passionately, she had a few qualms about his character. But then again, who of us had the right to judge a man who lived on borrowed time, fully aware of his death sentence?

Every Elder of the Jews and the members of his Council were mindful of the fact that their stint in power would be short and terminated at the pleasure of the commandant. While in power these men wielded nearly absolute authority within the camp, uncontested by anyone, bar the SS officers. To live with a death sentence, yet to have so much authority, brought out strangely dictatorial reactions in some of them at times. They knew only too well what awaited those they dispatched to Auschwitz for they would inevitably have to join them for an unavoidable execution. They were simply not eligible for forced labor commandos; once they were demoted they had to die.

For us, this shake-up in the Council threatened our existence. Dr. Tarjan, though not an integral part of the Council, was intrinsically connected to it. I was nearly certain that he would be among those marked for deportation. At the beginning, Dr. Tarjan had been sheltered as a member of the AK1, Aufbau Kommando. This privilege was later withdrawn and those still alive depended on other means for shelter. Dr. Tarjan, as the physician-in-chief, was closely affiliated with Edelstein's Council and their fates were intertwined.

Thus, the fall of 1943 ushered in the doom of Dr. Tarjan and, consequently, the loss of his protective Schutzliste that sheltered our family. We were about to lose our mentor, the man who stood between us and deportation to the east. From that day onward we would inevitably join the innumerable thousands of deportees. I became frantic, fearing our impending deportation to one of the eastern camps.

While these changes were in progress, we had already been there one and a half years. During that time, my grandmother, my sister, and Max had passed away. There were losses that deeply affected all of us.

I began to accept that we all were going to die, the only question was when. I lowered my original ambition of securing our survival to one of alleviating our misery. Following a lot of thought, I reached the conclusion that I did not have the wherewithal to do it by myself. With Dr. Tarjan potentially gone, I had to befriend an influential person within the camp's administration, one who could replace Tarjan and avert the danger of our deportation. The first step would be to decide who the correct person was and then somehow gain his friendship. But that was not at all simple. In the volatility of the camp, someone who was powerful only yesterday could become the victim of a Weisung deportation and pull down all his dependents. I was also painfully aware that I had little experience in handling men, for at 17 years of age, I was naïve and guileless. I did not think that I was in the same league as the many attractive women who were older, sophisticated and manipulative—they had skills that I sorely lacked. They all competed for the handful of men in power to shelter them from the horrors of deportation.

Until that time we had been fortunate. I could stay out of the world of rivalries because Dr. Tarjan's generosity secured our stay in the camp and managed to supplement our rations marginally. Now the situation would change. I would have to find some protector. It was not a matter of morality or even self-control; I just did not know any other way out. I thought that none of this could be debated with my parents who seemed old-fashioned, never acquiescent to questionable needs mandatory for survival. I thought they just did not get it, that the time dictated different methods than they were accustomed to. Perhaps I was wrong. Today I believe that they might have understood. Then I decided to seek advice from Dr. Tarjan, whose insights I respected and cherished a great deal. Often in the past I would seek him out in his little room where he lived as the privileged hospital chief. There we openly discussed our problems and the strategies needed for contacting Mr. Bleha, and we planned the barter of contraband—in short, all the illicit steps imperative to our survival.

This time, however, I was filled with apprehension before the visit. I did not know in what kind of shape he would be in, for he knew the score all too well. I was shaken and worried, seeking guidance from a man whose days were literally counted. But I could not fathom our future uncharted by his competent stewardship.

Even though he expected the call for his final journey, he appeared outwardly calm and composed. He still managed a vague smile, probably to hearten my sagging courage. He began by telling me that he fully expected me to manage without him but that I would have to rearrange our defenses within the camp, for with his deportation all the protection bestowed upon us would be withdrawn. He was not optimistic about his own survival, and though his hints about the mass annihilation in the east were unspecified, they did not leave much room for doubt. Again he returned to his conviction that we were doomed, that it was not a matter of if but a matter of when, who, and where. In his closing remarks, he suggested that if, by some unlikely miracle, we were to outlive the carnage, he would hope to meet me in a more civilized world. I was overcome by sadness and a feeling of great loss. I believed that without him and his sharp insight, I stood little chance to survive in this rough jungle. All along I had felt that he alone stood between us and certain death. No matter how hard I attempted to control myself, I still shivered with fear, taking leave from the one decent man who had sustained us for more than one and a half years. Dr. Tarjan and I were about to part, when he seemed to sense the naked panic reflected in my eyes. He embraced me, kissed me gently and whispered some words of encouragement.

I never left his room that night. I could not part from him, not just yet, not for this one night. I longed for some miracle that I knew was unattainable. It was not a rational decision to get involved intimately for the first time in my life with a man who was leaving for an almost certain death. It must have been an impulsive act of trying to avert despair and feel safe, if only for that one night. Until then I thought of him as a dear friend only. I admired his intellect, energy and indomitable spirit that were awe-inspiring. I trusted him implicitly, and his resolve was one of a kind. He had also provided all the answers, support and resolutions for most of our problems since our arrival in this miserable place. He was a perfect friend in those rough and dangerous conditions, where life was always on the edge and survival was unlikely. He had an uncanny ability to distinguish between those with a potential ascendancy to power from those who were about to fall out of grace with the mighty Germans. He knew how to navigate the rough and tumble waters of the camp and to manipulate the odds in his favor. That is, until now.

In the course of Dr. Tarjan's last week in the camp, when our relationship changed so abruptly, he devoted all the time he had left to me. I felt that without his assistance I could not single-handedly provide for my ailing parents. So he prepared me for his absence by tutoring me what I needed to know to manage without him. He warned me about many potential dangers. He introduced me to the few trusted contacts he cultivated in the camp. In short, he did as much as he possibly could to provide me with a manual for survival.

Time was racing by and soon the last night of his stay in Theresienstadt was at hand. On his last night in the camp, he continued to brief me on every contingency that might confront us in the future. One of the instructions he gave me was not to count on Mr. Bleha any longer for he must have been caught or denounced by someone for aiding and abetting Jews. Dr. Tarjan felt that if Mr. Bleha were alive he would have given us a signal. We knew that if Mr. Bleha had been caught or charged in connection with assisting Jews he would have been sentenced to death without a chance for a reprieve. He made me memorize all he said; nothing could be written down as such a scrap of paper could have fallen into the wrong hands and brought disaster to many. I tried to pay attention and memorize well all his admonitions but I was partially paralyzed by fear and dismay. His imminent exodus sent shock waves through my system.

I tried to take it all in as I listened to his calm voice, but all I could muster was the horrific thought that perhaps by this time tomorrow, he would be dead, gassed in Auschwitz. He did not stand a chance for he qualified as a member of Edelstein's clique who were all summarily branded with the infamous "SB" for Sonderbehandlung. Tarjan impressed upon me not to associate with the members of the incoming Council. He had some information suggesting that the SS commander, Burger, would be replaced in the not-too-distant future because his primitive ways were incompatible with some imminent changes that were in store for Theresienstadt. He hinted at some chance of an international inspection that would be preceded by major shifts of inmates as well as the members in the command post. It was only a logical assumption that the new SS commander would dismiss the incumbent Council and install a new one. Dr. Tarjan reminded me of the domino effect and its consequences.

Then, in the already twilight shadows of the fateful day, Tarjan gave me instructions for the eventuality of our deportation. Should I find myself in another camp, I should, if at all possible, avoid being loaded onto a truck or a lorry. I should always volunteer to march on my own, I should always state nursing as my profession, and, if there was some selection or inspection, to always stand straight, try to look wholesome, reply in a firm but polite manner to all questions directed at me. Tarjan emphasized the importance of a proper posture while in front of an SS man. I should stand straight but not to appear arrogant, when talked to I should look into his eyes, and if not addressed, direct my gaze at the tip of my shoes. He made me stand up and act out my bearing at a potential selection. I had to repeat it a few times before he was reassured that I had grasped the proper carriage. My mentor suggested that anyone who wore glasses or had a hunched bearing was a contemptible intellectual who would be deemed material unfit for life in the eyes of the SS. All that made sense to me; the Nazis hated intellectuals in general and loathed the Jewish variety in particular.

Respecting the steadfast rule of the camp, I never asked about the sources of his information because the less one knew, the less one could disclose if questioned under duress. But I always knew that among the many contacts Dr. Tarjan cultivated, some of them were in the German command post. There were substantiated rumors that the SS enriched themselves by brisk transactions in jewelry and hard currency which the desperate inmates smuggled in and were keen to exchange for food. The power of greed outweighed the apprehension caused by the grave risks of such perilous conduct. Some of the SS officers lined their pockets handsomely, but they were cautious, dealing only with a handful of trusted Jews. Dr. Tarjan was undoubtedly one of them. I will never know for certain but he always knew what would happen and his information mostly proved correct, even if sometimes it was not immediately obvious.

That very last night, in spite of all his serenity and reassurances, I felt as if an enormous pit was opening beneath our feet into which we would tumble and be buried. Only then did I realize how much I leaned on him and how helpless I would be in his absence. I tried to convince myself that if anyone had a chance of surviving, it was Dr. Tarjan. I wanted to overlook the fact that he would probably be gassed without selection, right along with the rest of the Council.

During our last session, Dr. Tarjan advised me to leave the hospital assignment if possible; it would no longer serve its purpose as a shelter from deportation. It was Dr. Tarjan who had passed me off as a nurse, highly important to the smooth functioning of the camp's hospital. Whoever was to replace him would not continue this charade. It was Dr. Tarjan's idea that I should try to get assigned to kitchen work to avert or ease our starvation.

On the gray morning of his deportation, we received one piece of consoling news. Dr. Tarjan was not included in the same freight car with the Council into which Edelstein was led, handcuffed, from his jail cell. Dr. Tarjan was deported with some other lesser officials. Perhaps that offered him a chance to go through selection and be chosen for hard labor? Given that chance, he would pass, for he was in good shape and looked like an excellent candidate for work in quarries. That would have been the best of all possible scenarios under those circumstances.

The hour for boarding the boxcars arrived and the deportees were pushed at top speed on the waiting train. The process was accompanied by the usual hysterical screaming whereby the Czech guards tried to impress or outdo the SS who had their guns poised. The SS officers were restraining the snarling German shepherds whose howling and barking only added to the eerie, frenzied atmosphere. All this elaborate performance was staged to intimidate and frighten the inmates, as if they were not sufficiently scared. All that was a show of what the Nazis believed was the proper conduct of a superior race, having to handle the lowest of the species.

I was hiding in a dark corner of the barracks and watched as the train was loaded. I saw the man to whom I owed so much, walking quickly towards the train. He looked so fit and so young that I kept on repeating silently to myself that he just might make it. Unfortunately, like most, he did not! After the liberation, I began the search for those I loved and who had not returned yet. In spite of my laborious efforts, I never came across a soul who could remember Dr. Tarjan at Auschwitz. The official card indexes of the Czech Jewish community, as well as the archives of the Kibutz Givat Chaim Ichud, claim he died on October 16, 1944, in Auschwitz. Does that indicate that he passed selection and slaved for some time in that inferno and only then died or was gassed? Or was there an error in the date of his recorded death and was he murdered immediately upon arrival as were all the members of the Council?

Most likely I will never find out. I often think of him with deep gratitude and I cherish his memory. If not for him my parents and sister would have died in the gas chambers in Auschwitz. And if it hadn't been for Tarjan and Bleha all four of us would have died in the mobile vans of Small (Mali) Trostenec in May 1942. My family were ill, malnourished and exhausted, but they were able to retain some of their human dignity. At least they did not die like Musselmen or exterminated like vermin. For all that I am indebted to Dr. Tarjan and Mr. Bleha, of blessed memory. For all those years that passed from the end of the war, I always found comfort in that one single advantage bestowed upon my loved ones.

Tarjan and millions like him do not have a resting place where one can go to pay their respects, remember and place a flower or a small stone. In lieu of a grave or a tombstone, I had placed a small plague on a wall of the Holocaust memorial in Toronto in honor of Dr. Robert Tarjan.

8

From Bad to Worse

It did not take long for the consequences of Dr. Tarjan's departure to affect us. The issues he foretold came to pass. We were enrolled in every transport to Auschwitz. Every day presented a new and more difficult challenge. I had to mount a valiant struggle to forestall our death. We had no valid pretext for being important to the German war production, the single most effective reason to stay in Theresienstadt. There was no member of the new Council to protect us; we now joined the pariahs of the camp, the anonymous mass targeted for deportation. Whenever I pondered a new avoidance strategy of the myriad threats looming over an inmate, I remembered Dr. Tarjan and how good we had it while he looked after us. I began to look back on the days of Dr. Tarjan as the good old days and, all in all, they were indeed better than the period that followed his deportation.

To make matters worse, my father's health continued to deteriorate in spite of my mother's valiant efforts extended to keep him going physically and emotionally. He suffered from recurrent kidney infections which resulted in lengthy admissions to the camp's hospital where Dr. Braun looked after him. On occasion, Dr. Braun would use the declining condition of my father to place him in the category of dying patients, unfit for deportation. On other occasions, Dr. Lotorejcik, another friend of mine, would provide some cover for us, arranging a stay of deportation, but our existence in the camp hung by a thin thread. I was haunted day and night by nightmarish scenarios of our being hauled to a boxcar on the way to our execution.

Our struggle to prevent deportation and avert death by hunger or disease was so all-consuming that there were days when I doubted the rationale of this fight, and often I doubted that I had the strength to carry on much longer. I thought that the best would be just not to get up, to remain in the bunk, lying there, wait for the deportation and accept the consequences. But I had two old, weak and dependent parents. It was but a fleeting wish, borne out of fatigue in our hopeless fight. I quickly dismissed such defeatism, got up and began to hustle for the means of securing our survival. Had I then met the Devil, I would have sold him not only my soul but my tired body as well. If only he would have helped me. Often I heard judgmental comments of what we should have done during our imprisonment, all the brilliant suggestions after the fact about how we should have defended ourselves. I rarely commented but I always thought, "How dare they? What do they know of all the pain and misery inflicted upon innocent civilians, unaccustomed to physical violence who could not appeal their death sentence?" The Monday morning quarterbacks are the most annoying individuals to put up with.

At one point I thought that I had found someone worth befriending on the new Council; Hans Braun, a German Jew, was interested in helping me. Several times he arranged our removal from the transport list to Auschwitz, just before we were about to be jostled into the freight cars. He had a difficult time, however, for he had no official reason why we should remain in the camp. He kept on insisting that I marry him which would have placed us in the category of those who were affiliated with the protected Council. I was so despondent and tired that I toyed with the idea of consenting but then I recalled the wise words of caution of Dr. Tarjan reminding me of the transient nature of this Council. It was my fatigue of this uphill battle which made me prone to give in to what appeared to be the easiest way out of insurmountable difficulties. But then came a more sane moment and I recalled the perils of becoming tied to a member of the Council of the Elders when a reshuffle of power might be imminent. I saw in front of me the sober and clever face of Dr. Tarjan, and, faithful to my resolve, I followed the route he had charted for me.

I should add a word about the camp's weddings. Marriages between inmates became a part of the sham of the Freizeitgestaltung, the so-called social and recreational activities. The weddings, permitted by the SS commandant, were basically unions of deaths. People decided to marry chiefly for the reason to leave the camp together. Another motive, usually futile, was the wish to protect the other, more vulnerable person from deportation. Some young couples nourished the foolish hope that if married they might be allowed to stay together. The Germans certainly loudly promised this.

While all married couples were separated upon arrival in Theresienstadt, it appears brainless in hindsight that many believed that there was a camp offering a nearly normal life somewhere. Humanity's wishful thinking and self-deception is boundless. It was in the interest of the Germans to lull us into believing that somewhere in the east we might resume a near-normal life. The more we hoped the less likely we were to commit acts of rebellion, punishable by death. Therefore, the Germans permitted several features compatible with civilian life such as a limited pursuit of recreational activities, marriages and, on a very limited level, religious worship. Germans not only permitted the ludicrous show of weddings, they also even allowed us to choose between a civil marriage and a traditional, religious version of one.

The civil marriage was just an official declaration of intent to marry: the so-called Eheerklarung declaration of marriage. The names of the bride and groom were placed on a joined card index of the administration and the couple was, for all intents and purposes of camp life, considered married and eligible to be deported together. The other version resembled a traditional ceremony under the chuppah (the canopy) officiated by a rabbi. There were always several rabbi-prisoners at any one time in the camp. I do not know how many weddings took place in Theresienstadt, but I suspect only a few.

Again, these recreational activities served as diversionary tactics to lull us into a false sense of security. There were few among us who knew for certain the horrendous truth—only the members of the Council of the Elders and some prominent individuals (e.g., Leo Beck, the former Chief Rabbi of Berlin). Even Dr. Tarjan, who knew full well about the extermination camps in the east, never admitted to it openly. Only to me did he hint at the truth. He repeated many times over the instructions on how to pass a selection successfully. He tutored me not to admit my age, but to say that I was 20 years old, healthy, fit for any work, a nurse by profession. He rehearsed with me how to appear to be an efficient slave. He stressed to me that I had to appear as neat as possible and to never, absolutely never, be attached to an older, sickly or unfit person! Never stand in proximity to a child who could be potentially interpreted as mine. During the selection I should not assist anyone; I should step in front of the selecting officer alone, polite and quiet, answering only when spoken to. Never was I to accept a ride on a truck or any other car if there was an option: the mobile vans were a death sentence. Dr. Tarjan refused to elaborate, and as I said before, and in camp one did not query. Dr. Tarjan always alluded to our only chance: the war in progress that might bring the Nazis to their knees before they murdered us all. Otherwise, he stressed that all of us would perish—there was no reprieve for the Jew.

I do not know how many of those who were affiliated with the Council knew the full truth. Many heard the shocking facts from the escapee from Auschwitz, Siegfried Lederer, who sneaked in to Theresienstadt, hid there and shared the ugly truth with others in the camp. He warned openly about the mass gassings in Auschwitz-Birkenau. The Council of the Elders wanted to hush this information. A potential rebellion staged by desperate inmates would have led to the eradication of Theresienstadt. Fearing German retaliation, the Council ordered Lederer to leave the camp's hiding place. Fortunately Lederer survived the war and testified to the abominable treatment by his fellow Jews who were concerned exclusively with their own immediate safety. Most of the inmates dreaded the truth, and in order to live for the day, most opted to suppress what boggled the mind. Council members in turn attempted to quash any circulating rumors. But I believe that they violated their integrity by preventing the truth from becoming known. The denial of the mass killings of the Final Solution remained in place until the end of the war.

Much later, when arguments and accusations were leveled against this suppression of the truth, those in the know tried to justify their position by arguing that they were motivated by the minuscule chance for survival of a few; in a rebellion everyone would have been killed. Were not the ghettos of Warsaw or Bialystok destroyed and the inmates murdered? Although that is true, I believe that we had the right to know and decide which way we wished to go.

The year of 1944 came and little changed in the bleak outlook for our family. Father's condition was dreadful. With pain in my heart, I had to admit that he was now a Sieche, an old man, done with life. Only Mother could not give up on him. It was painful to watch her stubborn efforts on his behalf which took such a terrible toll on her already weakened health.

She was extremely thin and suffered with recurrent bouts of fever. I worried a great deal about both of them and decided to follow Dr. Tarjan's advice and try to find an assignment for kitchen work. I needed to secure more food for my parents. While I was grappling with a multitude of personal problems, the revamping of the camp began in all seriousness. It was impossible to decipher what was in store for us upon completion of the remodeling. The transformation raised an inevitable question in all our minds: Why?

Why would the Germans encourage the formation of a soccer team? Or convert a ramshackle hut into a coffeehouse for the inmates? The changes were fantastic and hardly comprehensible. Then we learned through the grapevine that some commission would visit the camp and all the upgrading and improvements were meant to convince the world that we were treated well, that the nasty rumors about Jews being starved, tortured and killed were only malicious slander. This gossip really surprised us. Could it be that the world had awakened and really wanted to know how we were treated and, if so, why now? For the longest time nobody cared. Did they belatedly remember that there were once a people called the Jews—hardworking, well educated, intelligent and devoted to the good of the countries they perceived as their home? Could it be that now, in 1944, the world had woken up to the reality that our only guilt was the accident of our birth?

In the early months of 1944 few doubted the importance the Nazis placed on their new pet project: the beautification of the camp. It was obvious that everything would be subordinated to this—and, to us, a mystifying—undertaking. I pondered the enigmatic warnings by Dr. Tarjan who predicted all this several months ago. How could he have known all that was projected for the future? He foretold the changes months before. Only the Nazis were privy to these plans at that point so it follows that Tarjan had to have contacts among them.

The first victim of this metamorphosis was the commander, Anton Burger, who was so crude and rough that the SS felt he could not be entrusted with the camp's facelift nor could he be expected to welcome distinguished foreign visitors. No one regretted Burger's departure; only later did we realize that he was exceptionally lucky to be recalled at this time. He left for Greece, then Hungary and Germany, so it became his good fate that he disappeared after the war's end and eluded justice, a feat he could not have accomplished had he still been the commander of Theresienstadt. The inmates anxiously awaited the new commander and worried about his temperament and disposition.

Our family situation consumed all my concentration, preventing me from paying much attention to the dramatic improvements unfolding in the camp. Our food supply hit rock bottom. I searched desperately for a job connected with food handling, no matter how lowly. I no longer cared. I only needed a job where I could organize some additional provisions. Finally, assisted by some of my friends, my struggle paid off and I was accepted as kitchen help. It was to be hard work—I had to scrub the huge barrels and cauldrons—but I did not mind. I was happy, hoping finally to add to our diet. I started to believe that we had turned a page in our battle for survival; there seemed to be a glimmer of a chance to lessen our suffering. Even the dream which haunted my tired sleep in Theresienstadt returned less frequently. I used to dream that I got hold of a loaf of bread—a big, round, fresh and crisp one. I could have sworn that I even smelled the fragrance of the freshly-baked dough. This entire loaf was all mine; I could eat it all myself. But as I was ready to take the first bite, an invisible hand snatched it away and I was left empty-handed and hungry.

Back then, bread (even the mucky kind we were allotted in camp) was the unattainable luxury for I could not keep mine as this was the only bartering chip I had, allowing me to get something for my parents. This was the period of my incarceration during which I was always ravenously hungry in the worst possible way. I lost a lot of weight and began to fear that I might fall victim to starvation. Today it is difficult to adequately describe the level of hunger we experienced in the camp. Hunger dominated our minds and bodies. It became an all-encompassing need that drove us in search of something edible. Nothing else mattered. Hunger stripped away most inhibitions, the thin veneer of civility, forcing decent people to theft and later to violence. It overcame any other consideration, overwhelming and crushing its victims. In Theresienstadt, food was stolen whenever the opportunity presented itself, and later, when the death-march inmates reached the camp, people even killed for it.

In the hospital, the physicians discussed food, their favorite delicacies, the ingredients needed, in vivid detail. This physical and nostalgic longing masochistically increased their hunger pangs. Before the inmates sank into a stupor, when death approached their famished bodies, all they desired was food. Every fiber of our bodies seemed to scream for something to eat. It was the protracted starvation the Nazis inflicted upon us that reduced us to indescribable suffering before death mercifully released us from our bondage. Long-term starvation was the cause of the many ailments, ravaging the inmates' ranks. We all suffered with dysentery, endemic to the camp, and we had festering sores, carbuncles and furuncles that filled with pus caused dreadful pains. The lack of vitamins caused night blindness and many inmates developed pellagra. There was a host of other sicknesses we were afflicted with, most caused or aggravated by malnutrition and substandard living conditions.

The camp's famine generated yet another feature: the more visible presence of the remaining old German Jews who hung to life by the skin of their teeth. They offered a pathetic, heartbreaking sight. Unattached and unassisted, they suffered from terrible hunger which chased them out of the miserable attics and cellars where they lived, jammed with other old people. Their bodies were covered with fleas, bedbugs and lice. They staggered along, unsteady on their wobbly feet, holding on to the walls of the houses as they swayed, near death. The all-powerful hunger forced them to wait patiently alongside the long queues during the distribution of the watery soup. Although their clothes still betrayed a past elegance, they were unkempt and soiled. Most were emaciated and stooped; their faces could not hide their embarrassment. They were aware of their dripping noses and eyes and the fact that they had nothing to wipe off the trickle. Moreover, they knew that they were no good at beggary. This, then, was Europe's former intelligentsia: distinguished, illustrious university professors, physicians, lawyers, businessmen, and writers now reduced to derelict panhandlers begging for a spoonful of so-called soup.

Still today I can hear, ringing in my ears, their cultured German, as they asked those lined up their only question. They hardly looked into anyone's eyes, their heads slightly tilted, with an embarrassed expression, and they repeated over and over, "Nimmt der Herr die Suppe? Oder die Dame?" Loosely translated it meant, "Could the gentleman or lady spare the soup?"

The Germans must have rejoiced, for they deracinated and reduced the Jewish elites to beggary as a payoff for their dedicated devotion to and hard work for their much-loved German fatherland. We, the young, hardened by our suffering, thought of them as a nuisance. Some of us, however, would give them part of our tepid soup, something I simply could not afford to do. I only felt relief that my parents were not among them, and it strengthened my resolve to provide for them at all costs.

My new job in the kitchen nearly worked a miracle for our morale. Even Father smiled when I whispered intently into his ear that better days were on the horizon, for our fare might improve as early as next week. I was hired and asked to report for work immediately; the last remaining hurdle was my release from the services of the hospital, a mere formality, or so I thought.

I was in shock when the secretary of the physician responsible for health care replied to my polite request to leave with a flat "No," adding tersely that my demand was out of the question. For a moment, I believed that she had misunderstood me. Perhaps my lifelong habit of speaking at a fast clip had garbled my request and so I began all over again. She, in turn, sat there rather rigidly, let me rephrase my request and again replied with a curt "No." I felt my anger rising but I was well aware that exasperation was a luxury I could ill afford. Politely, I asked her to let me speak to Dr. Munk, the man in charge of the camp's health care. I was confident that he had overheard our conversation. The small desk which represented his office was behind a few planks next to the desk of his secretary, Ms. Jelinek, who so flatly rejected my request. He let me wait for quite a while, and when he stepped out I put forth my best effort to explain our catastrophic situation. I no longer asked him, I begged him to release me from my commitment to the hospital.

Erich Munk, in whose hands rested the fate of our family, was relentless. His face was stern and I could not detect a shred of compassion; his handsome features remained unmoved, as if carved from stone. In days bygone I had a good rapport with him and he always expressed satisfaction with my work. He was about 40 years old, very efficient, a good organizer, and an opinionated man. Erich Munk was a cold man in a cruel environment. There were moments when he was charming, exuding wit and ready with a clever repartee, but mostly he displayed a lack of empathy and compassion. As a powerful member of the Council, he was accustomed to being spoken to with a great deal of respect, but because of his position, his life also hung in the balance. Perhaps a man who knew that his days were counted was not given to kindness. He listened without interrupting me and then replied that what I was asking for was impossible to grant, it was out of the question. He continued to explain that the camp did not have any trained surgical nurses and that I, who had been working in that capacity for two years, could not be replaced. He added with some malicious irony, just as an afterthought, that I benefited from my work through Dr. Tarjan, who used this pretext of my indispensable performance as a shelter from deportation east. Then Dr. Munk's voice became cold again, impersonal and official when he reiterated that his only concern was the smooth functioning of the camp's health care, and he was not going to accommodate my private problems at the expense of functionality of the hospital.

I tried again, promising to resume my duties in the hospital if and when my parents' health stabilized. Then I begged him with tears in my eyes, losing my grip on the situation, all to no avail. He declared our conversation over, turned on his heel and left. Though my eyes were filled with tears and I was enraged, I still noticed that he was not quite at ease with his decision, but his secretary, Ms. Jelinek, flaunted a sarcastic smile, watching my frustrated misery. We sure had our share of mean wretches among us.

I still did not concede defeat. I just could not admit that I was so close to my goal just to get thwarted by Dr. Munk. I returned to the barracks, sipped my soup and tried to smile at Mom who looked worried, pale and far too thin. I racked my brain for a solution to this impasse. I had little time left for I had only two days before the start of my kitchen assignment. Then I had a brainstorm: perhaps the Elder of the Jews would help me. He might find compassion in his heart or understand my predicament. Without delay, I set out for the Magdeburg barracks, the place where the Elder had his office.

Soon I found myself sitting in the tiny corner in the office of Professor Epstein, talking to him about my problems and my confrontation with Dr. Munk. While I spoke, I watched his friendly smile vanish and I began to feel the chill—a portent of my impending failure to convince him. Then I fell silent, experiencing the tense fear of one who was about to hear a verdict of a death sentence. I looked searchingly into his face which again sported a friendly smile. Then he began to talk, saying how much he would love to help me, but it would be inappropriate to overrule Dr. Munk on health-care matters, a department that was his sole responsibility. Again I felt that these members of the Council were crazed with their power. How could he speak of propriety in a concentration camp with the unruffled voice of a board executive presiding at a corporate meeting? Was there not a shred of normality and compassion left in these Council members?

He must have noticed my frustration because his smile became warmer, a mixture of mockery and sympathy, and he offered his last-ditch advice: "A beautiful girl like you should not have to worry about food in a place like this. You must be aware that there are men who in many ways could take that burden off your shoulders?" While he spoke, he put his arm around my shoulders, perhaps trying to suggest that he would not mind being one of them. At that moment, I was so furious that I just got up and ran out. I hated Epstein, Munk and the entire crew of prominent and powerful men who tried to save only their nearest and dearest. Infuriated as I was, I could not distinguish then that perhaps none of us would have been different in their positions; the stakes were so high that it was impossible to deal with sentiments for others outside our inner circles. At the time, I thought that Epstein was living proof of Masaryk's truism, "Every nation has the Jews they deserve." In my anger he appeared imbued with all the vicious and base characteristics of his host nation: the Germans. In retrospect, I apologized for this cruel accusation. He perhaps was not a monster but only a man who had to narcotize and extirpate all sentiments lest he lose his balance.

The thought of giving up returned again but then I would remember the cautious words of Dr. Tarjan and his warnings that this Council would be a short-lived one and that it was likely the new SS commandant would choose another Elder. Perhaps the next administrator, I thought—still optimistic and naïve—might be a more considerate and compassionate man?

Our woes continued unabated but a few friends helped me to care for my parents. There was Josl, the simple boy from Ruthenia whose cunning and street smarts were unmatched, even in Theresienstadt, where these were the only life-saving skills. He secured for himself a position in the camp's bakery, the one which provided baked goods for the commandery, where he masterfully organized food that we inmates never got to see. On occasion, he would bring me a piece of cookie or fish—to us they were great luxuries. Josl was in normal days a skilled cobbler and he supplemented his sustenance by sewing the high boots for the SS. Josl did not suffer deprivation in Theresienstadt and he loved to assist me in my frantic hustle for food. But for my parents it was all too little, too late.

In February 1944, the new and last commandant of the camp arrived, Karl Rahm. He seemed a nonentity, and there were no rumors connecting him with brutality, horror and sadism. Still we were filled, as always, with apprehension about this new master of our destiny. All we knew was that he was a trained mechanic and that he hailed from Austria.

Early in 1944, my dad's health gave new reasons for concern. Father became gravely ill and was brought to the hospital. He was depressed and unwilling to continue a struggle which he believed had been lost long ago. While he was confined to the hospital bed, we were once more summoned for deportation: destination Auschwitz. It became almost routine; we were included in every deportation order. On that occasion, it was less complicated to claim our stay because Dr. Braun listed my father as moribund, and the rules forbade deportation of those whose life was coming to an end.

Mother was automatically exempted, and it was only me, then almost 18, who would have to leave. I did not succeed in getting my name removed from the list and I had to present myself at the loading station. It was with a heavy heart that I was readying myself. I knew when I kissed my father that I would never see him alive again and it was even more difficult to leave Mom, for she would have to shoulder the responsibility for Dad and I feared that she had neither strength nor health to do it. The dark thought crossed my mind: she too might not last much longer.

Carrying my few belongings, I reached the loading barrack and I noticed that the numbers called approached mine. As was customary for departing transports, all the inmates were pushed and jostled into the cattle cars. My bundle was already on the train as I inched slowly towards the boxcar. It was just then when I noticed, still some distance away, a thin female figure running, or rather trying to run, towards the forbidden site of deportees. Instinctively I knew that it was Mother. She waved her outstretched arm, bringing attention to a piece of paper in her hand. I realized immediately that it was the much-coveted reclamation paper which someone must have at this late hour arranged for me at the Council, granting me a stay of deportation. One more time I cheated death and escaped unscathed. For the moment I felt happy. Even in Theresienstadt there were moments of happiness, and this was one of them. I felt so relieved that I would not have to abandon my ailing parents in this Godforsaken place; they were so frail and defenseless. I felt as if a huge weight had rolled off my shoulders. All was gone—my meager bundle, my blanket—but it did not matter because, at that moment, we were filled with the joy of remaining together.

It was to be a short-lived happiness. In winter, transports were a frequent occurrence, relieving the camp of its congestion. Most of the unfortunate German Jews were dead by then. Yet the number of transports continued unabated, and I began to suspect that we would all be sent away and that the much-touted improvements to the place were destined for the returning, original Gentile population.

In Theresienstadt, there was always another blow just around the corner, and our next misfortune was the deportation of Josl, the boy who was so good to us. When he was deported, our pain from hunger and frost increased. The winter was bitterly cold, we had no wood to warm the barracks and we all suffered from repeated bouts of the terezinka, the bloody painful dysentery that tormented us all. The military barracks we were crammed into had large common lavatories, suitable for the military, but totally inadequate for thousands of women, frequently ill and in poor physical condition. There were long lines at the few available faucets for daily hygiene in the morning and even longer lines at the latrines.

Even the strictest orders and the best of intentions to maintain the barracks in an acceptable state were bound to fail. The hallways were always messy, though scrubbed frequently, for the unfortunate sick could not wait and hold off until they reached the latrines. It happened to me. A few times, I fainted on the street of the camps or in the barracks. It was so common that no one bothered to do anything about it. You either regained consciousness or your body was carted away, adding to the number of the day's dead.

Even today, if I close my eyes and concentrate, I can smell the stench of the barracks, which, together with the hunger, cold, hard work, infections, ever-present anxiety of deportation, noise and lack of privacy, soon wore down most of the inmates, leaving behind only the strong and young ones to endure more of the trials and tribulations.

There were many infections endemic to the camp and over the years I became subjected to nearly all of them. All were draining, painful and difficult to overcome. One of the many which racked my already weakened body was the recurrent deep skin infections. I was afflicted with large painful carbuncles and boils that grew on my body. Some of these boils would rupture but many kept on growing and spreading over large areas necessitating surgical intervention. No matter what I did, or did not do, this scourge would intermittently return to torment me.

I always hoped that perhaps this painful pestilence would burst open without surgical intervention but more often than not this would not come to pass. I would suffer, grind my teeth and wait. Later, when I no longer could stand the pain, I would brace myself and go to the infirmary where the surgeon on duty would open the throbbing, pussy boil. As always in camp, you had to be lucky; at times the infirmary had some ether or chloroform to put the patient under. On other occasions, nothing was to be had, not even the spray used for local freezing. On those latter days, the operation had to be performed fast, and somebody had to hold the patient firmly to prevent him from jumping off the table and darting off during the horrible few seconds needed for the procedure. In the early days, I was often one of the lucky ones for whom anesthesia was available, but during the latter years, no painkillers were to be had. I still have a few ugly scars, a reminder of the surgery on my back, where a large carbuncle had to be opened without any benefit of analgesics. Later nothing was to be found to dull the excruciating pain when the surgery of a large furuncle became mandatory, like the boil on my knee, another one on my thigh and some other smaller ones on my back.

Compounding the misery was the fact that most of the younger and more capable surgeons were no longer there—all of them had been deported. Some of my worse carbuncles were opened by an old man, Dr.

Heim, who had replaced the competent Dr. Viktor Kirschner. I still recall, with a shudder, the slow torturous incision he performed, his old hands shaking as he carved the opening on my back to allow the drainage of the infected site. Poor man, poor me! He knew that his surgical days were over; he did not like operating any better than I liked being operated on but there was no choice.

Following the surgery—during which we all screamed, no teeth grinding helped—you had to get off the table really fast, to vacate it for yet another unfortunate patient with a similar affliction. There were always long queues of people waiting their turn. The lesions were covered by paper or a rag, depending on what was available, if anything. Luckily, once these sores were opened, they discharged an incredible amount of pus but then healed relatively fast. At every occurrence I hoped fervently that this would be my last visitation by this plague, but on and off, I was tormented by it, up until the time of my postwar recovery.

In 1944 I began to have difficulties seeing, mainly after twilight. I was petrified that I might become blind, and I asked Docent Stein to see me. He took his time to explain to me that I was not about to lose my sight. My condition was night blindness caused by a lack of Vitamin A. Our protracted internment, aggravated by such abysmal nutrition, caused many chronic illnesses. As soon as the daylight faded, I could not see, only distinguish some shapes and shadows. The rest was a big blur, everything melted into an indistinct mass. Docent Stein, who felt badly for me since the night he had forced my hand into the joint killing of the newborn, tried to be helpful. Perhaps it was his way of making up for the trauma he had inflicted on me, forcing me to become a part of his plan to get rid of the unwanted baby.

He reassured me that my eye condition was reversible and would not plunge me into total darkness. He shared with me the news that he had just performed eye surgery on an SS man who had rewarded him with cigarettes and several boxes of sardines, which Stein requested for those afflicted by night blindness. He offered me one box and invited me for another check-up, and, if need be, treatment. I quickly grabbed the box, for we had not seen such an epicurean delicacy in years. I ran with this tidbit to Mother. She looked at it in disbelief. In normal times, not even a diamond solitaire would have stunned her so much. I made up some lies about my treatment and the need for her to take, as prevention, the dose of sardines. I do not think that she had much faith in my fabricated story but she had learned not to ask questions which would force me to make up more lies.

Later, I returned several times to Docent Stein who always commented about the stubbornness of my condition, which did not improve, the four boxes of sardines notwithstanding. I suspect that he too was well aware of my deceit, but he pretended to believe me. This condition also cleared up only after liberation.

From 1943, I had developed a skin condition called pellagra caused by deficiency of nicotinic acid. This disorder was manifested by brown, ugly and painless blotches and spots on the skin which bothered my vanity. It only worsened the diarrhea we all suffered with and made us fearful of potential mental disorders. Neither the night blindness nor pellagra were life-threatening conditions. Worse was my brush with jaundice, another epidemic spreading in the camp.

For a while I felt terribly ill and it was a close call. I had a near brush with death. I turned yellow, my skin was itchy and I felt that I was quickly losing the little strength and energy I still had. I was not even hungry any longer, a fact which was frightening, for those who stopped eating were doomed within a short time. But I recovered, though weakened and further reduced in weight. My enormous will and energy helped me to overcome almost certain death.

It was sometime in February 1944 when Dr. Braun informed me that Father's condition had almost miraculously improved and that he could not be kept in the ward much longer. I desperately wanted to move my dad into a better, smaller room, out of the huge hall he shared with some 500 other men in the Sudeten barracks. I did not want him to return to the horrible conditions in this mass dormitory. To find something better proved to be a complex task but eventually I succeeded in finding a smaller place for him. It took a few days longer than I thought it would but Dr. Braun obliged me and kept him in the ward for the time I needed. I felt good about my exploit, securing an improved shelter for my father, and with Mother I went to tell him the good news.

As soon as we entered the ward, we realized that something had gone awry. What happened? Father's cot was set asunder, and we were asked to wait outside. Mother seemed shaken and waited anxiously for an explanation. After what seemed a long time Dr. Braun came out, telling us that Father had suffered a seizure, a kind which they could not diagnose. Dr. Braun suspected uremia. Father was unconscious. We began a long vigil at his bedside. He rested peacefully and had I not known that he could not be roused I would have thought he was blissfully asleep.

Only slowly he regained awareness but he was never the same. He became a changed man; he did not return to reality. He believed himself to be either in Prague, in his office or at home in his study. He seemed to have forgotten that Eva passed away for he often spoke to her directly. He talked to Mom and me again but he appeared to have forgotten the happenings of the past six years or so. He seemed quite happy in his obfuscated mental condition, and we sat at his bedside, trying to adapt to his level of thinking.

We left him only for work and then we would rush back, wash him, try to feed him and make him comfortable. My heart ached for the man I once knew—the successful, proud lawyer respected and liked by all around him—who was lying here now, reduced to a shadow of his former self.

For the next few days he never returned to reality, and neither of us could blame him for having willed himself into another world, the kind to which he was accustomed, where men like him were recognized and honored. A place like Theresienstadt had no use for men like my father.

I sat there ashamed, recalling how often I had resented his unwillingness to fight, to adapt to the camp's mores, to learn to steal and cheat. Belatedly I understood that he could not do it. As he gradually drifted away, I looked at Mother who held his hand, trying to give him a drink of water, wiping his forehead, gently stroking his cheeks, and I wondered how she was going to accept the loss of the man she loved. Would she ever learn to cope without him? She still was reeling from the huge heartbreak, Eva's death, and now she would be forced to weather another shock.

It was Sunday, March 5, 1944, when he passed away, liberated from the hunger and infamy of the concentration camp. Death came to him gently and peacefully, more like a friend than a usurping foe. There was no struggle or mortal fight. His shallow breathing simply stopped, and he appeared asleep and in peace. Death understood him better for he was a gentle and serene man, thrown into violent turbulence with which he could not cope.

The very next day, my mother and I walked behind the hearse as far as the camp's fence, from whence the corpses made their lonely journey to the crematoria. I tried to support Mother who tottered unsteadily. She seemed so thin, so devastated. Upon our return to the barracks we had a long talk. We tried to comfort one another and strengthen our resolve to persist in spite of all the pains and enormous odds. Mother agreed with all I said but her eyes were full of tears. Her thoughts were with Eva and Father, both lost to us within one year. With a heavy heart, I tried to come to terms with the destruction of our family, and I was deeply worried for Mother, whose ravaged appearance gave serious reasons for concern.

9

The Incredible Selection

It was during the winter of 1944 that a new infection spread among the inmates, killing some and maiming others. Inmates began to complain of headaches, dizziness and unsteadiness on their feet. Following some clinical investigation, Dr. Kral diagnosed numerous cases of encephalitis. There was little anyone could do for those who succumbed to the illness which soon assumed epidemic proportions. I was fortunate for when I came down with the symptoms, unlike others, I did not become gravely ill. Dr. Kral advised me to stay away from work but within a few days I returned to the chronically understaffed hospital. Many of those who were affected had lifelong neurological deficits but I had hardly any complications.

Only a few weeks had passed since the death of my father when Mother became ill. Initially, it appeared to be another bout of fever, only this time it did not subside within the customary few days. The previous fall, mother came down with pleurisy which needed some weeks to clear up. But she seemed to have recuperated, at least on the surface, and had only a few more bouts of fever. Her condition now gave more cause for concern. She ran a high fever, sweated profusely and lost her appetite. Unlike her previous febrile episodes, her condition did not clear up or even improve during the course of the next few days. The barrack's physician believed that her condition was to a degree psychosomatic—had she not just buried her husband? But I knew better than that; it had to be some physical condition. Her heartbreak had not left her since the death of Eva; it was not then and was not now the cause of this feverish, debilitating disease.

Because she did not improve, I began to press for her transfer to the camp's hospital, where I hoped to offer her better care. I knew most of the physicians well and there was no doubt in my mind that they would do their level best to help. A few days later I brought Mom to the ward in the camp's hospital. The physician in charge of the internal medicine department, Dr. Erich Klapp, tried to establish a diagnosis. There were few diagnostic modalities but he was an excellent diagnostician, and soon he made an unequivocal diagnosis. Mother was afflicted with tuberculosis of the lungs which had spread to both lobes, with little chance for improvement, considering the reigning conditions in the camp.

The news hit me like a ton of bricks. I knew about the root causes of TB from my training, and although we lived in privation and penury, crowded into filthy and cold barracks, I was not anticipating tuberculosis as Mother's affliction. Soon I steadied myself by believing that Mother had a chance if only I could supply the proper nutrition. I bolstered my faith by reflecting on Max's mother who had recuperated from a bout with TB (so much so that after Max's passing she was deemed fit for deportation to Auschwitz).

Until now, I had always tried my best to mitigate our suffering, but with Mother's illness, I became even more obsessed with the urgency to turn back the tides threatening to engulf my mom. In my hustle for food I contacted all my friends, promised, and did everything anybody wanted in return for helping me. I took risks by delivering contraband, cigarettes for the sentries, jewelry in the underground passages, all for the reward of some morsel for Mother. At the end of the day, I would run to the hospital and bring her what I managed to collect. Mom always greeted me with enthusiasm, pretended to savor what I brought along, only I knew that she did not really enjoy it. But I stubbornly believed that it might help anyway; her body needed the strength to heal. Or was it my wishful thinking? I was driven by this illusion.

While mother was hospitalized I moved to different barracks. The health-care workers were all supposed to live in separate barracks. I always maneuvered myself out of that directive for it would mean leaving Mother in the Hamburg barracks alone. Now, due to changed conditions, the administration relented and guaranteed Mom could move there with me right after her hospital discharge. The new ward was a great improvement. It was less crowded, had only two-tier bunks and, due to lesser congestion, was also easier to keep clean.

During Mother's illness I had a self-imposed routine which forced me to rush a great deal. I had to work, organize the supplies and then run to the hospital to spend time with Mother, who always waited for my arrival as the highlight of her day. One evening in late March, I stepped quickly into the barracks, carrying my liquid supper with the intent of drinking it, collect what I managed to hoard for Mother that day and then go see her. In the barracks, there was a bench near our bunk, and I noticed that there was a visitor sitting there.

The first thing that struck me how much his hair resembled Max's. Only the stranger's shock of hair was light brown unlike Max's darker shade. I thought that he had a handsome face, clean, open and friendly. He was neatly dressed and he resembled the boys from days bygone, not the Theresienstadt kind who were either nebbishes on their way out or vultures.

Immersed in these thoughts, I likely smiled, for the young man returned a friendly grin and introduced himself. He added that he was waiting for my bunkmate, Edith.

We had a brief chat but I was pressed for time. I was about to leave when all of a sudden he offered to walk with me in the direction of the hospital to give us a chance for a longer chat. On our way we passed by the new coffeehouse, just opened by the SS—another feature designed to contribute to the camp's facelift. I had not been inside; an inmate needed a ticket, and these were by no means easily attainable. My escort mentioned casually that he could show me the inside of the new facility. He had two tickets and we would not have to stay for long. I became curious. I had heard of the unbelievable metamorphosis of the new Theresienstadt but I had not seen many of the improvements from within. The SS had built a pavilion for children in the park, the old building of the Sokol association was converted into some kind of a club, some shops were opened and adapted, and even some prisoners' barracks were improved.

Now in the company of this pleasant man, who had a relaxing influence, somehow easing my now permanent state of high tension, I decided to make a concession and spend a few minutes in the coffeehouse. Though I chided myself for such frivolity, I reflected on the fact that it was an eternity since I afforded myself a casual conversation. All my efforts were directed to plan, get, or, if needed, "organize" some food, prevent deportation or come up with some other strategy for our basic maintenance. I persuaded myself that I still had an entire evening, even if I indulged my interest for a few minutes to visit this new feature of the camp.

We entered the place and sat at one of the tables in this packed, shabby room. There was nothing edible in sight but soon the program began. Two accomplished cabaret performers sang charming couplets, the musical accompaniment was provided by an accordionist, Kurt Mayer, and a violinist, Otto Sattler, who presented a medley of melodious, soft tunes, mostly upbeat. Soon I forgot my nagging pangs of hunger and the myriad worries, and I began to enjoy this high-class fun. It was a grand performance; all the participating artists were professionals and internationally acclaimed performers. Even today I recall a few lines from the ditties performed that evening. A few rhymes presented some cryptic aphorisms aimed at our oppressors, trying to ridicule their Teutonic grandeur. The wit of those songs would have punctured many holes in their armor—that is, if anybody had had the gumption and opportunity to present them in the commandery.

The show lasted nearly an hour, much longer than I had planned to spend there. I really got carried away; it was a long time since I heard or enjoyed anything like that hour. We walked briskly the short stretch to the hospital where I took leave from my companion who introduced himself by an abbreviated form for his name, Arthur; he liked to be called Turek.

My mom's reaction to my late visit was just the opposite of what I expected. She was glad to hear that I had spent such an enjoyable evening and she encouraged me to go again, if an opportunity were to arise. She always fostered in me faith that the better days of our past might return, if only we resisted and persevered in our struggle to outlive the present evil.

For the next several weeks the young man all but disappeared from my sight. I only briefly recalled the evening of fun and wistfully remembered the witty, friendly young man. The one hour of fun spent with him in the coffeehouse gave me a new lease on life. With the passage of days I began to believe that he had likely been deported. This was a routine happening in Theresienstadt; people came, stayed for a few brief moments and vanished into the bottomless pit somewhere in the east. It came as a great surprise to me when one day I caught sight of him. He waited in the corridor of the hospital. I quickened my pace to catch up with him and say hello. We both were glad that we could see each other again. He offered to accompany me during my lunch break. We stood in the long queue, waiting for the distribution of the soup that would be ladled into our tin dishes. Meanwhile my new friend began to tell me something about himself and his family. It became evident that he was one of the late arrivals in the camp.

His special privilege was due to his engagement in the group of Salo Kraemer's who was in charge of clearing the apartments of the deported Jews. Thus he only left Prague in the summer of 1943. He likely noticed a hint of disapproval on my face. We did not appreciate the Kraemer action which we perceived as a pack of vultures feeding on Jewish carrion. Work in the Kraemer unit delayed the workers' deportation until most of the Jews of Prague had been sent to various concentration camps. The Germans did not wish anything to hinder the smooth collection of their loot. Short of killing Jews, the second most important task was the theft of our possessions. Such were the priorities of the Nazis. Arthur, or Turek, as he preferred to be called, hastened to explain that he accepted this work only because he wanted to protect his elderly mother, a widow of many years. In addition and perhaps more importantly, he devised a scheme for smuggling medical drugs to Theresienstadt. Under Kraemer (who, like Turek, hailed from Ostrava), he was put in charge of warehousing drugs and medical supplies in one of Prague's largest synagogues. The Nazis confiscated all medications in their original packaging from Jewish homes and medical offices for their own people. Medications not in their original packaging were supposed to be discarded. Instead, Arthur and his helpers devised a scheme for channeling these drugs via the underground network to Theresienstadt to provide us with rare medical supplies.

The Germans disqualified all containers that were tampered with for fear of sabotage, contamination or decay. Under Arthur's leadership, the group of workers in the drug depot devised a courageous plan. They took it upon themselves to interfere with the sealed containers, removing small parts and in doing so disqualified them for use by the Germans. It went without saying that it was an extremely risky project. The Germans patrolled and inspected the premises of the storerooms and if a Jew was caught tampering with "German property" he would be punished by death. This lengthy disclosure impressed me for I not only knew the risk but also the camp's dire need for any such help.

Gradually, Arthur became nearly a daily companion of my lunch breaks. He told me most of his future plans that he was convinced he would achieve. He planned to study medicine as the pharmacy course was only a steppingstone to his final objective. He chose this circuitous road because his father's small textile store experienced considerable difficulties and nearly went under. That crisis had taken place when Arthur was choosing the course of his university education so he enrolled in the college of pharmacy which ensured he would remain in Prague and be finished in two years. It was Arthur's fervent hope to continue his medical studies at a later date, for once he became a fully qualified pharmacist, he could earn his income manning the night shifts in some pharmacies in Prague. The medical course, a longer and costlier one, was beyond his father's financial situation. I listened silently, disbelieving my ears. Here was a man who made plans for the future; he honestly believed that we had one. There were moments when I silently questioned his sanity or at least his veracity. He was perfectly credible when he spoke about the past; it was only when he made designs for the future that I doubted his sense of reality. To my mind, the future consisted of the next hour, and with some luck, perhaps another day, but this man devised plans for the days after the war.

I much preferred when he spoke of his family. His father had died, leaving behind a widow and three children. Turek had a sister in Theresienstadt and his much-adored mother was also an inmate. They arrived with him. He had a much younger brother who was fortunate, for he left Europe with the last group of Aliyah Noar destined for Palestine, sponsored by the youth branch of a Zionist movement. At the time of his deportation, Arthur was recovering from surgery on his duodenal ulcer. The daily aggravation and stress of his job while he tried to despoil some of the German booty worsened his condition so much that surgery was deemed necessary and was performed in Prague's Jewish hospital by Dr. Paul Wurzel. It was a good decision for Arthur spent at least a part of his recovery in Prague where the nutrition, though inadequate, was far superior to the camp.

I listened and marveled about the different fates of different families.

While all of us had a rough time, those who had personal connections had it much easier. I was reminded of the only man we knew upon our arrival in Theresienstadt, Dr. Tarjan, and even him we befriended in an oblique way. It demanded deliberate efforts to make connections and enter the inner sanctum of those in charge of the camp. Arthur, a lifelong member of the youth Zionist movement, seemed to have scores of friends; he knew all those who mattered and then some. He never ran out of people in right places. Most of the men with clout were the onetime members of the Zionist movement, and they remained quite clannish, only helping one another. Often

Arthur Schiff's homemade baggage tag, 1943.

I quietly raged against their closed brotherhood which I only began to understand and perhaps forgive many years later. It might have been only human to try to save those connected to them first and foremost but it was certainly unjust to the multitude of unaffiliated, assimilated Jews. Perhaps they justified their stance ideologically: survival was the privilege of those who would carry the banner of Zionism into the future and win the battle for Jewish independence by achieving statehood for the homeless, dispossessed Jew.

At that time, I hardly understood that the purpose of the defenders of the Zionist movement was to make sure that the Jews would no longer be unwanted guests among other nations. While I want to believe that they had this lofty goal of securing the final victory in mind, during our imprisonment I could not see past my own misery. I had no vision or ambition, bar the one to ease the suffering of our family. Even today I am uncertain if those in charge had the God-given right to promote their own over the resented assimilated Jew.

Arthur, for instance, had to work, like any other inmate, the 100 days of compulsory menial work, the Hundertschaft, but then he got an administrative assignment as the keeper of the camp's drugs. It was clearly an artificially created position for a man who had to be protected. There were no drugs to be administered in Theresienstadt; the post was meant to shelter Arthur from outside drudgery and suffering.

With time, our brief meetings became a welcome highlight of my days. I could tell him all about us, and in turn I would listen to his concerns. Ours was an honest, open relationship, of which there were only a few in the camp. Neither of us could have offered any advantage to the other in the material sense but emotionally our affinity was rewarding and smoothed our daily harassment. I found myself looking forward to seeing his smiling face and when he did not show up I was greatly disappointed. And so gradually we fell in love. He became my companion, and, with time, the only highlight of my existence. Unlike Arthur, I did not plan some illusionary future; I was happy to be with him now and here, experiencing for the first time the magic of love. Unlike my relationship with Max that was rather a childish story and never blossomed into consummation, Arthur soon became the love of my life.

In Theresienstadt, Arthur called a bunk in the men's barracks of Hanover his home. Most of the barracks in the camp were named after German towns. I never knew why; were the Germans really so proud of the camp and its creation? The hall where Arthur lived housed about 100 men, sleeping in the customary three-tier bunks and, as only men lived in the large ward, it was even less tidy than the barracks that housed women.

In one of the many rows of bunks was the place Arthur called his camp-home. When I saw it for the first time I was taken by surprise. The barracks and this crowded room exuded the stench of too many poorly washed bodies cramped together but Arthur's space was a clear proof of his imagination and inventiveness. Never in my three years of incarceration in Theresienstadt did I see anything remotely resembling Arthur's creativity with which he transformed his narrow cot.

As for myself I did not make any efforts to beautify my bunk. I had neither the time nor the inclination to improve the space allotted me. I spent only brief periods of rest there. When I first visited Arthur's bunk I could not believe my eyes; I was truly impressed. He really performed a small miracle in the narrow, confining space, on the very bottom of the three-tier bunk. His creative improvements merit a more detailed description.

No one who was relegated to live in such a tiny space could imagine what it took to improve on the use and looks of it. Arthur had paid a high price of two cigarettes which, in camp life, was the equivalent of two bread rations for one full week, for a piece of cloth; from this cloth he fashioned a roll-up enclosure, offering him a modicum of privacy which was almost an unimaginable luxury in this crowded mass of men. He had enough left to cover the planks above his head, the ceiling of his bed. This protective baldachin layer was particularly helpful because those who slept in lower bunks bore additional affliction: bedbugs, fleas, lice and other trash from the inmates occupying the upper level rained down on those in the lower tiers. To exacerbate Arthur's frustration, in his case the upper bunk was occupied by a cobbler who supplemented his rations by repairing the shoes of his fellow inmates. This work augmented his fare but numerous nails and tacks fell down on those below. In Arthur's case, the protective cloth caught this debris and so sheltered Arthur at night from inevitable disturbance.

The next impressive feature of this sophisticated bunk was a short row of small wooden cupboards built within the inner side of the bunk, one of which could have been locked, and Arthur even owned a key. This in itself was an unheard-of luxury. This allowed him to set aside food without exposing it to theft, which was rampant. The starving inmates could not resist stealing anything edible within sight and, therefore, veteran prisoners like me never kept anything. Not that we owned much, only perhaps some disciplined inmates could divide their bread which was distributed for three days at a time or the spoonful of sugar, doled out once a week or less often, or the spoonful of jam (a creation from beets), given twice a month, if lucky. Most of the inmates swallowed whatever they were given as soon as it was distributed, relishing the delight of the moment, never having a storage place or the slightest inclination to keep it.

Basking in my shock, Arthur unlocked his cupboard and took out bread and jam. He readied himself to treat me. For years I never knew anybody who saved his rations, apportioning the supply for days to come until the next bread distribution, much less was there a soul who would keep the spoonful of sugar or jam. I was flabbergasted; he was a model of normality and civility in this crazed madhouse. It took me a while to regain my composure.

Arthur had yet another invention which made his daily life a bit easier. He had constructed under his bunk a narrow, wooden railing to hold a sliding wash basin. This contraption enabled him to fetch water in the evening upon returning from work, at the time when the pressure around the faucets was at the lowest. In the early morning, when all hell broke loose around the dripping faucets, all he had to do was to use his filled basin and wash himself in the comfort of a nearly empty room. Arthur was also in possession of a handmade portable toilet seat, manufactured from some "organized" wood. Its use protected him from the filthy facilities of the camp.

The next innovative upgrade of his bunk made me almost envious. Arthur had taken the grave risk of "borrowing" electricity from the one naked bulb of the hall which gave out only dim light, suspended high from the ceiling. If he had been caught that one transgression would have netted him the death sentence right then and there. But most of our attempts to make it through the day carried risks of severe punishments. On the bright side Arthur's illegal source of light allowed him to read. Unbelievably he brought a few of his favorite books with him to camp. These were in no danger of being stolen; few were interested in printed matter. Right then and there I knew that if anybody had the mettle to survive the war, it would be Arthur.

On one of my daily visits, I was recounting to Mother the extraordinary qualities of my boyfriend. He was the epitome of creativity. He knew how to improve the camp's conditions and had the God-given talent to make the best of the worst. I likely gushed so much praise that my mom began to understand that I met a man who meant more to me than I was willing to admit. Mom, always sensitive and concerned with changes in my life, asked me to bring this new friend of mine to visit her. This request was highly unusual: Mother never wanted to meet any of the men I associated with, be it at work or elsewhere. The only man she ever acknowledged was Max. I did not know how to interpret this demand because it was so out of character for her. Was it connected to her failing health? Did she want to get to know him because she felt so ill? Did she hope to see me with someone decent, someone she could relate to? Did she hope he was someone who would have fitted into the world we left eons ago, a person who would be around for her little girl, just in case...?

My heart began to race a mile a minute; my stomach knotted with fear for her life. Was she on the verge of death? But I promised to bring him; I would have done anything within my power to offer her comfort or a moment of joy. Rumors seeping through the permeable walls of the camp had it that the Germans' war efforts were failing and that the tide was turning in favor of the Allies. I kept praying and trying to pull Mother through with the hope there were better days in store for us after all. Somehow the indomitable optimism of Arthur began to rub off on me: was it possible that we might have a chance of life?

The next time I met Arthur, I asked him to join me during my visit with Mom. He agreed without batting an eye. Mother and Arthur seemed to get along well and were engaged in a lively conversation when she suddenly asked me to fetch a glass of water. I was not happy about that errand. I thought I knew why she wanted to be left alone with him. The thought frightened me for she had just met him. I believed that she was about to ask him to stand by me if and when she passed away. Though her wish angered me, I complied. I went because we were not used to talking back to our elders, and much less would I do it now, when she was unwell. Although neither of them ever told me what was discussed in my absence, I am sure that I was the topic of conversation because I suspected that Mother solicited Arthur's help and assistance for me, just in case.

Upon my return, Mom looked tired and worn. I placed the glass in front of her but she did not even take a sip. Soon thereafter we took our leave from her. During my visit the next day, she said: "The young man who came along with you yesterday is very pleasant, too bad that your temperaments and ages are so different." That was her way of saying she liked him but did not believe that we were compatible or were meant for one another.

In April we saw intensification of the serious upgrades, improvements and innovations of the camp. Children's rations grew in size and, sure enough, they began to gain weight and strength. Our rations could be supplemented by the "Theresienstadt spread," a strange concoction of mustard and vinegar that had a sharp acidic taste. The Germans introduced this spread during the preparatory stages of the camp's beautification. It was and remained the only item purchasable with the camp's money, distributed at the place of work. The camp's currency elicited little interest because nothing could have been purchased with it except for the spread, and few wanted this acidic mixture that failed to fill the stomach and only intensified the hunger pangs.

Certain parts of the camp underwent a thorough cleaning; the Nazis demanded that restoration and painting take place. The commandant ordered repeated rehearsals of the presentation planned for the arrival of the international inspection. Evidently the SS men were seized by near panic for in some parts of the camp they left no stone unturned. Tension permeated the camp for the Germans clearly placed high stakes on a successful outcome of the inspection. Certain parts of the camp underwent thorough scrutiny. Were these the chosen sites where visitors would be taken? We, the inmates, hoped and wished for the inspection to be thorough and usher in lasting upgrades of our day-to-day life.

Often I remembered Dr. Tarjan and marveled over the accuracy of his predictions some eight long months ago. Suddenly, in May, when things had been improving in the camp, we were hit with another calamity. The commandery issued an order to clear the camp of all sick inmates in general and the TB patients in particular. The order was not negotiable; all

TB-affected inmates had to be deported forthwith. The order stated categorically that one and all had to be assembled in a large hall in the hospital and from there they would be carried to the Hamburg barracks and then on to departing trains. No exceptions would be considered—not even members of the Council of the Elders were to be spared. The objective was to rid the camp of all sickly patients whose looks betrayed their condition; the Nazis didn't want the inspectors to have any evidence of the inmates' malnutrition or privation. The visitors should not have to look upon the unseemly sight of consumptive patients. Hence, before the illustrious guests were to arrive, all those affected by tuberculosis would have to be deported to Auschwitz.

I reached my 18th birthday during the distribution of the summonses. Panic stricken, I would have probably forgotten all about it if not for Arthur who came to congratulate me and bring some generous gifts. He surprised me with a toothbrush, toothpaste and a bed sheet—items I had not seen in a long time. I had lost the last of my personal belongings during my last reprieve from deportation when I was unexpectedly released shortly before loading. Later in my life I received many gifts but obviously these presents have a special place in my heart and memory. First of all they came from the man I loved and there were also a reminder of my past life. How long was it since I owned a toothbrush and toothpaste?

Mid–May was the target date for the deportation of the frail and sickly. These were the last touches in the beautification project, the final steps that paved the road for the arrival of the international inspection. Three transports left in rapid succession, removing a sum total of 7,500 people. No sickly inmates would be permitted to scar the face of the "transformed Theresienstadt," for Theresienstadt had to live up to the German propaganda which advertised the place as "the town the Führer gave to the Jews." Here the Jews enjoyed a peaceful life, where they learned to work and fend for themselves and where they attended cultural events, visited coffeehouses and other amenities while the heroic German army was engaged in an armed struggle for life and death and bled for a better tomorrow for mankind!

My poor mom was enrolled in the last of the three transports. Her condition had deteriorated so much that she had to be carried to the yard of the Hamburg barracks on a stretcher. Arthur fashioned one for her; it was just a thin blanket stretched between two poles, items Arthur had to purchase for his bread rations. Once in the yard of the gathering place I had to defend her right to remain on the stretcher; the rest of the deportees were thrown on the bare ground. That yard in the Hamburg barracks was the last station before the deportees would be loaded onto the box cars for the insatiable gas chambers.

From the moment of the round-up of the tubercular patients I knew one thing: I could not let Mother go alone. I had to join her; she was way too ill to go through her last steps unassisted. The May transports did not include any able-bodied inmates who might be eligible for selection. My decision to join Mom was not a simple bureaucratic move. As I was not a consumptive patient, I had to apply for the right to get enrolled alongside my mom.

In Magdeburg barrack, the place of the camp's administration, my request was met with incredulity. No member of the Council wanted to listen, and my friends believed that I had taken leave of my senses. They all agreed that the deportees were doomed and they labeled my request a suicide mission. Though I agreed with them in principle I knew that I could not let her go alone. I would not be able to live with myself wondering about her last days or hours were. I felt that I could not abandon her in the worst hours of her life, no matter what the cost. Then the thought occurred to me that even if we were going to be gassed, it was probably our destiny sooner or later. Besides, if I were to survive alone without my family, such a crippled existence would hardly be worth living. I would be tormented and haunted by images, rightly or wrongly, seeing her leaving this world all alone, with no one to wipe the sweat of her forehead or support her during her frequent bouts of coughing that seemed to tear her lungs. By that time all of us were accustomed to the probability of death. Perhaps I was too tired, worn by the long, seemingly futile fight for survival, the nagging hunger and hopes that were always shattered. I honestly did not know; I had no time or inclination to analyze my motives. I was only sure that my mother would not leave this damned camp alone on a journey to yet a worse one.

Once the Elder of the Council realized that I was determined and adamant about my decision, he granted my wish. What an irony! For years I had fought against our deportation and, at the end, I had to fight for permission to join the transport of the doomed. If life in the camp was not full of absurdity I don't know what was. The Elder of the camp heaved a sigh and with repeated oohs and aahs consented to accept me as a transport nurse. I was given an armband with a red cross indicating my official function, and I realized that I could be of help to my mother because I would be able to move among the patients and so perhaps secure a better site for her. As a nurse I might be able to hustle for some dry straw which would help ease her suffering. Mother remained impassive, lying on her stretcher in the courtyard. I moved as little as possible away from her side. She ran a high fever and was only partially conscious, and on occasion she opened her eyes and then tried unsuccessfully for a smile.

Somebody whispered to me that loading was to begin at around 10:00 p.m. Most of the trains were filled and readied in the late evening and departed at night. I found that appropriate: maybe even the SS felt that their nefarious deeds could not bear the scrutiny of daylight. Probably it was something more prosaic and practical such as a suitable timetable for the trains or the fact that at night the exhausted inmates could not think of hiding and were readily shoved in the waiting cars. Perhaps the Teutonic psyche simply enjoyed the darkness and loved to perform their evil rites at the hour of the devil. Whatever the reason, loading was set for 10:00 p.m.

Earlier in the day Arthur had come to say goodbye. It surprised me just how difficult it was to part from him. Though I had known him for only two months I had become fond of him—more than I realized in the course of those troubled, hectic weeks. As always, he was encouraging and warmly sympathetic. For a moment, a naïve thought crossed my mind: how different it would have been had we met in another time and another, kinder world. I regretted that I would never see him again but I genuinely hoped that he would survive and get out of this mess healthy and in one piece. I bade him goodbye, clearly feeling the pain of yet another loss. Arthur, downcast and subdued, kissed me and whispered that he would wait on the upper level of the barrack and watch the proceedings in courtyard. He would see us off with a prayer for a miracle. His kiss left a salty taste; I was not sure if the tears were his or mine as they mingled in our last embrace. I felt a stabbing pain in my heart. Why, God, does it have to hurt so badly?

It goes without saying that anyone mixing with the deportees at the time of loading of the train would be immediately included among them and driven into the car for it was forbidden to be present in the area of departing transports. For that very reason Arthur could not stay with us in the courtyard; even the upper floors were not safe. But there were a few hiding places, almost secure, right behind two heavy beams in the corner of the corridor. Shortly after he left us, I caught a glimpse of him hiding behind a pillar, waving furtively in our direction. Suddenly something was set in motion in the yard; something changed the dynamic of this huddled group on their way to hell. Immediately on high alert, I counted on an advanced loading, but to my surprise, I saw a few of the officials responsible for the orderly departure (Transportleitung) carrying a table straight to the center of the yard.

One of the men, an acquaintance of mine, whispered as he was passing by, that the SS commandant, Karl Rahm, was coming to the barracks to supervise the deportation and that he would perform a quick selection. It would be possible to address him, provided the inmate had a sensible reason to petition for a stay in Theresienstadt. This was certainly another inexplicable new occurrence, never experienced before or during the dispatch of a transport. Never—to my knowledge—did an SS man talk to an inmate and any attempts of a Jew approaching a German, never mind an SS man, would have been met with a bullet to the nape of the poor fool's neck. My first instinct was to think that this was a drunken joke on the part of Rahm who perhaps thought it would be a hilarious diversion to listen to these dying Jews whose end he was about to facilitate and perhaps accelerate.

Much later I learned that, although Rahm was drunk, he was under orders to screen the departing transport for the presence of some individuals who could enhance the image of Theresienstadt for the impending visit of the Red Cross commission. The complexity of the conversion of a camp to a nearly functional small town, even for a day only, presented difficulties of epic proportions. There seemed to be a lack of healthy young inmates and so there was a dearth of normal-looking townfolks. The SS hoped they could salvage a few from those destined for transport to the east.

The moment I heard of the unexpected screening by Rahm, my mind began to race a mile a minute. I understood instantaneously that I might have a last-minute chance for a reprieve. I began to concentrate, feverishly plotting what to do. I came to realize that I had an unexpected opportunity, and I made up my mind at once to beseech him to grant permission for my mother to stay in Theresienstadt. I prepared two short sentences with great care, searching for words that might soften the heart of an SS commandant. I hoped to emphasize that Mom only had a short time left, a fact he could see with his very own eyes. I thought to solicit his compassion, pull on his heartstrings, provided he had some.

Within seconds I put together a polite entreaty in the best German I could muster. I understood that I must not be long-winded: the patience of an inebriated camp commandant was limited, especially in the middle of the night. I decided to address him with following words: "Sir, I beg of you to grant a stay of deportation to my mother; she is dying and has only a brief while left." I memorized it quickly, concerned that the presence of the SS commandant could throw off my concentration. I glanced above and saw Arthur's encouraging signs. He too likely guessed what the commotion in the yard was all about.

Those inmates whose physical condition allowed them to take advantage of this opportunity were ordered to line up single file and wait for Rahm's arrival. Quite a few attempted to wait in an orderly fashion as demanded but many dropped out, unable to muster the strength. A short time later we heard orders shouted from the gates for the inmates to clear the way and remain silent. This was the customary introduction for the arrival of the SS who would not walk or pass through or mix with throngs of Jews—the road had to be wide open for the Superman. A few moments later I saw Rahm, in the company of several SS men, as he tried to walk swiftly to the center of the courtyard to the makeshift selection post. His gait was somewhat unsteady and I prayed silently for his perseverance, at least until my turn. Seconds after his arrival the screening began. The queue of inmates began to move at a snail's pace and I worried that he would get tired of this charade and order the loading of the train.

In my state of high tension all seemed to move agonizingly slowly and simultaneously too fast. I wanted the chance to address the SS commandant but I felt hopelessly inadequate. How to convince him to let us stay? And all I had for this most important task were a few short seconds.

The procession of the condemned barely inched ahead and I found myself closer to the middle of the yard and caught a glimpse of the place of our last judgment. There was the table where Rahm stood, leaning heavily on it for support. He was flanked by a few SS men and Dr. Erich Munk, the deputy of the Council responsible for the care of the sick. Most of the inmates were, following only a cursory glance, sent to the right side and led away in the direction of the train. Only two people were singled out for the left side; they were considered wholesome enough to pass the examination and allowed to remain in Theresienstadt. All my instincts and faculties on high alert, I took in the scenario silently, rehearsing my speech. Soon I found myself only one man away from Rahm. Beseeching the Almighty I whispered a prayer, took a deep sigh, and stepped in front of the man who was to pass a verdict of life or death for Mother and me.

I breathed in and noticed the strong smell of alcohol wafting from Rahm and his cohorts. He lifted his eyes and looked at me, and I began to present my entreaty that I had committed to memory. It went quite well. I remained calm, humble yet emphatic, at a volume audible enough, yet unpretentious. I concentrated painstakingly on the tone of my voice and on speaking slowly and distinctly. I wanted to avoid his irritation by talking too fast. He appeared to have listened and, when I fell silent, he asked sharply where the rest of our family was. I answered that all had died already which seemed to please him, for he turned to Dr. Munk and asked him if I was a competent nurse. A wave of panic swept through me for Dr. Munk was the man I had had the bitter row with only a few short weeks ago when I had asked him to release me from the hospital assignment and free me for a kitchen job. I thought all was lost but only for the second it took him to reply, and while I tried to look composed, all inside me trembled with fear.

I did not need to worry. Dr. Munk was not a vindictive man. During this ominous hour he tried to support my chance. I heard him praising my diligence, devotion, competence and dedication. I sensed Rahm's hesitation as he contemplated his verdict. Well aware of German expectations when within eye contact of the SS, I cast my sight demurely on the ground.

Rahm's bark informed me that I could remain in the camp; there was no need to have a nurse accompanying a transport of consumptives. Dr.

Munk, well informed that I was a volunteer and not an assigned caretaker of the ill, asked for permission to add an explanation. Dr. Munk most likely feared that I would anger Rahm by refusing to step aside if I didn't get permission for my mother to stay with me. Now he took it upon himself to clarify the point that I was a volunteer, wishing to go along with my ailing mother. I was not certain that Rahm's brain, awash in alcohol, took it all in. There was another pause but then, rather impatiently, he raised his voice, saying, "Step aside, both can remain behind, get out of my sight, next, quick!" I doubt that I have ever felt greater relief and gratitude, in such intensity and depth, as in the moment I stepped back from Rahm.

I honestly believed that I was experiencing a miracle, a stay of execution for the two of us. I was convinced that the Almighty had swayed the decision of this man to spare us. Never before or after did I feel so anxious, never ever had so much hung in the balance as when the SS commandant pronounced his verdict, commuting the death sentence for the both of us. Before he or anyone else was able to interject something that could have changed his mind, I moved aside to the left of the table where I became the third and last one to be exempted from certain death.

Shortly after midnight, Rahm declared the selection concluded. On that night he surveyed less than half of the deportees. He and his entourage left as abruptly as they had arrived. They were in a hurry to take what they no doubt felt was a deserved rest following a hard day's work. As soon as the upper SS echelon withdrew, the lower ranks of the SS unit, aided by the Czech guards and the group of Jews responsible for expediting the transport on the appointed time, began to push the deportees onto the train. The delay caused by the unexpected selection was intolerable to German punctuality, especially in such important matters as the timetable of trains carrying the condemned cargo to the gas chambers. The men responsible for the expeditious dispatch of the transport had to work at double time to meet the timetable.

I tried not to look at the jostling of the inmates. Most had to be carried or dragged towards the train for they were too weak to march at the expected speed. I concentrated on Mother's condition: she was lying on the stretcher, looking drained, probably because of her spiking temperature. She shivered under her thin blanket though the mid–May night was temperate. Soon the lower rank of the SS men sealed the wagons, silencing the screams and cries of the prisoners who were thrown helter-skelter in the box cars. The loading had to proceed faster than ever to make up for the time spent during the selection. The sudden silence was eerie. The commando responsible for the dispatch left, all were keen to get some rest, and there I stood all alone with the stretcher on which Mom laid exhausted and listless. But help was on the way. Soon I was joined by Arthur who had watched the dramatic happenings from his hideout. He came running, overwhelmed and overcome by the unexpected turn of events. He found it hard to talk; it was not easy to find words when one encountered and was touched by a miracle.

Together we carried the stretcher to the now vacant hospital room, all of its previous occupants having been deported. We placed Mother on her narrow cot. She could only manage a faint smile. I forced her to take few sips of water for I feared that she might be dehydrated. She obliged me and whispered I should get some rest. I gladly complied. I was bone-tired and hungry but momentarily relieved of an enormous burden. In parting I blew a kiss to Arthur, thanking him for all his help, and, having reached my bunk, I dropped off into a deep dreamless sleep. The next day, my friends and I had a hard time believing what had transpired. Never before or after was an already determined group of deportees offered another selection right at the embarkation site.

Theresienstadt, purged of the unappealing inmates whose looks disclosed the true face of the camp, underwent further improvements and facelifts. All the groups assigned to participate in this make-believe presentation had to rehearse their parts frequently. All had to be orchestrated and choreographed to perfection. No slip-ups would be tolerated for this had to be a flawless, grand show. The timing of the marching groups would be honed to the second. It would put Count Potemkin and his rather simplistic attempts to create non-existing villages to shame. While Potemkin's fake villages may have impressed Czarina Catherine the Great, the distinguished guests who were about to visit Theresienstadt would be treated to a much more sophisticated show.

While this was the talk in the camp, I had other worries to deal with. Mother's health continued to fail. She was so thin that even I had to admit that she was starting to resemble a Musselman. However, she remained alert. I kept on hustling food, hoping that she might live until the end of the war. Daily I reported to her the rumors about Germany's imminent defeat; on all fronts the odds were stacked against the Nazis. I even embellished the hearsay, just to strengthen her faith and her will to fight the illness. But it was the honest truth that the fortunes on the battlefields were beginning to tilt against the Germans. We inmates never really knew what was going on in the outside world but we hoped that the gossip was true.

The Russians were advancing; we heard rumors about the opening of another front by the Allies in the west. I was quite skeptical about the hearsay because I understood people's capacity for self-deception; however, I felt that all these circulating reports had to have a kernel of truth in them.

Perhaps we had a chance to outlive the terror but for the time being I dreamed of my loaf of bread. When June arrived, the hectic preparations for the arrival of the Red Cross inspection reached its feverish peak. On June 23, the Germans would try to dispel all the disparaging accusations about their mistreatment of the Jews. There was no truth in the reports given by escaped prisoners who spoke of atrocities and genocide on an unprecedented scale. This day would exonerate the reputation of the Herrenvolk, documenting how a civilized nation treats the Jews under its jurisdiction, despite the burden they imposed on the German economy and war efforts.

10

Beautification—
The Great Charade

From the Nazi perspective, the Red Cross inspection of the camp turned out to be an enormous success. The German master plan unfolded without a hitch. On the day of the big show, inmates scrubbed the streets on which the guests would be walking one last time. Those who did not look healthy enough were hurriedly dispatched and confined to their bunks: they were not to ruin the peaceful, rustic harmony of the town with their emaciated faces. The Czech guards were ordered out of the camp for the day so that their uniforms would not intrude on the friendly atmosphere. Even the weather cooperated: it was a beautiful late-spring day with lots of sunshine.

The Germans treated the Jewish actors on display with elaborate courtesy and friendliness. No one, least of all the three members of the inspecting team, could have guessed what a regular day in the camp was like in its unadorned reality. Nor, I suspect, did they want to notice any elements which would disrupt the idyllic picture of this quaint Jewish town. The Germans went to great lengths to make Theresienstadt look its best. Some of their ideas were totally ridiculous. One of those was a long row of water basins with brand new faucets attached to the outside of one of the barracks. The only problem was that there were no pipes nor any kind of plumbing whatsoever within the walls. Had the visitors tried to turn the faucets on, not a drop of water could have been squeezed out.

Epstein, the Elder of the Jews, was renamed the mayor for the day and dressed in a dark suit; his limousine was chauffeured by an SS man who bowed politely while opening the door for him. The three inspectors, accompanied by SS Obersturmführer Rahm, his assistants, and Epstein began their stroll through the camp. As if by chance a group of the best-looking girls in the camp passed by, singing simple, pleasing tunes and cheerfully swinging their rakes. In a corner, white-gloved bakers unloaded bread, the kind which we had never been seen or tasted here. In the camp's

141

center an orchestra played popular, internationally known tunes in a newly built summerhouse. A little farther on the newly opened sports grounds built for the commission's benefit, a soccer game was in progress, and when the refined visitors happened to pass by, one team scored a goal. On yet another site, workers unloaded green vegetables, which, even on the day of the inspection, were not destined for us. In the middle of the central square, on the new grass-covered playground, children frolicked, closely supervised by white-clad nurses. As the visitors came within earshot, the children belted out the line they had memorized and rehearsed for the past few months: "Uncle Rahm, please come and play with us!" The benevolent uncle smiled warmly and replied gently, "On another day, dear children, today your uncle has important visitors."

The bank was the next feature which deeply impressed the guests. The manager of the newly opened bank engaged the Red Cross representatives in a spirited conversation about various monetary systems, trading and stock markets. Right on cue an SS officer offered cigarettes to the guests, the first one to the "mayor," Epstein. Another obliging SS man sprung to action, offering to light their cigarettes, starting with the Elder of the Jews. Such deferential politeness was extended to the Jewish representatives of this lovely town! In Theresienstadt, on any other day, not only smoking but even possessing a cigarette butt could result in the death penalty.

On a secret signal, the orchestra switched to play a swift march while a group of inmates dressed in neat suits debated serious topics. The one-time Jewish intellectual elite were divided into small groups, debating a host of high-brow issues.

The scriptwriters made sure they employed a number of the young-sters: the Nazis had to nix the ugly gossip that children were gassed without exception. Therefore, the show included as many healthy children as possi-ble. Near the debating groups, only steps apart, more cleanly scrubbed chil-dren approached Rahm with another well-memorized one-liner: "Uncle Rahm, do we have sardines for lunch again?" They asked the question in a bored, dissatisfied way, one supposed to imply that their lunches were rep-etitiously filled with sardines. Rahm answered softly, "No, children, your uncle has arranged a better fare for today. I know you have had too many sardines." The poor kids, of course, had never heard of or tasted sardines.

The visitors were duly impressed. Was this not a beautiful, charming, clean little town where the Jews finally learned to fend for themselves and became useful members of society, all under the benevolent auspices of the Germans? The group of inspectors consisted of a representative of the Dan-ish Foreign Ministry, a member of the Danish Red Cross and a representa-tive of the International Red Cross. They never asked a probing question, never attempted to look around and walk in any other direction but the one suggested by the German hosts. They never saw the real housing, the crowded hospital, the starved and dirty inmates: they never wanted to see the reality of Theresienstadt. They wished to have a clear conscience, comforted by the memory of the peaceful, pastoral life afforded to the Jews by the generous Germans.

Following the walk through the streets of the camp, the distinguished visitors retired to the commandery to be treated to a lunch accompanied by a performance of Verdi's "Requiem" presented by the inmates under the baton of Raphael Schaechter. Eventually they were treated to a sampling of the children's opera "Brundibar." They left duly impressed. The show was such a success that the eager Nazis decided to keep the image for posterity. What better way than to capture it on film? Thus they decided to make "Der Führer gab den Juden eine Stadt" (The Leader Gave a Town to the Jews). Kurt Gerron, a famous movie producer from the days of UFA (Universale Film Ateliere) during the German heyday of movie production in the Weimar Republic, was entrusted with this task. Gerron, once a toast of Europe, was offered a deal he could not refuse: make a movie we will be satisfied with and you will live. The Nazis promised that if the results were up to their expectations Gerron's life would be spared. Gerron jumped at this offer, his only chance at life.

He embarked on his assignment diligently. He tried to capture the camp in the best possible light by filming scenes from the coffeehouse while the audience was enjoying some of the wittiest cabaret ditties. He captured many of the charming scenes designed for the inspectors' consumption and then some. He added scenes of swimming and diving into the nearby Ohre River. As soon as the movie was completed and the commissioners long gone, the Germans disassembled the stage, took away the props, and sent Kurt Gerron to Auschwitz, marked S.B. (Sonderbehandlung), and our lives returned to their previous misery.

The movie made in Theresienstadt, or at least the part that is preserved in Yad Vashem in Jerusalem, will hopefully remind the current and coming generations of the gullibility of those who wanted to believe in Germany's integrity. My father's favorite truism was proven correct: "Mundus vult decipi ergo decipiatur" (The world wants to be deceived, so let it be deceived). I did not take an active part in the beautification project that unfolded in the central square. Those of us who worked to care for the sick had neither the time nor the energy to spare. As always, the camp was awash in sick and dying inmates.

The brief conversion of the camp into a lovely, quaint little town was but one of many peculiarities in the inmates' existence. Many aspects of our lives in the camps involved contradictions. Some Nazi ordinances were prosecuted with utmost severity while others were conveniently overlooked. For instance, smoking was a major offense which could be punishable by death but cigarettes were actively traded on the black market and were the camp's universal currency. Not only did the Germans know about it but they also participated in this trade and lined their pockets handsomely by doing so. Cigarettes, jewelry, hard currency, all found their way into and out of the camp. Profits accumulated by the black-market profiteers provided a cozy nest egg for some Germans and Czech guards who engaged in these risky but lucrative exchanges. There were several inconsistencies tolerated by the Germans when they suited their objectives; sometimes it was to enrich the Nazis and at other times it was meant to keep the inmates hopeful.

With the farce of the Red Cross commission over with, life in the camp returned to the dreary routine; my life had hardly been interrupted or affected by all the hoopla connected with the Red Cross inspection. I did notice—gratefully—that prior to and during the time of the "distinguished" visit, our bread rations were more generous. Nevertheless, I had to continue my hectic pace of food hunting, working at my job and trying to build some cover for the next deportation order which was always just around the corner. I knew that another exemption by an SS commandant was highly unlikely.

During July and August, Mother's condition did not improve. Both her lungs were affected by the spreading tuberculosis; she was feverish and her body wracked with bouts of coughing that left her exhausted. Following some of those attacks she would be so tired that I had to wipe the bloody spit from her lips. At times, she sweated so profusely during her sleep that, by the early hours of the morning, her shirt was soaking wet. I changed, washed and dried her clothes as quickly as possible. The washing and drying was a complex task. We had so little water and a shortage of space for hanging the laundry. To keep her dry, I had to barter some bread rations for additional shirts to prevent her from lying in wet clothes.

On my daily visits, Mother would insist that I listen to her repeated instructions as to the whereabouts of our hidden possessions and money and what I was to claim following the war's end. From her sick bed she had reached the point of trying to direct my life after the war. She would repeatedly stress the need for me to study and remain faithful to our family values. To minimize my distress she would add, "Well, it is all meant just in case…." My heart ached while I listened to her; I was well aware that she was preparing me for the eventuality of her death. She insisted on my attention, though I would have given anything not to have to do so.

All my painful worries left me little spare time, and, with the exception of Arthur, I hardly met anyone else. Arthur would join me on occasion for a short lunch break. He never failed to radiate optimism, sport a warm smile and bring some optimistic rumor about the impending German defeat. I kept on hoping that the end of the war was imminent and my mom would live till that time. I hoped to find some good sanitarium specializing in lung ailments where Mom would be restored to good health.

August 4 seemed just another day. The previous evening Mom seemed in much the same condition. The only thing that startled me were tears in her eyes. As I kissed her goodnight, I noticed the strange sheen in her eyes. That was highly unusual for Mom; she always kept her emotions in check, retaining her brave optimistic front. I bent down one more time and inquired if anything was amiss. She categorically denied any discomfort and encouraged me to get some sleep.

My shift the next day was an early one. I took my lunch break as early as 11:30, and as on any other day, I rushed to the TB ward, #90, (once again) jammed way above its capacity with consumptive patients. Already at the doorway I noticed that something was not right. Indeed the change in Mom's appearance was shocking. Mother was in obvious agony, gasping for air. Her face was covered with sweat; her hair hung in matted strands alongside her pale face; her eyes were burning—resembling Eva's during the last hours of her life. Mother choked and coughed in fitful spells which left her totally exhausted. There was bloody foam around her lips; she could not talk and appeared in extreme distress. For a moment I froze, shocked by the sight in front of me. While Mother had been sick for a long time and even appeared somewhat unnerved the previous evening, she had never been in such a critical condition. In the last 12 hours her condition had taken a sudden turn for the worse. What triggered this deterioration? I tried to ask her but she couldn't answer. She did not have enough air to muster a reply though she clearly understood my alarmed questions.

I wiped her face, kissed her and ran to find a physician. I found Dr. Wein, but to my surprise, he was well aware of the ongoing crisis. I listened, unsteady on my feet, to his long-winded explanation. He explained to me that Mom was subjected to a treatment—at her own request—an invasive procedure called an induced pneumothorax. She had been informed and warned of the potential complications and dangers of such a procedure.

The young doctor was ill at ease; he did not look in my eyes and he obviously wished to conclude our conversation as quickly as he could. Following a brief pause he continued telling me that some time ago another patient in the TB ward had received the same treatment and improved somewhat, and Mother must have drawn hope from that case. To say that I was stunned is an understatement. There were so few diagnostic tools in the camp; it was nearly impossible to determine what and when to apply, bar the very basic critical treatments. In late 1944 it was folly to subject a patient to any invasive procedure for all medical and technical means were so inferior that most interventions only created unwarranted risks, dangers emanating from all aggressive treatments exceeded most potential benefits. Most experienced physicians had been deported long ago, the little equipment left was broken, rusty and mostly useless and there were no drugs of any kind. Only a lunatic or a patient bent on suicide would undergo a procedure of such gravity, considering the prevailing conditions.

I was so upset that I was unable to utter a word but my face must have disclosed my painful question: was he insane or unscrupulous? He must have read me well for he began to elaborate on the allegedly explicit wish of Mother not to consult me or inform me about her decision. He added that he did not pretend to believe in the success of such a procedure and that Mother knew that. She was supposedly told that even a slight improvement was highly unlikely. He then suggested that Mother must have been tired of her long suffering and had perhaps wanted to hasten the inevitable, in her own way. He reminded me that the outlook was grim and likelihood for improvement very remote. I gnashed my teeth, refusing to lose self-control. I was no fool. I knew how serious her illness was but I hoped to keep her alive till the end of the war. I shared this wish of mine with all the staff. Only then, in a specialized hospital, she might have had a chance to partially or fully recover.

I knew my mother as a decisive, energetic person who thought about her decisions for a long time and rarely wavered once she had made up her mind. She was adamant and single-minded in the pursuit of her goals. If what Dr. Wein shared with me was the truth, she must have believed that the intervention would be helpful. Perhaps, though, the physician was a lowly liar, treating her as an experiment, a lost cause, good enough to practice on. I was aware of many cases of procedures on moribund patients for the sake of expediency and practice. One thing I knew for certain: she would never have committed suicide no matter what pains and torment befell her. Under no circumstance was she a quitter. Given her condition, I was unable to ask her or verify the explanation I received from Dr. Wein. In normal times Mother was many things to many people within our family and the large circle of our friends, but to all she was known as the ultimate fighter. Her prodigious energies were always channeled and spent in efforts to promote the harmony and respectability of our family. In addition, she was deeply religious although she practiced few rituals and was only partially observant; she would never abandon the tenets of our faith. Her faith in the ethical side and moral precepts of Judaism never wavered. She would never have committed suicide.

Later I discovered, hidden among her few earthly possessions, two little pads which she used as her camp diaries. She confessed her innermost thoughts in short, dated entries. Repeatedly she expressed her hopes for at least a partial recovery. Moreover, Mother would have never abandoned her duties to me. Her brief notes are filled with anxiety and worries about the fate of her child, if I was left orphaned.

Her hurried comments in her little diary echo her fervent wish to live. I thought then and still do that the physician gave her some reason to believe that the pneumothorax (the air insertion into the cavity of her tubercular lungs) would help. Perhaps he had genuinely wanted to assist her, perhaps it was not a malicious hoax. In camp ad hoc treatments were not even considered, and while life had little value to the Nazis, the physicians faithfully observed the Hippocratic Oath. Could it be that the doctors misjudged the gravity of her condition or perhaps there had been a technical error? Did all his solicitous explanations result from his guilty conscience? I realized that I might never have my answers but I sensed, filled with cold fear, that, barring a miracle, she would not recover. But I was no longer the young girl who prayed at Eva's bedside and genuinely hoped for a last-minute supernatural reversal of her fate.

I shuddered, imagining the damage to her ravaged lungs by the pneumothorax—likely the last affront to her dire condition. I returned to Mother's bedside. The day dragged on without a change. She gasped and choked, fighting for air and, when she caught some, she would look at me and try to smile. She could no longer talk; her air supply barely allowed her to live. The camp never had any oxygen tanks to assist patients in pulmonary distress. We had no drugs of any kind to dull her pain. I kept my lonely vigil, holding Mom's hand, wiping her forehead, fluffing up her pillow, and all the time fighting back my tears and total despair.

On occasion, I noticed Arthur peeking in. He sat outside waiting for me, but I was afraid to leave her for fear any of those labored breaths were her last. So I continued sitting there, holding her hand, wiping her sweat, changing her soaked shirts as often as they dried until the late night switched into the next day. I did not pay attention to the passing hours for I prayed and prayed, knowing only too well that no matter how fervent my supplications, no supreme deity would change the course of her path. I watched the mortal struggle of her emaciated body, unable to help, trying to brace myself for the worst. The intervals between her fitful spasms for air became longer and longer. But she fought as if she could not let go.

She was cold and clammy and yet she continued her struggle for breath. The end came in the early hours of Sunday, August 6, 1944. She gasped one last time and then her hand, clasped in mine, became limp. Her face had been contorted suddenly relaxed into peaceful tranquility. Her suffering came to an end. It had to be my piercing cry of pain that carried throughout the ward. I tried to wake her. I kissed her. I was no longer rational. I was overwhelmed by despair yet I could not let go of her. I felt as if I was going to fall into a pit of insanity. I was holding her, waiting for her to breathe again. I hugged her, stroked her wet hair, unable to let go.

Arthur waited all those hours outside the ward for what he knew was the inevitable outcome. He must have feared my reaction for he had somehow organized a shot of sedation that mercifully knocked me out. I must have been out for some time because the next thing I could recall was Arthur's voice telling me to get up and join the procession accompanying the hearse loaded with the corpses, all of whom had died the same day as my mother. I followed like an automaton, only half-conscious and totally heartbroken.

In a short time span of slightly more than two years I had lost all my immediate family. I buried all those I loved and I felt as if everything that made life worth living had been taken away from me. I really wanted to give up, join my loved ones and leave this ugly world where people continuously inflicted pain and suffering upon each other. It was a warm August day when I buried my mom, yet I shivered as I reeled and stumbled within the dense throng of grievers. I was totally engulfed in the darkest, blackest hopelessness. That August day was one of the worst, most painful days of my life.

Arthur never left my side. He walked alongside, gently supporting me, softly whispering words of comfort, promising that soon all would be over. It did not seem to matter that the burial would be concluded soon. All I wanted to do was to lie down, rest my head and sleep—preferably forever.

The next few days I spent in kind of a semi-twilight zone. I was left alone and I slept and slept some more. Whenever I woke up, it was with a sharp jolt of feelings of guilt. My first impulse was to jump up and bring some food to Mother. How could I forget my duty? I could not dilly-dally like that, indulging in a long sleep. A second later, it would all come back to me, sinking in with a devastating impact. I had nowhere to rush to; Mother was not hungry, not now or ever. I had no one to care for anymore. The stabbing pain in my heart told me that my family were dead and that I was now alone, totally orphaned. So I put my head back and beseeched the Almighty to take me too and allow me to leave this vicious world.

My prayers were not answered and I continued to awake. On one occasion I felt ravenously hungry as I woke up, for I had not eaten since Mother's death. Then the thought crossed my mind that it would hurt my parents to see me as a defeated, suicidal quitter. I felt a wave of anger rising and for the umpteenth time I asked myself who had given the Germans the right to perpetrate all their evil crimes. How was it possible that they were allowed to shovel heaps of suffering on us without responsibility or punishment for their wicked misdeeds? Perhaps there might come a day of reckoning, of judgment, when society would call the Germans to answer for their deeds

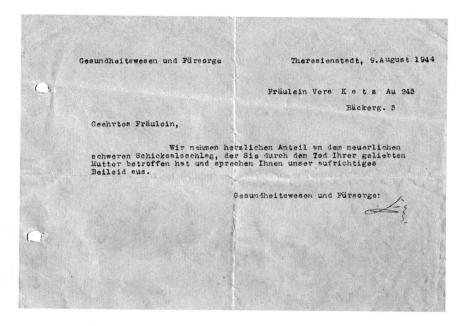

Gesundheitswesen und Fürsorge   Theresienstadt, 9.August 1944

                              Fräulein Vera K e t z Au 245
                                    Bäckerg. 5

Geehrtes Fräulein,

          Wir nehmen herzlichen Anteil an dem neuerlichen
schweren Schicksalsschlag, der Sie durch den Tod Ihrer geliebten
Mutter betroffen hat und sprechen Ihnen unser aufrichtiges
Beileid aus.

                              Gesundheitswesen und Fürsorge:

A condolence message from the camp's healthcare system to Vera about her mother's passing.

and I felt that I would like to be there. I knew that absolutely nothing would bring back those I loved but I began to feel the urge to avenge them and to help indict the Nazi criminals, if at all possible. There had to be some tribunal that would call the Germans to answer for their crimes. The world had to see the truth and render a verdict on what the Germans had done to us Jews and humanity at large. Only then would justice be served. I decided to try to live for the day when the murderers were called to account.

Later, Arthur dropped by and told me that he had looked in on me several times but he had not tried to wake me up for he believed that my strength would return faster if I had a thorough rest. Even the hospital covered for my absence, and that was quite exceptional: the only cause for not working in Theresienstadt was one's own near-death state. But then I was perilously near death, even though I was not physically ill.

The next day, I returned to work and joined the living but with many misgivings and reservations. I felt as if a big part of my heart died and was buried right along with my mom. The Jewish faith stipulates that the mourners gather and sit for seven days, comforting each other, trying to come to terms with the loss of a loved one. No such piety was practiced in a camp. Few had any family left. I did a lot of soul searching, pondering the question of the value of the struggle. Often I remembered the anger that I felt when my father had reached the conclusion that everything was lost and all we could do was to spare ourselves future torment. I was near that state myself at a time when news seeping into the camp gave reason for optimism. Wasn't it my duty to try to live until the liberation, if for no other reason than to see the retribution?

Often during this phase of my life I felt like giving up the nonsensical battle for my survival. Hitting rock bottom, I would pull out my mother's camp diary, and I would read and reread these few pages written in her small handwriting on cheap paper with a blunt pencil, smudged with her and my tears. Every time, I drew strength from her instructions which she so carefully charted for me. I safeguard this tiny memento as a precious treasure, the only souvenir my mother left me. I have carried it with me through three continents and that many emigrations. Even today, I still read her words for they always offer me strength and direction.

For some time, I avoided people; the only person I was in touch with was Arthur who still joined me during my brief lunch breaks. He became my lifeline and my emotional crutch. In later years he told me that I would not have pulled through this phase if not for our relationship. I always denied that emphatically. I wanted him, our sons and even myself to believe that I alone had the fortitude to carry on, but now, as I review my past without pretense, I believe that most likely he was right. I might have gone under without his encouraging and optimistic attitude. Arthur was one of the few men who never doubted that he would survive Hitler's murderous orgies. I never knew the source of his incredible optimism. At times I thought him naively hopeful; perhaps the strength of his conviction was based on his deep religious faith? I don't know what was at the root of his unswerving certainty but I know that his confidence never wavered. Not only was he convinced of it for himself, he also believed in the reunification of his family; his mother and sister were also in Theresienstadt and the youngest member of the family was then in Palestine. And we would need Arthur's confidence to face the challenges yet to come.

Every year in the fall, in September or thereabouts, the Germans prepared some infamy to torment their captive Jewish victims. It likely had some connection with Jewish High Holidays that are observed at this time of year. The autumn of 1944 would not be different despite wartime reversals.

That year Theresienstadt was singled out for a major deportation. It created a cataclysm for the camp. The intense speculation forecasted an impending series of liquidation transports out of Theresienstadt. Only a handful of prisoners were to be left behind to disassemble the camp and prepare for its dissolution. Eventually the remnant too would be removed to one of the eastern death camps. This time I did not panic; I remained almost indifferent. In the past I would scramble in a hectic search for some protective means and arrangements to avoid deportation but in September 1944 I did little to secure my stay. I felt neither anxiety nor the need to prevent the final tragedy, the journey to Auschwitz.

I did not attempt to find out who were the main targets, young or old, ill or healthy, artisans or the crews who toiled inside the compound. I was at peace, almost relieved that I did not have to search for someone for help. Until that moment I had never anticipated a major deportation with near indifference.

As for Arthur, I had full confidence in him: he was so well connected and resourceful. Few men had his talents, ability to improvise quickly, and find innovative approach to all problems. He knew all too well about Auschwitz-Birkenau and I trusted that he would find an escape hatch out of this upcoming wave of deportations. According to the grapevine, things would be more difficult this time because the numbers of deportees would be staggering. As on other occasions, all the dire predictions soon became a reality. The end of September brought about the first calls for deportations which continued for two months without interruption.

Transports to the east left Theresienstadt during the better part of September and October. About 18,000 prisoners were sent to Auschwitz-Birkenau, ravaging the infrastructure of Theresienstadt and paralyzing its functionality. When all was over there were about 3,000 of us left behind, mainly old folks deemed only good enough for dismantling what the Nazis thought of as a redundant camp. This massive deportation was to be the last one, hence referred to as the September transports. Arthur was included in the second round-up of the young men fit for hard labor.

11

Theresienstadt in Its Death Throes

Most major deportations were preceded by a reshuffle or demotion of the Council of the Elders. These transitions always shook the foundations of the camp. They had a ripple effect on most inmates' existence. September 1944 followed the customary path.

Early on it became evident that Professor Epstein and his entire Council would be deported. Professor Epstein was arrested and secretly taken to the Small Fortress jail where he was tortured and eventually shot. The other members of his Council received the standard S.B. designation and so were destined for immediate execution by gas when they reached Auschwitz. Once more, the tragedy of yesterday's mighty and powerful being condemned to death played itself out in the camp. The wheel of destiny made another 360-degree turn.

Rahm, who was Austrian, wanted to get rid of Epstein and replace him with an Austrian Jew. My friend Helen, a mistress of Epstein, was included among those marked for deportation with the S.B. designation. Her relationship with Epstein brought about the end of her young life. Helen's deportation also pulled in her estranged husband and his girlfriend, who also perished. In their relentless pursuit of killing Jews the Germans cast their nets far and wide. They sure lived up to their reputation for thoroughness and efficiency which sped up our undoing.

The choice of Dr. Benjamin Murmelstein as Epstein's replacement was another affront to the sensibilities of decent people. The new Council was installed, chosen from Murmelstein's cronies. Dr. Murmelstein had a reputation for being a pig and he looked the part. He was nearly obese in a camp where inmates were starving. His facial features were all but obliterated by fat; his eyes were but narrow slits in his rosy-complexioned face. If he had had an apple in his mouth he would have looked much like a pig in the butcher's shop window.

There was no doubt in the inmates' minds that Murmelstein would cater to Rahm's infamies and add some of his own. He did not disappoint us. Dr. Erich Munk, who had refused my transfer to the kitchen assignment but who had supported me during Rahm's selection when our lives hung in the balance, was among the members of Epstein's council who were dispatched to death. He was replaced by Docent Richard Stein.

Although I believed that I was desensitized to pain by now, I shuddered when Arthur's deportation call came. He was his typical confident self, exuding optimism and comforting me. He assured me, sporting his bright and cheerful grin, that he would not die. He definitely was going to live for he would pass any selection and return at war's end, which was at hand. As I listened and looked at him, I almost believed him: he looked well and more importantly he maintained his terrific attitude. Such courage and optimism should get him through the most fastidious screening. His persistence amazed me. I used to compare his stubborn tenacity, half seriously and half in jest, to a bulldog. All these characteristics and qualities might help him to face down the angel of death. One more time we rehearsed the right poise, facial expression and gait to get him through the selection for forced labor.

Arthur was included in the second transport, assigned to load at the Hamburg barracks as was customary—the same place four months ago he had watched and silently encouraged me to plead with Rahm. It seemed like so long ago.

Just before the loading time, I went to bid him goodbye. As soon as I saw him I noticed a major change in him for the worse. He looked unwell, his skin was hot, his eyes had a strange sheen and around his lips was a noticeable red eruption. The change in his looks came about quickly and, bar a reversal, would disqualify him from hard labor. In this form he did not have a snowflake's chance in hell of passing selection. But Arthur's luck did not run out on him yet.

The physician responsible for the health probity of this transport happened to pass through the corridor. He gave Arthur a cursory look and asked him to step near the window so he could better see his strangely patterned rash, as the barrack had little light. Arthur complied with little enthusiasm but only a moment later the physician concluded his examination with the diagnosis of an acute case of scarlet fever, a disease always quite common in the camp. Many infectious illnesses were rampant in the camp and all inmates who came down with one had to be kept in an isolation ward. They were automatically exempted from deportation. The Germans were petrified of spreading epidemics. As the trains traveled through some densely populated areas, inmates' diseases could spread to the civilian population. Any inmate diagnosed with such an ailment was automatically confined for six solid weeks to the isolation ward of the hospital, no ifs, ands or buts.

While Arthur's diagnosis made me very happy, he was troubled by the thought that most of his good friends were included in the departing transport. He feared that, following his recovery, he would probably be grouped with strangers and that was risky indeed. Friends in camp were invaluable; they often made the difference between life and death. Yet Arthur had no luck bargaining with the physician who was not ready to imperil his own life in order to accommodate Arthur's wish to leave with his friends. What a lucky strike that was!

There was no denying that he was ill. His face betrayed his illness; he would have never passed a selection. As matters stood, he was dispatched expeditiously to the isolation ward where he was kept for six weeks, according to the rigidly enforced orders. Most people who knew Arthur suspected his illness was self-induced. Even years after the war, many queried the strange coincidence. All believed it was the doing of a very ingenious man who knew how to infect himself with the Streptococcus and time it perfectly so that the symptoms sprang up at the right moment. But the truth of the matter was that it was not artificially inflicted, it was the real McCoy. It was, if you will, God's will.

One transport was dispatched on the heels of another one. There were only short intervals between the transports carrying away thousands of inmates. Only three days after Arthur's hospitalization, the next group was summoned, and this time it was my turn.

I was ordered to present myself in Hamburg barracks, the usual gathering place for all departing transports. For the first time, I decided not to fight the deportation order. It was a common knowledge that most, if not all, would have to leave and I knew that I didn't have a chance to get out of this summons. I packed the handful of items I owned and I walked the few steps to the place where I was to join the group enrolled in the same transport. I was convinced, like the rest of us, that the mass deportations augured the dissolution of Theresienstadt; there could hardly be a functional camp with most of the young workforce gone. It would be impossible to maintain the last shreds of the basic infrastructure or functionality of the camp.

Upon my arrival at the deportation site I was given a number. I was soon joined by another nurse, Blanka, a one-time girlfriend of Arthur who he dated during their university years. Though Blanka and I worked in the same ward, she never seemed approachable but under the circumstances it was perhaps understandable. Now we met again to share the ordeal of deportation. To my surprise, she drew near me and, in a hushed voice, disclosed her plan to hide during the night of loading, for she was promised an exemption paper for the next day. But she was scared of being shot if she was found hiding. Although any delay during the massive September deportations was only a deferment of a few days at most, she feared the German wrath if discovered behind the heavy beams where she hoped to find shelter for the night. She asked me to join her in her overnight hideaway. In case her contact failed to secure her stay, we would both automatically become included in the next departing group. I was intrigued though I sensed Blanka was prodded by fear, that misery liked company. I liked her plan and agreed to go along with it. We decided to hide in a corner where there was a large pile of planks in front of the heavy beam. The otherwise neat corridor was less immaculate during the confusion of mass deportations. Someone must have left the heap there, perhaps with the intent to hide there just before the call up. We tried not to stir up suspicion of any passersby and we were particularly concerned not to draw the attention of the men charged with finding missing inmates.

We were the targets of an intense hunt during the night Blanka and I were supposed to leave for Auschwitz. The search parties passed by many times, calling our numbers, even aiming their searchlight in our direction, but they never attempted to inspect behind the pile. These men ferreting out hiding inmates were members of the Transportleitung, Jews made responsible for gathering the full complement of deportees and herding them to the loading site. They were not armed and did not present a serious threat. While the Germans were always armed, they remained in the open courtyard during the entire duration of the preparations for the train's departure. The Germans loathed dark corridors and secluded places; they preferred to stay in wide open places that offered greater visibility.

If missing inmates were not rounded up, the officials picked the remaining numbers from the reserve. Every transport had a sizeable reserve on hand, for just such an eventuality. Above all other considerations, the exact number of inmates had to be pushed on to the train. The same routine was followed in our case. When we did not respond to the hollered exhortations and refused to leave our hiding place, two people were picked out to make up the complement. This routine was always followed; the culprits who did not show up were flushed out after the transport left on time.

After the last shouts and screams fell silent, the train left Theresienstadt and the commotion was replaced with eerie silence. That was our signal to climb out from the hiding place. First we dashed to relieve ourselves and then we confronted the transport organizers who gave us a weary look and immediately issued us the first two numbers for a transport leaving two days later. They did not bother to threaten us. They knew that we had no choice but to present ourselves: we had no ration cards and hunger forced us out.

Blanka and I parted, and, after a short nap, I decided to use the opportunity to visit the isolation ward. I knew that at best I would have a chance to speak with Arthur through the barred window but any chance to see him was a treat. On my way I had to smile, imagining Arthur's surprise to see me. Because he believed I was on my way to Auschwitz, it would almost be like a visit from a ghost.

According to the rules, I was to remain in the barracks at the deportation site but not much was enforced during the mass deportations. The turmoil affected everything and gloom blanketed the showpiece camp of only two months ago. I was so lackadaisical that I did not bother to remove the number hanging around my neck, marking me for the next departure.

Upon my arrival, someone called Arthur to the window and, as I anticipated, he was initially shocked to see me, but he quickly composed himself and proposed our instant marriage. According to the camp's rules, his six weeks' confinement protected him and would extend to me if I were his wife. Again I had to smile: in the doomsday mood of the camp's mass deportation I would not be able to find any official who would marry us, no matter what my answer was. Besides, I was a defector from a transport and was no longer listed in the ledgers of the camp. I thanked Arthur for his concern but I explained to him that not even in a dream could I find anybody who would perform such a task while the camp disgorged all its inmates. I promised Arthur to try to act upon his suggestion and I pledged to return, provided I still had an opportunity. It might not be any time soon.

Then events took another unexpected turn. The situation was fluid and changed rapidly. Life in the turmoil of mass deportations was full of twists and turns, few of which favored inmates' chances of survival. As I trudged towards the Schleusse (the deportation barrack), I ran into Docent Stein. Only hours ago he had been promoted to run the health care of the camp. Now the new top man of the camp's health division, he seemed pleased to see me and mentioned that he was looking for me. He continued, in his curt way, telling me that this very night all the employees of the hospital were to be presented to Rahm. We were to line up at 8 p.m. in front of the commandery. I replied to Docent Stein that I was no longer included in the camp's census; I was already well on my way out so that the order did not affect me. He motioned that I shouldn't contradict him and almost rudely ordered me to show up where and when he told me. He stressed that my noncompliance would have grave consequences.

I could not fathom what ill effects my disobedience could bring about and I rather hoped to get some much-needed sleep, but then I decided to follow his orders and present myself at Rahm's office. One more sleepless night would not matter all that much. Soon I believed I would sleep for a long, long time. I did not ponder the new quirk of fate, nor did I believe it was important. At twilight I walked to the commandery where I joined a growing throng of anxious folks who were queuing up in an orderly fashion.

I knew most of them; we all worked in some capacity in the care of the sick. The line began to move at about 9 p.m. at a very slow pace. Evidently Rahm took his time deciding, whatever it was that he was sorting out at this juncture. I reached his office after midnight. I was worn out, slowly inching up the staircase towards his spacious office to which we were admitted one by one. When I finally faced him I felt so tired that I barely stood upright. I had not had a decent rest or something to eat for several days and nights in a row.

He lifted his head from some papers on his desk and then asked about my position in the hospital. While I formulated my reply, he suddenly seemed to remember something. He asked me when and where he had seen me before. He appeared pleased with himself and almost looked friendly. If he were not an SS man, I could have sworn that he smiled at me. I obliged him and recounted the transport of May 18 when he had approved the stay of deportation for Mother and me. He showed good recall for he asked me about the condition of my ill mother. When I told him she had passed away about one month ago, he continued probing by asking about the other members of my family. He seemed quite pleased to hear that I had no family members left. I believed that he was done with me, but he added, almost as an afterthought, if I had another request. I must have smiled, unprepared for his question, but then I shrugged my shoulders and answered, "No, not really, Herr Kommandant." His surprised face did not disclose irritation but his voice gained some volume when he sharply asked, "Do you want to be deported or would you rather stay here?" Seizing the opportunity, I quickly said, "I would like to remain in Theresienstadt." My answer met with his approval. Again I thought that some vague grin softened his features. Turning to his aides, he said, "I want this one to stay behind. We still have to keep the hospital functional." He dismissed me and simultaneously freed me from the deportation order for the next day. That nod and wink sealed my fate: I was to stay in Theresienstadt till the bitter end of the war.

Later, in 1946, Rahm was tried by a special People's Court in nearby Litomerice, where he had to answer for his genocidal activities as an SS officer and Theresienstadt's last commander. He was found guilty, sentenced to death and hanged. Though I was certain that his punishment was well deserved, I could not get rid of feelings of unease. I could not help remembering the fact that I owed him Mother's reprieve and my life. He had exempted my mother from death in the gas chambers. He consented to my plea, thus allowing Mom to die in Theresienstadt. All the tubercular patients enrolled in the May 1944 transport were summarily gassed without selection and we—but for Rahm's compassion—would have been among them. Later he took my name off the deportation list when I was registered for transportation to Auschwitz. At times I wondered why he saved my life twice without an ulterior motive. Was there some kindness left in him? Did I remind him of someone he was fond of? With the typical ambiguity of the bizarre times we lived in, I cannot help but be grateful to an ogre without whose intervention my death would have occurred on May 19, 1944.

Unbeknownst to us the fall deportation would be the last one. I only knew that October night that I would have to re-enter the camp records. According to the administrative routine I had been stricken from the register the night before. I discarded the cardboard square indicating my transport number with gusto, and returned bone tired, nearly at dawn, to the almost empty barracks. I returned to work the next day.

On that night Rahm sent most of those he screened to Auschwitz, leaving only a handful of people behind to minister to the remaining population the camp. When the deportations finally stopped at the end of October, the sheltered Danes were left behind, a few young women and even fewer young men; most of the remaining inmates were old people, expected to pass away quickly. In the fall of 1944, there was somewhere between 3,000 and 3,500 inmates in the camp. This number later swelled with the newly arriving transports from Slovakia and the Jews whose mixed marriages were not dissolved; these groups arrived in December 1944 and January 1945, respectively.

There is a gruesome addendum to the final transport, which left on October 28, 1944. Rahm personally assigned 20 young men to a special carriage which was uncoupled near Theresienstadt. There these unfortunate inmates were ordered to discard the ashes of previously cremated prisoners into the Ohre River. If that was not appalling enough, the next order was even more ghastly. The 20 men had to dig up the corpses of those prisoners who were executed in Theresienstadt and were buried in mass graves. These remains were dispatched for cremation. Upon completion of their macabre task, the group was taken to the nearby Small Fortress prison where they were beaten to death, probably because they had seen too much. The news of the fate of the 20 men reached Theresienstadt the next day, and we all shuddered, trying to absorb this depravity.

I saw Arthur regularly; he made giant strides in recovery from the scarlet fever. While he was recovering he worked on maintenance and improvements to the ward where he was cooped up. He picked up many other outstanding jobs. There was a great need for able-bodied inmates for a lot remained undone as most of the manpower was gone. Every pair of hands made a difference. I too gained some strength, becoming less tired and drained. Now I had all my rations for myself, inadequate as they were, and there was more food in the camp. We became the beneficiaries of some rations designed for those who had been deported.

In December 1944, the first Slovak Jews arrived. Additional transports from Sered and Vahom and Novaky reached us in January, March and April of 1945. All brought horrid tales of mass extermination by gas in Auschwitz and other death camps. Incredibly, even at this late date, some inmates refused to accept the unpalatable truth of genocide in progress.

January also brought a new class of inmates: the Jews from mixed marriages and some descendants of those unions who had been protected from deportations until now. These were the very few Jews whose Gentile spouses had braved the dangers and did not divorce them. In spite of the fact that the fortunes of the war no longer favored the Germans—and even we were aware of it—they continued to deport more Jews. They found the time and used trains needed to supply men in uniform just to kill Jews. Everything was invested into the top priority of the Germans: the destruction of all Jews. Obviously at that point, the annihilation of the Jews was deemed more important than winning the war. What a dubious distinction!

Arthur was one of the few young men who remained in Theresienstadt to the very end. He owed this to the lucky whim of fate in the form of the well-timed outbreak of scarlet fever. His confinement to the infectious ward lasted six long weeks and came to a conclusion at about the end of October, after the last transport was dispatched from the camp. This was also the time when the new Council tackled the task of the camp's functionality. Having lost well over two-thirds of its workforce Theresienstadt was paralyzed. The work force had to be restructured for the camp to remain even marginally operational. This was a gigantic task for which the new members of the Council were hardly qualified.

As mentioned, while still a patient, Arthur helped out in the ward. He filled in for the man who was responsible for heating the water and hospital maintenance who had been deported. After Arthur's discharge, Docent Stein asked him to continue his work in the hospital because his previous privileged assignment could no longer be justified. The original "stoker and baths" attendant, now gone, had built, with tacit approval of his superiors, something resembling a roomette high up in a corner of an attic. This imaginative and wonderful creation became Arthur's inheritance. Arthur in turn had a very developed sense of upgrading and improving his environment, facilitated by his exceptional manual dexterity. This unexpected windfall stimulated Arthur's imagination and ambition to expand on its practicality and looks. From our present vantage point it is nearly impossible to explain how a dusty, tiny corner in a dark attic was converted into an almost cozy place. For the first time we had a semblance of a room just for the two of us. There were quite a few planked-up small garrets left in the half-emptied camp, for many inmates had built up these secluded corners into quasi-private mini-dwellings. We called them mansard.

For me, leaving the crowded barracks, even if unofficially, was a great relief. The long time spent in the packed, noisy, messy and smelly halls was weighing on every inmate. Here in our roomette, there were no fights, tears, pains or memories of others to endure. Nobody's nightmares or sobs disturbed our sleep. As for myself, I felt as if we had moved to the Garden of Eden.

By a quirk of fate, my personal situation was upgraded. Totally unexpectedly I met an old acquaintance of my dad. One day while we lined up for soup I met Mr. Roubicek, an invalid from World War I. He had arrived in the camp with the mixed-marriages group that removed the Jewish spouses from still-existing unions. Though the Nazis hated all Jews, they gave a temporary reprieve to the invalids who had fought in the 1914–18 war for Austria-Hungary or Germany. These people were assigned to easier work and so Mr. Roubicek, my father's friend, was ordered to clip the coupons from the ration cards and indicate to the distributing cook the number of portions the inmate was collecting.

Mr. Roubicek suggested a simple plan: I would join the queue where he was posted and he would inform the cook that I had submitted coupons for two inmates instead of one only. The cooks hardly ever checked, knowing that few would take the risk for fear of punishment. The hazards were considerable had Mr. Roubicek been caught but spot-checks and controls in the near empty camp were rare and perfunctory. The scheme worked well, though I was careful not to abuse it. From the end of October 1944 to February 1945 all deportations came to a standstill and Theresienstadt experienced one of its calmest periods.

Transports were arriving but none left; starvation abated somewhat and the crowding was eased greatly. In early February hearsay had it that some Jewish inmates would be swapped for German prisoners of war; the transaction would be mediated by the Red Cross. The Council of the Elders asked for volunteers. Few believed the proposed exchange would take place. Most of the seasoned inmates were convinced that Rahm, who had personally ordered this transport, would be following the tragic strategy used to dispatch the children from Bialystok. We became less certain when those who took the chance and enrolled were given nice, nearly new luggage; no numbers were issued to them and, wonder of wonders, they boarded a passenger train where each had a seat. We tried to decipher the enigmatic ruse, suspecting some new deceit. We were all proven wrong. Sometime later postcards arrived, mailed by the members of this transport, from a place we thought impossible for them to reach: Switzerland.

Though we had reasons to believe that Germany's defeat was not far off we had some very serious concerns and issues to consider. There was one question on everybody's mind: "How will the final act unfold?" We did not believe that the Nazis would let us live; we were sure that they hatched plans to do us in. We watched with great unease the strange happenings that unfolded in front of our eyes. The camp commandant ordered a mysterious construction in the underground passages to be completed. It had to be done in an exact timeframe. Openings in the walls were bricked up and a ventilation system was installed. The completion of the structure was supervised by the SS officers exclusively who brutally pushed for a swift finish. Another passage of Theresienstadt's fortress was walled up with only a narrow entrance left. Though the building was off limits to all inmates except those who were ordered to work there, nothing remained hidden to the rest of us. Just in case, if there were some individuals who doubted the purpose of this structure, the final order for an iron grille and air-tight doors persuaded everyone that a gas chamber was being built. The fact that Rahm forbade the use of hydrogen cyanide for disinfection and personally took the key from its storage was further proof that we were going to die soon, by the time-tested methods of the Nazis: gassing with Zyklon B.

We all lived through a veritable roller coaster of emotions. Daily we dipped down and swung up, vacillating between hope and despair, life or death. Only after the war did we figure out that the contradictory incidents were due to a fundamental schism among the Germans. The Nazis realized that they were down to the wire, the war was lost and time was running out. On one hand a faction of the SS wanted to complete the annihilation of the Jews and gas all those still alive as a last hurrah before retreating into their Valhalla. They were opposed by a group of more pragmatic—though no less criminal—SS men. They reasoned that preservation of the camp could become their ticket to freedom; if they were to hand it over to the Red Cross then they might buy some goodwill to ride out the storm and preserve their personal safety. The infighting of these opposing groups of SS officers caused the dichotomy of actions during the last days of the war. On the one hand, the Germans were hastily constructing gas chambers, and on the other hand, they were sending some inmates to Switzerland.

The work in the hospital did not ease. It remained backbreaking but I had more energy, thanks to Mr. Roubicek supplementing my daily rations. Arthur and I kept close watch following the rumors of the imminent completion of the gas chamber. As we faced this prospect, Arthur began to devise contingency plans such as building a hiding place for us.

We had to prepare for all eventualities. Arthur decided that in case of mass execution by shooting, we should find cover in the huge sterilization room of the hospital. Arthur worried about the length of time we would have to hide in case of gassing. Always a handyman, he dug out an

underground cubicle next to the boiler in the ward reserved for sterilization. He removed a few planks in the floor, adjusted the ground underneath
so that we could stay there for a few days in the event of a final onslaught.

Soon another doomsday verdict began to circulate. We heard that
the Germans were going to flood the underground passages as well as the
large pond. They would herd all the inmates in there and drown one and all.
There was no end to speculation, some real and some imagined, all taken
seriously and hotly debated by the inmates. The flood of rumors of our
impending end obliterated other considerations, bringing our anxiety to
new heights. I relinquished all contingency plans to Arthur. He was highly
competent, seemed to be confident and well prepared for all eventualities.
I did not share his optimism. I thought that the odious Nazis would find a
way to pull us down with them in the final hour of their defeat. While we
waited on death row, another piece of gossip hit the camp: there might be
a chance for another group of Jews to be exchanged for POWs and sent to
Switzerland.

This alluring prospect might offer a chance for life. Arthur snooped
around and found out that we had a better chance if we were married and
applied as a couple. I had no objections. I just thought that it was bizarre to
marry amidst all the death and destruction but Arthur met my sentimental, outdated considerations with a condescending smile. With his characteristic tenacity, he embarked on preparations for our camp wedding. All
was settled within a day or two. Arthur chose the traditional religious ritual
which was more meaningful and compatible with his upbringing.

My only task was to find a dress. At that stage I only owned the gray
smock in which I worked and wore every day of my life. One of the girls
I worked with, Herta Kraemmer, quickly volunteered to lend me the
only dress she had left from her better days in Vienna. It was a creation
of a famous house of high couture. On my wedding day, March 6, 1945,
I donned the elegant pitch-black dress, created by one of the best Viennese fashion designers, and I walked to the Magdeburg barracks, the center
of the camp's administration. There, in one of the rooms, was an improvised chuppah, the traditional canopy, imperative for a Jewish wedding. In
reality, it was only an improvisation—a semblance, if you will—of the real
thing: the drapery fastened above our heads was a threadbare blanket supported by four sticks, rather wobbly and unsteady.

Compensating for the shabby exterior was the impressive presence of
the officiating rabbi, Dr. Friediger, who, though a prisoner like us, was a
member of the privileged and prominent Danes. He enjoyed an illustrious reputation for wisdom and integrity, so rare a commodity in camps,
where most inmates had to rely on their cunning. Arthur did not stop
there: my indomitable groom arranged for a musical accompaniment. At

some point he befriended Hambro, the fine Danish violinist, whose mastery of the violin filled the drab room with enchanting sounds of melodious compositions.

According to tradition I circled around my groom seven times and I also received a wedding band. Only God knows how he got hold of a simple silver wedding band that he placed on my forefinger, repeating the ancient prayer of a groom consecrating his bride in marriage according to the ancient Jewish laws. Rabbi Dr. Friediger also improvised; he substituted black coffee for the wine we were supposed to sip. In spite of several extemporizations the ceremony was dignified and to me very meaningful.

The transport to Switzerland did not materialize but there were some negotiations with the Red Cross. To that end the camp hosted a much-feared guest. Theresienstadt was visited by the notorious Adolf Eichmann who ordered the destruction of incriminating evidence and some improvements within the camp because there was another visit of a Red Cross commission in the offing. Likely the Nazis were panicked that time was running out for their thousand-year reich.

Then I had no time to reflect on the peculiar coincidence that in the worst time of my life I had met and married a man whose unwavering optimism offset my bottomless despair. Arthur brought love and hope into my life. I admired his strength and emotional—as well as physical—fortitude. Perhaps it was his inner core, not diminished by a personal tragedy, which helped him to retain the confidence that I had lost long ago. While I viewed every hour as borrowed time, Arthur thought of the spring months of 1945 as the time of new beginnings. Though the outline of the postwar years was not visible yet, it was readily imaginable to his mind. Though I did not want to dwell on my despondency, I could not shake the feeling of dreary loneliness. At this time I suffered still another personal tragedy. While I never ceased hurting for the loss of my much-loved family, the demise of my would-be first-born hurts on a different level. In camp all pregnancies had to be interrupted or the woman was sent to die in Auschwitz. Nobody could have saved our baby: it was doomed, its hour of conception was wrong; it never had a chance of life.

One day, during a surgery, I felt ill and fainted. The physician was puzzled. I seemed so much physically improved lately that having ruled out all else, I was sent to Dr. Klein, the camp's obstetrician. The diagnosis was fast in coming: I was pregnant, some three months plus, and I had to have an abortion as fast as possible. Arthur and I were surprised and heartbroken about this turn of events. There was nothing anyone could do for us to change the situation. We had only one evening to come to terms and accept that our would-be first-born had to be killed.

It was not even that Arthur and I were careless, far from it. As was

Vera and Arthur's ketubah from their camp wedding, March 1945.

the case for most women prisoners, my ovulation stopped long ago. I was assured by Dr. Klein that protracted starvation could only be reversed by normal diet and improved living conditions. Dr. Klein was on record as doubting that the fertility of women who were affected by so much deprivation might ever be restored, even when normal nourishment and care could be provided. I never thought that my much-improved rations from August

1944 could rebuild my hormonal balance so quickly. There was no percep-
tible evidence to suggest any reversal of my condition from the last three
years and the last thing I thought about was the danger of getting pregnant.

Arthur and I spent a sleepless night, trying to come to terms with the
bitter fact. In the early morning hours, I entered the endometritis ward.
Dr. Klein tried to provide me with some ether to put me under, but in spite
of his best efforts, he managed to organize only a few drops of it. Whatever medication there was before was all gone—all was bare and empty.
The excruciating physical pain of the procedure was nothing in comparison
to the emotional anguish I had to come to terms with. The procedure was
short but to me it lasted an eternity. Afterwards, Dr. Klein sat on my bunk.
He supported my forehead and wiped my tears. The ether, which failed to
put me to sleep, had some effect after all. I kept on choking, retching and
feeling so miserable that Dr. Klein did not dare move from my side.

The very next day I returned to my hectic work which offered, as
always, the chance to forget all pains. I mourned my unborn child in a special way. I still do. It would have been our first born and it became another
victim of Nazi hatred. Later Arthur and I never spoke about this tragic
event but I know that we both mourned that loss in our separate personal
ways.

The month of April ushered in sensational rumors in Theresienstadt.
The favored Danes would be allowed to leave the camp and return home.
At first nobody paid attention to such incredible gossip, but when April 15
came, the astonished inmates woke up to see the camp's central square filled
with white Swedish buses. We all rushed towards the shiny mirage which
we could only approach from considerable distance. For years we were
used to seeing inmates leaving, always with a bundle, and always pushed
onto box cars. Now we witnessed a miracle: Jews, albeit Danish Jews, being
treated like valued citizens. Men in white uniforms stepped out of those
buses; some of them were drivers, others sent to accompany the inmates
about to be released. To us the shimmering white images resembled heav-
enly angels from some child's tale. And quite like the emissaries of mercy,
they began to distribute gifts to the amazed Danish Jews. The Danes, previously ordered to the central square by the Elder of the Jews, were totally
bewildered as they received food and the camp's taboo: cigarettes. To say
that they were overjoyed was an understatement. They were ecstatic about
their good fortune. They were filled with gratitude for the miracle. It was
the crowning achievement of their brave, dedicated king, Christian X, who
never abandoned his Jewish subjects.

The rest of us watched the extraordinary display with rising spirits,
happy for our Danish co-religionists, wishing them well, and for the umpteenth time longing to be one of them. The camp's orchestra was on hand,

playing Danish songs as their departing salute. Quite unexpectedly an SS man appeared. I believe it was SS Heindl, one of the meanest tormentors of the inmates. He walked quickly in the direction of the buses and was about to enter one of vehicles. Then, to us, another near miracle happened. A tall, hefty Swede spread his arms, barred his way, stared him down and announced loudly, for all of us to hear, "These buses are here by the order of the Swedish Red Cross to pick up and return the Jewish Danish nationals. By an explicit order no one else is permitted to enter! The buses represent Swedish territory."

We listened with tears in our eyes and looked with malicious joy at Heindl as he walked away like a beaten dog. This was the same Heindl who had kicked and trampled a boy to death, perhaps only ten years old, who had sneaked out of the camp and tried to steal a few cherries he plucked from a tree. This was the same brute who was famous for sneaking up behind workers and ordering them to empty their pockets. Anyone who had a cigarette butt or contraband became the target of Heindl's ire. He would whip and beat the offender long after the unfortunate victim had stopped breathing. Now the ogre shrank in size, humiliated in front of us—his victims of long standing. The first signs of poetic justice were being sketched, on display right before our eyes.

Once the Danes had safely boarded the coaches, they made a point of showing off the rights and privileges of their freedom. They ostentatiously lit cigarettes, regardless if they smoked or not. It was their message to the watching SS men, the joy of flouting the Nazi prohibition of smoking, only yesterday punishable by death. Indeed, April 15 was the first happy and proud day for all inmates of Theresienstadt! We bid farewell to the Danish Jews and thought of the great humanitarian, the Danish king Christian X.

A few days after the departure of the Danes another event shocked the camp, only this one sent waves of outrage through the ranks of the inmates. The death marchers began to arrive. The Nazis had ordered the evacuation of inmates from camps scattered in the archipelago of the many concentration camps. Most were located near the shrinking battlefronts. From the west and east the Allied forces pressed on and were closing in on most of the notorious death and labor camps. The Germans embarked upon the removal of the last living witnesses to a place still under their control: the most inland camp, Theresienstadt. The plan called for the liquidation of the remaining witnesses of Nazi atrocities. The only place that it could have been accomplished was in a camp still under Nazi rule: Theresienstadt. It would be completed in the newly built gas chambers, thus no inmates would survive and none could testify to the atrocities perpetrated by the master race.

Throughout the last throes of a lost war, the Germans did not give up on their main goal: extermination of all Jews. One means of doing this was the death marches for the remaining prisoners. There were new horrors on the roads of Europe: stumbling shadows of men and women forced to march on the frozen highways as the Nazis retreated. They stumbled on, without food or drink, without warm clothing or footwear, in the bitter frost of winter months for weeks on end, most falling by the wayside. The accompanying SS guards would shoot anyone who fell down; others froze or were left to die from exhaustion. Only a handful managed to escape this final nightmare, hide in some remote farmhouse and wait for the fury of the demons to subside. Thirteen thousand shadowy skeletons reached Theresienstadt in the last two weeks of April. Most of those who got to Theresienstadt died there—succumbing to the spotted fever epidemic, malnutrition or a host of other illnesses. The final weeks of World War II gave a new meaning to the word "hell": Dante's Hell could not compare to the Nazi version. The roads of central Europe reflected the ultimate nightmare of ruin and devastation. This, then, became the final legacy of the Third Reich.

Among the first returnees were some of our friends who had left Theresienstadt perhaps only six months or a year ago. They were changed beyond recognition, converted into the strange apparitions we called Musselmen. They were tragic caricatures of human beings, no longer living creatures but not quite dead. This was but the beginning.

The death marchers were coming day and night by the thousands, emaciated, covered with sores, some half naked, others clothed in dirty, torn rags, infested with lice. They were dropping like flies, dying on the road, soiled beyond imagination. But that was their least concern. They had lost all traces of human dignity; they never even noticed the feces dried on their stick-like legs. They were obsessed with one thought alone: food and drink.

All Theresienstadt's remaining work force was ordered to try to help this incoming flood of unfortunates. Our resources were so totally depleted, inadequate in all aspects. The most we could do was to try to bury the dead, and that soon became an impossible task. Not unlike the fall of 1942, corpses were everywhere. They decomposed and rotted, filling the camp's air with the horrid stench of decaying human flesh.

One afternoon, I happened to pass by when yet another group of living dead had stumbled into the camp. Suddenly I thought that I recognized a friend, Dr. Schapp. I reached into my pocket where I hid a small piece of bread. I thought of throwing it to him. But with his last strength he mouthed the words: "Don't do it, Vera. They'll kill me for it." I saw him clasp his hands, as if in prayer, and I refrained from my ill-advised charity. He was right, of course; many had died, trampled by a headlong rush of starving Musselmen who had reason to believe that there was a piece of bread

or a potato peel around. With their last bit of frenzied energy the totter-
ing Musselmen fought for anything edible, summoning more strength than
we thought their skeletal bodies could generate. Whenever anything edible came in sight of the Musselmen, they suddenly came to life, energized,
fighting tooth and nail in ferocious attacks to grab whatever they could.
The Nazis could have been proud of their handiwork: they had turned the
remnants of European Jewry into savage animals. And the floodgates of
the Musselmen never closed. They kept on coming, worn to death, keeling
over and dying everywhere, on the grass, the pavement, heaving one over
another. Their bodies' skin and bones, their bulging eyes and yellow complexion, the silent testimonies to the torturous months they had to endure.

   Although we seemed to work day and night, we did not make progress
eradicating their misery. There was no food, medication or disinfection;
the delousing stations could not clean up this quantity of sick and dying.
And they just kept on coming and coming. On one occasion, I went to the
attics to bring some soup to the few we managed to bring inside. I went
with Dr. Braun, a young and still strong six-footer. We carried a cauldron
with soup. I tried to walk on an elevated plank that separated the floor of
the attic into two separate parts. I thought that I could best help by feeding
some of them but it proved impossible. To my surprise they rose like shadows from Hades. With their last ounce of strength, they lifted their hands
high enough for me to see, hoping to draw my attention to their plight. All
they managed to do was to scratch the skin of my legs.

   A few moments later I looked down at my ankles and calves, noticing blood oozing down my legs. I bled badly, the blood mixed with the dirt
from their grimy fingernails, but I did not feel the pain. The physical discomfort was overshadowed by my anguish watching this wild nightmare. I
looked transfixed into their huge, death-marked eyes. I remember thinking
that we were witnessing the true Gehenna.

   It was in those days that little Jozsi was brought to Theresienstadt. By
then we had next to no children in our midst; most of the youngsters had
been gassed long ago. We were all surprised when a small, skinny boy, perhaps six years old, was carried into the hospital. At first, I noticed a pair of
large, dark eyes, those of a suffering sixty year old. His little face was contorted with pain. He did not cry, he had not enough strength for that, he
just whimpered like a badly hurt kitten. I tried to place a dressing on his
back, or rather what was left of it, after an air-raid hit. Little Jozsi had been
deported on a truck that was the target of an air raid. Both his parents were
killed, and Jozsi sustained grave injuries when the gunfire strafed the poor
little boy. The machine gun from a low flying aircraft tore half of his back,
exposing torn flesh covered with caked blood that dried up long ago and
where a myriad of flies and insects were feasting.

We knew that we could not save Jozsi. That was heartbreaking enough, but to make matters worse, he fixed his burning eyes searchingly on me. He did not even cry, he just whined softly while his big eyes were filled with despair, their expression speaking volumes. I could not put him back on the floor among the other patients. I kept on holding him in my arms, rocking him gently, softly repeating over and over again the only Hungarian sentence I knew: "Nem Fai, Jozsi" (It does not hurt, Jozsi). I did not know if he understood my Hungarian but he reacted to the universal language of compassion and gentleness. He sensed my attempts to soothe his pain and give him tender loving care and warmth for the last time on this earth. He clung to me for what comfort I was able to provide. A while later, his eyes closed, and his breathing turned increasingly shallow. Then it slowed even more, soon stopping completely. Jozsi was liberated from his suffering. His little body, racked with pain only a while ago, rested limply, wilted in my arms. He had attained his peace. I caressed his little face, crying for a lost life, shattered by inhumanity of the war. Sometimes Jozsi comes back to me in my nightmares that force me to revisit the past.

The death marchers were covered with lice and most suffered from typhus and other illnesses. Soon these plagues spread through the rest of the camp. One morning I woke up feeling ill, running a high fever. Clearly it was my turn. But mine was a strange variant: I had a high fever for three or four days, which then subsided, only for it to come back within a week or two. The physicians called it "febris recurrens" and, true to its name, it came back at regular intervals for one year with undiminished intensity.

At this time, I was ordered to work with Dr. A. Guttman, a skillful and indefatigable surgeon. Dr. Guttman was a young man, a recent arrival, for he was one of the protected Jews, married to an Aryan. As a newcomer to the camp, he had a limited understanding of changes wrought on inmates by their lengthy internment. While he had difficulties understanding us "old-timers," he was at a loss to grasp the mentality of the Musselmen, who hung on to life by the skin of their teeth.

To illustrate what I mean, I will relate one typical incident. It demonstrates the different plane on which we moved then and later, separating us from other people. The episode was in itself unimportant; it was something that unfolded in camps many times every single day. It happened on the ward where patients were jammed tightly. Some had cots; others were lying on the bare floor. One morning I heard some altercation. It proved to be a fight over the theft of a piece of bread by one hungry patient from another one. The thief, a wisp of a man, was recovering from a surgery on a large abscess. He sneaked up to the bed of another man who was semi-conscious, hoping not to be seen, and broke off a piece from his bread ration. No one who had been in a camp any length of time would have been surprised.

Food was routinely snatched by other inmates. Camps were governed by laws of the jungle: every man for himself. The inmate who did not learn this principle early on had a very short life expectancy. This particular petty theft did not go unobserved, for Dr. Guttman saw it from a doorway. The tiny, withered thief trembled and cried out in fear when Dr. Guttman grabbed him by the collar of his smock. With his feeble, raspy voice he repeated in Yiddish—a language Dr. Guttman did not understand—that he had not pilfered the whole piece; he had only broken off a small chunk. By camp standards (such as they were) he was really a considerate fellow, for he had left some bread for the rightful owner instead of snatching the whole piece. He must have feared that the man who had caught him would kill him or beat him to a pulp. That was the usual punishment meted out by Kapos to inmates who stole from another one. I still can hear his whining words, "Ich hab nue ugeschnitten."

Dr. Guttman was light years away from hitting a patient; he only scolded the thief and gave him a lecture, delivered in his elegant German, about some principles of civilized behavior. The little schlemiel neither understood the language nor the educational methods of the surgeon, but he understood the rules of the camp: the right of the stronger man to brutalize the weaker one. I watched this episode unfold and I turned to Dr. Guttman and said abruptly, "You are a fool; let him go, you make me positively sick." The good doctor was taken by surprise, so much so that he dropped the offender who quickly scrambled to safety in the most distant corner of the ward. Dr. Guttman, still bewildered, asked me if I condoned thievery and he seemed genuinely amazed by my answer. I replied that he would understand if he too would have been an inmate of long standing. Had he suffered starvation and deprivation to the extent we had, he would have understood. Prisoners in Nazi concentration camps had to adapt to the laws of jungle. We lived by a different set of rules—those that helped us exist in this particularly vicious, depraved outpost. I added that even if he read volumes of books, it would not help him to grasp the rules of this subdivision of hell.

It was the first time that I felt that few, if any, would later understand what it was like to live under the German whip in their concentration camps. Few could grasp the impact of long years of life on death row—the death sentence hanging above our neck suspended like Damocles' sword on the thinnest of wires. To watch the demise of our loved ones and experience brutal hunger for years on end: how could the outsiders appreciate the impact that this wrought on our outlook on life? I believe that the self-imposed silence of the survivors, which lasted well over ten years after the war, was based on the reasoning that no one would or could comprehend, even in the unlikely event of being interested. There was no sense in trying to explain what was beyond the pale. It might have been a mistake but we were convinced that we had endured an experience that defied understanding by other, more fortunate mortals.

Later I was proven right. Few wanted to know. Most people were uncomfortable in our presence as if we were stained by some invisible mark of Cain. I am not certain why our experiences during the war years made people feel ill at ease when the very same people would discuss with morbid curiosity the latest bloody crimes or street brutality. Was it perhaps some vague feeling of guilt? The indifference was not so readily explicable among the younger generation who were not around at that time. Perhaps they felt some embarrassment for their elders' palpable indifference while this world plunged into catastrophe.

During the last painful spasm of Theresienstadt, I only had the occasional glimpse of Arthur. We spent our days and most of our nights trying to take care of the death marchers who were streaming in. Though we knew that the task to consolidate the chaos was above our capabilities, we still kept on trying. Sometimes, when I paused for a breath of air, the thought occurred to me that there must have been some enormous crime in our past that we had perpetrated and for which we had been sentenced to death en masse. Why else would the world remain indifferent to suffering on such an unprecedented scale? Were our elders, parents, and teachers sworn to conspiratorial silence, having hushed up these crimes to their offspring? Later, I just smiled about my own stupidity, but I was then only 19 years old and three of those years were spent interned in a camp.

The nightmarish days of April slipped almost unnoticed into May. Only the lovely weather helped to ease the hardship of people lying outdoors, helter-skelter, exposed to the mercy of the elements.

12

Liberation

Early in the morning of May 8, I got a message from Arthur to come down to the sterilization room as soon as possible. My first reaction was one of trepidation. I was concerned for Arthur's health as he had badly injured his knee just two days before while assisting some of the newly arrived. He walked with a great deal of pain. I rushed down and to my relief Arthur did not seem worse for his recent injury.

What was surprising was the company he kept. With him was a death marcher, one who appeared in slightly better condition than most. Arthur appeared pleased as he explained that the man was the fiancé of his sister. That piqued my interest for I had heard many tales of Ann's childhood sweetheart. Now Kurt L. returned, surviving the death march. He arrived with a cube of sugar and two cloves of garlic in his pocket. That was a feat. The man must have been extremely disciplined to restrain himself from devouring these items. Later, he told us that he chewed daily on the garlic clove, hoping to boost his strength. His presence and his remarkable tale of survival brought much joy to the Schiff family, and other than meeting Kurt, the morning of May 8 was not particularly memorable. We tried to follow the whispers about the imminent German defeat, and though our confidence grew, we could not differentiate what was exaggeration and what was truth.

There was chaos in the camp. We still worked around the clock but the conditions seemed to deteriorate by the minute. At midday, however, the corridors of the hospital began to resonate with unusual shouts urging those who could walk to run to the fence. Most of us were not sure what was afoot, but I joined the crowd.

From a distance we could hear the heavy rumbling of trucks, armored vehicles, artillery and tanks. Someone exclaimed that the Russians arrived; others thought Americans were approaching the camp; and a few skeptics warned that the sounds might be motorized German units. The latter utterances were viewed as undue pessimism and were quickly silenced by those who argued that if the Germans were still in charge, they would have shot us while we ran and gathered around the fence, for approaching it was strictly forbidden. A few dauntless inmates tried to break an opening in the fence, cheered on by the others. It took a short while and the banging yielded a big gaping hole, the first glance at the world outside. I dashed through the hole and I was outside the camp on a highway I had never seen before. For the first time since my deportation, I stepped out into the free world. I had spent the last six years of my teens and adolescence trying to avoid death, a strange preoccupation for a youth. The last three years, I had been confined in a tightly sealed camp, overwhelmed by hunger, illness, violence and death.

Nearby were villages and small towns where people existed under nearly normal conditions, only marginally affected by the consequences of the war. It seemed as if we lived on two different planets, though physically close by; we were light years apart.

My first moments on the highway were wonderful: the air seemed intoxicating; the thought of freedom was dazzling. While all these thoughts raced through my mind, the distant rumbling sound was getting closer and louder. And then we saw them: the Russian tanks, manned by young soldiers. Before we saw the soldiers we could clearly see the signs of the Soviet Union: the hammer and sickle painted in red on the tanks. The men in the turrets of these tanks appeared to be angels. We could hardly believe our own eyes. They were approaching at a fast clip, coming closer and closer to where we stood. We all wanted to welcome them; gathering our last strength, we broke into cheers for our liberators.

When they reached the fence we made out their faces; they were so young and boyish and they looked at us and our enthusiasm with uncertain smiles. They seemed astonished to meet such a motley crowd: some of us wore prisoners' striped uniforms; others had torn civilian clothing, mostly dirty and raggedy. We were all skin and bones, and though we cheered with joy and delight, we still had the looks of worn, longtime inmates. Not only did the Russian soldiers seem uncertain about whom or what they had encountered, they also appeared in a great hurry. But we, who had waited for so long for this hour, would not be deprived of the best hour in our lives. We yelled and shouted that we were no ordinary prisoners; we were innocent Jews, held captive in the camp right behind us. I do not know if they understood or if it helped any, but the column began to slow down, looking at us with some curiosity.

Their conclusion must have been that we needed food. The Russian boys were not naïve, they had their experiences with the Nazi camps; they knew the devastation that Nazi rule wrought on its victims. We must have been the last camps to be liberated by the Soviet army. It took a long, bloody war to break the back of the Nazis. They could hardly comprehend what the sight of their young, well-disposed faces meant to us. To us, even their tanks, marked with the Soviet emblem of the sickle and hammer, were signs of redemption and salvation.

The Russian soldiers did not need a long time to make out that we were a starving crowd and they decided to do something about it. They began to toss down bread, meat and potatoes to us. That was the worst, if kindest, idea they could have conceived. What ensued could best be described as pandemonium. Someone screamed the word salami, others shouted chocolate—there was no stopping the ensuing chaos. People began to push and jump over one another. Overcome with intoxicating euphoria, most failed to notice that the tanks only slowed down their speed, never coming to a complete halt.

When the uproar subsided, a number of people had been hurt. I looked at the injured: it was foolish to take such chances on the day of our liberation. But we waited so long for this hour, often losing hope that we would ever experience it; when it finally arrived, the bedlam was surely understandable. We carried the hurt back to the camp where we cleaned and dressed their wounds, pains which were overshadowed by the miracle of the day. We all were indescribably happy. Afterwards I went to see Arthur who was immobilized by his dislocated knee. I reported the day's happenings to him which still seemed unbelievable. I feared that it was a dream and that we might wake up to another day of Nazi-dominated reality. Not Arthur; he was radiating happiness and repeated that he always knew that we would outlive our tormentors. This was the honest truth; he never lost faith in the ultimate victory and our survival. Since I first met him he maintained that he would live to see the end of Hitler's infamous rule and it is equally accurate that I often thought his belief naïve and outlandish but I never failed to be impressed by his indomitable optimism and faith.

The days that followed the wondrous elation of liberation brought more disarray. Theresienstadt had no food or medicine for the death marchers who kept on pouring in and the epidemics reached such proportions that it swept through the entire camp's population. In those final hours it seemed as if death might prevail after all. Would not it be a supreme irony to die already liberated? We hoped for some immediate humanitarian help but there were no signs of anyone coming to our rescue.

The handful of survivors who pulled through the Nazis' murderous spree teetered on the brink of death. Our stamina long depleted, we had no strength to cope with the myriad of infections all around us. The greatest threat was the raging epidemic of typhus, the spotted fever, and the spread by the innumerable lice. Thousands died in the first days of liberation, succumbing to the pestilence of many epidemics that ravaged the lives of the few survivors. In fact, some took their last breaths, never knowing that they had lived long enough to witness Germany's defeat.

The first days of our freedom then were less than pretty. At this point, the entire expanse of Theresienstadt was littered with corpses. We had no strength to bury them or even cart them away to the crematory. They were scattered all over, rotting in the sun, exuding an unimaginable stench. Eventually the health authorities in Prague became sufficiently alarmed to dispatch a preliminary emergency medical unit. At the helm of the contingent was Dr. Raska who stated upon arrival in Theresienstadt that his main concern was to assist the Czech prisoners in the nearby Small Fortress; his heart was not with the interned Jews. His announcement caused consternation among us. Will there never be an end to the insults and discrimination, even now that the Nazis were vanquished? Obviously anti–Semitism was alive and well; the Nazis sowed the bacillus that sprouted even after their demise. Not that Czech anti–Semitism was unknown but it was mild compared to Hitler's virulent brand of hatred. This first message from Prague emissaries had the familiar tone of bias and discrimination.

The dangerous epidemics had to be brought under control, and the Russians helped consolidate our efforts to battle the outbreak. Fortunately the Soviet army medical corps rose to the occasion. In mid–May the Red Army took over. Once more Theresienstadt became sealed from the outside world. The Soviet medical team began to stabilize the hazardous situation.

In cooperation with the Russians, Docent Stein decided to vacate some barracks and transfer the typhus patients to this makeshift isolation station. I was ordered to report for duty in the newly opened typhus isolation ward. At first I wanted to comply but then something within me rebelled. I felt that I had my share of misery within the walls of this camp. The Red Army's medical corps was comprised of healthy, strong and efficient medical and paramedical professionals. They were well qualified and had the experience in handling pandemics. I felt I had neither the strength nor the will to stay. I was drained physically and emotionally. I wanted to go home.

I shared my decision with Docent Stein who voiced his disapproval but he used words and tones which gave me reason to believe that he understood. Arthur could not join me. His knee injury was not mending well at all, and he was for all intents and purposes immobilized. We agreed that I would go home alone and come back to fetch him after taking stock of the situation in Prague. I took my leave from Arthur and neither one of us gave a second thought to the fact that I did not have a home anywhere, least of all in Prague. It was typical of those times that we did not bother to plan trivial details. In the course of all those years in the camp I thought of home as the apartment in Prague we used to live in. It never occurred to me that it might not be there for me. Perhaps it had been destroyed by Allied bombardment but I thought of it as loose ends, not warranting my concern. That was where I wanted to return to, that was my home. The next day, early in the morning, I went to the main road, where I hoped to hitch a ride to Prague.

There was another hitchhiker waiting with the same aim in mind. He was not an old-timer; he was deported to Theresienstadt from Sered only in December of 1944. His relatively short internment was reflected in his overall condition and clothes and I was not even surprised when he took exception to the strange whitish smock that I wore. He wondered loudly if people would not stare at my bizarre outfit. I patiently responded that, had I something more seemly, I certainly would have worn it, just to look more presentable on my first steps to freedom. We waited for a short while and then we noticed a military jeep driving at a great speed from Prague, in the opposite direction we wanted to go. We did not try to flag it but the vehicle stopped on the order of the officer who sat next to the driver. He inquired about our strange looks and about the fenced-off town. We communicated in three languages: Russian, Slovak and Czech. Luckily, all the Slavic tongues share many words. The officer seemed touched and moved by our narrative, and he weighed his options about how to assist us. He told us that he was a colonel and a Jew and he was appalled by the horror of the camps the Soviets had liberated. He hesitated for a moment and then ordered his driver to turn the jeep around and told us to jump in. He was talkative. We heard that he was on his way to Munich but that he felt he could justify this delay. He asked us many questions, listened attentively and seemed genuinely shaken and pained.

Moments later he became concerned for we had told him in answer to his question that we had no cash. The friendly officer reached into his pockets and began to grope for money. He pulled out fistfuls of the interim currency, then issued for the military. It was used during the early days of transition from combative state to armistice. When he noticed that I had no pockets, he offered his kerchief, into which I placed my sudden windfall. Soon we reached the suburbs of Prague. He ordered the jeep to halt and told us to get out. He had to rush back to his assignment in Munich. He wished us well and waved off our thanks. We stood there as the jeep spun around and left at a fast speed. As it vanished into thin air it raised a cloud of dust and smell of burning tires. I had returned home.

13

Prague—1945

As soon as I got off the Russian jeep, I sensed that Prague had changed greatly. I remained standing on the pavement, trying to take in the new sensation of freedom at home. Only it did not feel right, as returning home should, and as I used to imagine it would. In the last few days I indulged in dreams, picturing my homecoming and the accompanying joy. As I stood on the pavement I did not feel any of it.

That particular day in May was lovely: the sun shone and the passersby seemed to enjoy the first resplendent spring of freedom. I looked around for familiar sights and the friendly atmosphere of my hometown. This was the place where I grew up, was bred and nurtured, yet I could not see or sense any familiar sights or commonality. Prague appeared irreparably changed. Or was it me who was different? There were the immediate signs of the postwar destruction, wrought on the city by its needless last-minute rebellion. The entire insurrection had lasted only a few days but had inflicted much havoc on the city. The public transit did not function; the tracks were disrupted, in some parts torn out of the ground. Pavement was broken up; there were large gaping holes, many of the cobblestones were missing, having been used for the erection of barricades. All around me there was evidence of the damage caused by the war. The barricades built by the rebels gave the city the look of a beleaguered fort. I felt alienated, as if I stood in a strange place, one I had never set my foot on before. Even then, I sensed that more had changed within me than in this town and that more was broken and crushed inside me than the pavement of Prague.

Longing for familiar warmth and sights, I decided to walk to Letna, the district of Prague where we lived before the war. But then suddenly I was hit by an epiphany. Then, and only then, it occurred to me that I did not have the keys to the apartment, and I realized that, more likely than not, someone would be living there, perhaps even some Germans. The next notion was still worse: suddenly I understood that not one of my family members would be there, and that even if the apartment was vacant, I would be in the large flat all alone. That awareness nearly brought me down;

it felt as if an iron fist hit me in my gut. The crushing realization nearly brought me to my knees.

Momentarily I was unsure of where to turn or where to go. Then I noticed that passersby were looking at me with some astonishment and I became painfully self-conscious of the smock I was wearing. It did not look like anything people wore, even in the aftermath of a six-year war and a recent rebellion. Unsure and ill at ease, I decided to find a change of clothes of which I had a rich supply at the Vrzak family flat. I knew that road well. Eva and I had walked it so many times while we were carrying our belongings there for safekeeping. I could have walked it with my eyes closed. This time, though, I had nothing to carry, only the handkerchief with the money given to me by the friendly colonel. I felt unwell, burdened, old, tired, and full of doubts and insecurities. I tried to give myself a pep talk, with marginal success.

Then it occurred to me that I needed to make some concrete plans. This was a new obstacle. For years I had not planned beyond the next hour because the camp situation was always unpredictable and volatile, and nobody had any future, much less plans for one. I would have to readjust to my changed circumstances. Many thoughts raced through my mind but somehow I was unable to concentrate. Unlike my usually decisive disposition, I remained vague and unsettled.

Slowly I reached the district and eventually the street where the Vrzaks lived. I hesitated for a brief moment and then I began to climb the stairs. Soon I was out of breath and had to wait for a moment to recuperate. Finally I reached the flight of stairs where the Vrzaks' flat was located. I was relieved to note that the familiar name plate was still affixed on the door.

I paused for few moments, my misgivings rising, unsure what I might encounter once I rang the bell. A few moments later I plucked up my courage, scoffed at myself for my anxiety and rang the bell. Nobody answered. I became apprehensive, beginning to panic, suddenly realizing that they might have left Prague. Many of Prague's denizens fled the city, fearing the rebellion and the German reprisals. Unable to come up with some alternate plan I stayed put, standing in the stairway which was filled with the pungent, stale odor of cabbage and onions—the usual smell of working-class high-rises. I did not move for what seemed to me an eternity. Finally, I wanted to move on and it was then that I heard some shuffling sounds behind the door. I spotted an eye looking through the peephole. But to my disappointment the door remained shut and all fell silent again. Once again I rang the bell. This time someone returned faster and partially opened the door which was secured by a bolted chain. An angry voice of a woman asked me who I was and why I insisted on bothering them. I introduced myself into the dark crack at the doorframe. Mrs. Vrzak cried out almost hysterically for her husband who must have been somewhere inside the apartment. "Father, come fast, someone insists on telling us that she is Veruska. Come here to see for yourself; she does not look anything like Vera used to. It must be an imposter."

I did not budge from the door, awaiting the next move from within. I glued my eyes at the peephole hoping that Mr. Vrzak would confirm my claim. Three years are a long stretch of time to affect a teenager's appearance but it was hard to believe that I had changed beyond recognition; then again, life in the camp had taken its toll. Mr. Vrzak arrived, obviously excited, opened the door a crack and looked at me probingly—appearing unconvinced and almost suspicious.

I noticed that he had aged, was much too thin and stooped. He squinted as he searched for familiar features in my face. He had a hard time finding any. Evidently uncertain, he pulled me into the dim hallway and began to question me, mainly about my family and our past. Soon I saw that I gained his trust and that the news I brought hit him hard. He became upset, shocked and deeply saddened.

He put his arm around my shoulders and led me into the living room. He must have noticed how tired and worn out I was, for he offered me a chair and asked me for more details about our family. Over and over he mumbled, "Such a tragedy, this is incredible." While I related the story of the last three years, I could not help but look around the room and notice they were using the tablecloth and napkins and many other items from Eva's trousseau. It did not bother me; my poor darling sister would never need them. Mrs. Vrzak wore Mother's housecoat; the walls were adorned with our paintings. It felt strange surrounded by our belongings. Wherever I cast my eyes I found familiar objects. Our towels were in the bathroom; everything in the kitchen bore the monogram E.K. Though it was ours, I was strangely shy to touch any of the relics. Instead of conveying feelings of familiarity, these scattered possessions surrounding me caused my heart to bleed.

Mr. Vrzak pulled himself together first. He invited me to stay with them until further arrangements could be made. He then realized that more likely than not I was hungry and he encouraged his wife to offer me something to eat. I believe that he was embarrassed by her passive, almost inhospitable acceptance. I don't think that she was indifferent or unfriendly. I believe that she was shocked by my looks and overwhelmed by my narrative. Mr. Vrzak was apologetic about the use of our possessions, but I told him truthfully not to worry. How could they have stored so many things without some being in sight? Their apartment was not spacious, it was an unimpressive flat located in one of the old-fashioned buildings in a working-class district. While he spoke I felt another recurrence of fever creeping up. The familiar chills and fatigue were unmistakably the first signals of a repeated attack.

I gratefully accepted their invitation. They let me use a narrow niche in the kitchen where they kept a spare bed. They offered me an excellent meal and the luxury of a warm shower and sent me to sleep. The Vrzaks were good to me; they fed me well, let me stay with them while my mysterious fever returned and incapacitated me for several days at a time. They put up with my drenching their linens with night sweats, my screaming during the nightmares that haunted me. They never hinted that they felt burdened by my moving in with them. I certainly was not an easy visitor, yet they graciously opened their door and hearts to me.

Later they even returned most of our linens, blankets, clothing and silver to me. Some of it they kept and I forced them to take more, for I hardly needed it all. The years I spent in a concentration camp divorced me from those things I thought were essential before the war. Only later I came to reevaluate my disdain of materialism. I was genuinely grateful to the Vrzaks for their concern and help. Other friends of my parents who willingly offered to safeguard our valuables refused to give back any of them. All had some handy if hardly believable explanation such as having been robbed or found out by the Gestapo harboring Jewish possessions, having sustained damage by fire, flood or other lies. Most of these "ex-friends" of my parents were affluent people but greed got the better of them. They were seduced by the once-in-a-lifetime opportunity to appropriate some valuables, antique jewelry and costly works of art. It did not bother me particularly then that I was robbed and shortchanged; right after the war our mindset was not yet adjusted to acquisition of material goods. It was the thought that my parents had trusted such unworthy people that was so painful to me.

When the first attack of my illness subsided, I got up and set out on a search for my uncles, aunts and cousins. In the early postwar days, no one knew who had been deported and where to, or if anyone had survived the years of horror. At first, I followed the example of other repatriates and began leaving notes on the bulletin boards at the offices of the National Council. This organization sprang into existence for law enforcement in the chaotic flux of the war's aftermath. The original blueprint called for the council to administer properties abandoned by the fleeing Germans. But many of the bureaucrats deviated from their official duties; they too wanted a piece of the action. While their authorized function called for sealing the vacated dwellings and awaiting legislative decree, many violated the order and stole what they were supposed to safeguard. In the postwar disorder few were caught and hardly anybody was charged with theft and violation of the office. In a way they "set the wolf to mind the sheep."

The Germans who did not flee in time suffered no major retribution in Czech lands. Although hated by the long-suffering population, only a small number were chased after and executed in the streets. Most remained unharmed as bloodshed was not the favorite pastime of the Czechs. I wished I could say the same about their greed and envy.

My top priority became the acquisition of my own place, and I submitted a petition for the return of our apartment at Letna. It became vacant, deserted by the German family who had used it during the war. Because my thinking had not yet adapted to normal times, I worried little about the steep rent. The council responsible for the district settled my case expeditiously. I was encouraged to return within a week and take possession of my own apartment.

In the meantime, I pressed on with the search for any surviving family members. The number of returnees began to rise and they congregated around the buildings of the former Jewish community of Prague. We were a motley bunch, most had no hair or just newly sprouting crew cuts, were clothed in mélange of donated apparel, skinny and often unsteady on our feet. We stuck out as sore thumbs but we could not care less.

Soon we got into the habit of leaving notices on the walls. Every day while returning to the Vrzaks' flat I nursed a flicker of hope. Tomorrow for sure would bring some news; some of my many relatives would be back. We also used the many Russian tanks scattered throughout the city as forms of communication. The soldiers who manned those tanks allowed us to stick small notes with messages indicating our identity and whereabouts. The Russian soldiers were by and large congenial, singing, laughing and drinking vodka. They developed strange hobbies. They would demand watches from civilians passing by and they would attach them on their forearm. It was a common sight: a Russian boy with watches tightly placed on his wrist up to his elbows. That might have been comical. We laughed less when we heard of the many rapes the young soldiers were accused of.

Almost daily I set out to check if anybody looked for me or added new names to the list of returning survivors. So far I did not find any response but I remained hopeful. Many were returning; a number of survivors were gravely ill, dispersed in hospitals near the camps where they had been liberated. The Allied command set up clinics for the ill and many were in no shape to be transported back to their original homes.

The Western powers hurriedly established the displaced persons' camps, all within the German and Austrian territories. My relatives could have been at a number of different locations and there could have been just as many causes for their delayed return. Every single day I told myself in no uncertain terms that today would be my lucky day: I had to bolster my sinking optimism. I knew I was in for a long wait. News reached us that the "displaced persons" camps might be maintained for a long time because some Polish Jews no longer wished to return to the anti–Semitic environment they had lived in prior to Nazi invasion.

Many Polish Gentiles feared that the handful of surviving Jews would demand their possessions back. A new wave of anti–Jewish sentiment arose in Poland. The Poles staged a pogrom in July 1945 at Kielce. A handful of Jews were repatriated to Kielce and attempted to reclaim some of their possessions. The irate population, angered that a few Jews were left alive, sought a pretext and found it: when a young boy went missing, his family blamed the local Jews for having kidnapped him. The boy had gone to visit friends and concocted the story to escape punishment. The Gentiles assumed that the Jews needed the blood of a Gentile for Passover Matzoth. Ugly superstition reared its head and served as a pretext to attack the Jews. This absurdity was incredibly convenient for the citizens of Kielce. No one paused to think that it was July, and Passover always coincided with Easter, now long gone. What ensued was a murderous spree. In the back of the minds of the aggressors was the thought that dead Jews could not reclaim what the Poles had usurped.

The handful of assaulted Jews called for police assistance. As used to be the custom in Poland, the police deliberately delayed arrival until it was too late. Many just-liberated Jews were murdered; scores were wounded. The few who saved their skin ran for their lives to neighboring Czechoslovakia, and to the credit of the Czechoslovak government, they were not only admitted but helped and allowed to stay until they could arrange their immigration papers, either to the United States or Australia. The Poles had blotted their postwar record with the only, and hopefully last, pogrom on the European continent.

Initially the Czechoslovak government was considerate and compassionate in addressing our plight. All repatriates were issued identity cards, describing our status as liberated victims of Nazi terror. The owner of such a card was entitled to the use of the many emergency food distribution sites, free and preferential medical care, free use of trains and streetcars and many other essential services. The public, government-sponsored kitchens were scattered in most districts of Prague; they prepared nourishing food, offering meals to the repatriates throughout the entire day. During those days we walked the streets of Prague savoring tasty food, consuming one tasty meal after another, relishing in the long-forgotten sensation of an appetizing meal.

The Czech social agencies provided us with clothing so that we no longer looked like raggedy beggars. We got regular shoes; we no longer wore footwear full of holes or the abominable wooden clogs common in the camps. Every office was ordered to prioritize the needs of the liberated victims. We were encouraged to return to school where the teachers were ordered to provide help for those who had to terminate their education prematurely. We basked in the kindness that we had missed for such a long time.

My physical strength was improving, though I experienced more relapses of my feverish condition. Still, I felt better and began to regain confidence in our future. But just as our physical health improved, emotional problems began to manifest themselves, as if to defy our bodily recovery. We began a new phase of emotional, psychological and behavioral adaptation which proved to be much more complex than the physical recovery.

It is my belief that most Jews, indeed most decent people of that era, were changed, for they had witnessed the impossible become reality. What we, the seasoned inmates of those ghettos and camps, did not perceive immediately was that the experience marked us for the duration of our lives. Our initial struggle following the physical recovery led us to integrate back into the fold of the nations in which we believed we had an integral place and played an important role.

To our surprise we found out that hardly anyone wanted to hear about our experiences. Few asked questions, and if the subject came up, the conversation was quickly redirected to another topic, more general in nature, not specific to the Jewish calamity. As a result of the obvious unwillingness of the general public to know or even listen politely, we became shy and more alienated. The topic of the Holocaust was taboo in the aftermath of World War II, at least in Czech society; the Czechs wanted to believe that their privations, mostly economic in nature, were the worst possible suffering and we should turn the page now that the war was over. Most people wanted to forget their pain and make up for lost time.

We were glad not to revisit our pains for all the wounds were still open and we wanted little else than to forget as fast we could. Then we knew little of the lasting effects of the trauma we had suffered. We wanted to become just like the others, not realizing that it was an unattainable goal. We tried to imitate others by adjusting to their values and discarding our habits acquired in the camps. We tried to relax to no longer be on high alert. The ingrained vigilance of the camp's life had to ease up; we had to appear more relaxed to be socially acceptable. Then there were the social niceties: we had to learn how to create a polite smile instead of a grimace which most of us produced. We had to re-learn to respond to signs of friendliness with some degree of confidence. It took a long time before our laughter became genuine. It was harder than most believed to cast off fears of men as a potential danger or carrier of ominous news. It took a long time—and for some it never came—to reach a state of mind where catastrophe did not loom just around the corner.

Even little things were new to us. I remember how surprised I was breathing in fresh air instead of the stench of unwashed bodies, decompos-ing cadavers—the detritus of humanity that was part of camp life every sin-gle day. For years we had been forced to look at scenes from hell.

Very slowly I discovered the pleasures of a walk through a park. The first time I saw a flower I stopped and admired it, taking in its lovely scent. I remember that I squatted near the lawn and gently touched the bloom, almost fearful not to harm it. I marveled over its glorious colors, the crim-son and the fresh green. How long was it since I had seen such lively shades? It dawned on me that in the camp everything was shades of gray, black or dirty brown. In camp all was wrapped in drabness and ugliness; we almost forgot how lovely nature can be. How long was it since I last enjoyed the sight and scent of a flower? There were no flowers in Theresienstadt; it was a revelation after such a long time. Only then did we realize how much we had forgotten about normal life.

Much of our adjustment involved a readjustment of our values. In particular, we had to reestablish our social contacts with children and the elderly. We had to experience children not as automatic victims of the next transport or selection for gas but as delightful creatures who had bright futures ahead of them. As for the old people, in Theresienstadt the "Siechen" were seen as a burden that the few functional inmates had to drag along. Now we had to come to terms with the fact that the elderly are integral parts of a normal family. We had to adjust to the reality that oth-ers had extended families while only a few of us had living relatives. We were not supposed to appear bitter, sad or downcast; others in the post-war world expected our gratitude and good cheer. And we did play the role; we did not want people to hate us again even though it was extremely hard on us.

We were never permitted to grieve for the loved ones we lost. In the camps we had no time to pause, and when we were liberated, we were expected to be in a celebratory mood. We had to show flexibility and adap-tation, which, in retrospect, seems very cruel. It was hard not to obsess about food; it took us a long time to throw out anything edible, no matter how rotten it was. These were but a few of the immediate adjustments we had to make to reintegrate into society. Many others had to be made later on in our lives.

But let's turn back to the events of May 1945, and my first confrontation with normality. I went to claim my apartment. At the promised time, the paperwork was ready and I was invited to sign on the dotted line. Accord-ing to the rules I had to be accompanied by one of the guards on duty at the National Council. It was his task to officially open the apartment and hand the keys over to me. He was a friendly man who enjoyed the role of Santa Claus, distributing priceless gifts. He talked a mile a minute and could not understand why my replies were monosyllabic. He thought I was extremely lucky and I should be overjoyed but I was tense and apprehensive.

We reached the building of Ovenecka 19, my last prewar home. The elevator came to a stop at the fourth floor and my escort turned the key in the lock and, with a broad smile, he motioned me to enter. What ensued was totally inexplicable to me, let alone to him and I did not find words to make him understand. As he flung the door wide open I was expected to walk in. Only I could not. I froze in the doorway, certain only about one reality: I could not live there; I could not even enter the place. Suddenly I saw from every corner the faces of my dear ones. I knew that I would never be able to call it my home again. I realized that I had to leave right now or I might lose my composure. Quickly I turned on my heel and ran back to the office of the National Council. I did not consider for a moment that I violated the regulations stating that it was my duty not to leave the escorting guard alone in the apartment, forgetting all about the warning of the clerk who issued my paperwork. I left the man there, his mouth agape. He could not understand my reaction any more than I could explain it to him. When I arrived at the office, out of breath, exhausted by my frantic run, I found a handy explanation.

I informed them about my inability to pay rent for such a large apartment; I did not need all the space anyway. I remember the incredulous looks of the men behind the desks who likely thought me a lunatic. They tried to explain to me that I could sublet it or exchange it for a smaller place privately. They were all convinced that I had flipped my lid and did not appreciate my good fortune. They tried to persuade me but before long they realized that they were dealing with a stubborn mule and drew the appropriate conclusion. They voided the paperwork; they sent me to find a place which would meet my needs. This proved to be an almost impossible mission. There were few apartments left. Some were allocated to genuine repatriates but others were grabbed illegally by some using forged documents stating that their original home had been damaged in the war. Morality had hit rock bottom; theft and forgery were rampant.

Everybody wanted a piece of the pie, to benefit from the reigning confusion, improve their lot and be compensated for shortages and scarcities endured during the war. Prague is a city which has always suffered from a dearth of apartments, and some fast operators sensed the opportunity to enrich themselves by the quick acquisition of a dwelling. Moral turpitude was everywhere, and everybody seemed to be on the take. I had to hunt for quite some time before I found what I was looking for.

My search was hampered by yet another recurrent attack of fever. I felt worse than ever—very drained and weak. I was forced to stay put in the kitchen corner of the Vrzaks, shivering with fever, totally exhausted and depressed. I felt I was an imposition on my kind hosts. I was convinced that I should free them of my morbidity and less than cheerful company. To give credit where credit is due, the Vrzaks never even hinted that they were tired of taking care of me. With the passage of time I also began to waver in my belief that some of my relatives survived and would come back. I hoped fervently that I would be reunited with some relatives so that we could recreate some semblance of family.

As soon as I became mobile again, I intensified my search for a flat of my own, thinking I would recover better if I enjoyed some privacy. I thought of Arthur's optimism; I missed him and his encouraging attitude. I had to regain my emotional balance. I sensed that my feelings of sadness were getting the better of me; I was losing my emotional grounding that was not too firmly rooted yet anyway. I had to reunite with my husband and go from there.

Finally my hunt yielded results. I found a small garconniere in the same district of Prague where we had always lived. It was a tiny place indeed, but I could not find anything better. My new dwelling consisted of a small room where one secluded corner served as a kitchen counter. These mini-flats were then quite popular with low-income young singles or childless couples. My new dwelling was relatively clean and was sparsely furnished.

One more time the wheels of bureaucracy began to grind, more paperwork had to be drawn up and the same procedure was followed. A guide walked with me to the assigned address but this time all went well. Here, there were no ghosts to haunt me. I looked away as my escort rifled through the drawers, filling his pockets with some of the contents. I could not watch this petty thievery; it was so awkward and embarrassing. I did not say a word, and the man did not even blush.

My move into my new dwelling was completed quickly. After all, I only had what the Vrzaks returned to me. I even convinced them to keep more of Eva's trousseau. I really felt indebted to them for all their care and the inconvenience I had caused them.

On one lonely evening I decided to return to Theresienstadt to see Arthur, check on his health and report to him about my half-successful attempts to integrate, the mixed feelings of sadness and dislocation, and my intense search for relatives that had not yet yielded results. I did not know why I felt so downtrodden. Where were all the glorious feelings I imagined would accompany my new freedom? At the time I perceived it was my problem only. Later I realized that I was too emotionally wounded, too changed to fit in with those who had spent the last years in more or less normal circumstances. My daily shattered hopes to reconnect with some of my relatives began to slowly get me down. I felt like a stranger in a foreign country.

Frequently some kind soul would relate the difficulties the war had imposed on the citizens of Prague. Everything (meat, poultry, flour) was rationed; quantities allotted were minuscule, they had to barter their valuables for food, and so on. While I did not doubt their words, I felt like screaming, remembering our fate. Instead I listened politely. I had to remind myself that they were the normal ones, we were the weird breed. No sense trying to explain the inexplicable.

Returning to Theresienstadt was not simple. I had to hitchhike. The transportation was still chaotic, within cities as well as interurban. Though I set out early, it took almost an entire day for a trip that should not take more than two hours. When I reached the familiar sight of the camp, the daylight was fading, replaced by a dimming dusk. There I had to overcome a new hurdle, an unexpected obstacle: I could not get in. Though unwell, I could not help but find it funny. For three long years I could not get out and now the reverse situation complicated my purpose. But this time there was a perfectly sound reason: the Russian military had ordered the camp hermetically sealed, trying to confine the raging epidemics and the spread of lice infestation within the boundaries of the camp. Typhus, cholera, dysentery and many more infections ravaged the inmates: the harvest of death was still on the rise. I stood in front of the rebuilt fence and tried the best I could to convince the soldier guarding the gate to let me in. I was not an imposter; I was an inmate who was outside by error. All I said was the truth but the sentry seemed in a foul mood. He looked at me menacingly; he was unmistakably drunk and dangerous. He was holding his cocked gun pointed in my direction, clearly not a man to antagonize. His presence reminded me of the unsavory reputation of the Russian soldiers who were supposedly in the habit of shooting first and asking questions later. If the encounter was with a female, she might be raped, a common practice of the liberating army, brutalized and hardened by the war. Allegedly the only way to extricate yourself from such an impasse was to present the soldier with a bottle of vodka, one which mollified the many drunkards in the army.

My problem was that I had no vodka or any other alcohol. Therefore, my only logical tool was to convince him that I was ill, very ill, that any contact with me would endanger his life and that my place was within the city. My efforts were hampered by my lack of conversational Russian and I had to use a lot of mimicry and body language. Finally I must have convinced him though he grumbled and scowled but he finally unlocked the gate and let me in. I was hit by a feeling of familiarity, taken by surprise that a place as miserable as Theresienstadt could provide feelings of comfort almost as a home. I remembered having read somewhere that long-term prisoners find jail familiar and comforting. Was I that far gone?

All around me were visible changes. The Russians had brought order to much of the earlier confusion: the filth and the piles of dead bodies had been removed and the putrid stench of decay had been replaced by the strong odor of Lysol or some other disinfectant. The Russian medical corps brought in much needed changes. One of the first reforms affected the diet of the ex-prisoners. They imposed a strict diet, imperative for the rehabilitation of the ex-inmates. Initially the only food permitted was cereal, dry potatoes or bread. The amounts were liberal and were gradually increased. Though the cereals lacked spices, they offered a nourishing start for those trying to return to a normal diet. Many inmates were voraciously hungry and rummaged for additional food, disobeying the rules of the medical staff. More often than not they paid for it dearly, sometimes even with their lives; the weakened digestive system of the long-term malnourished inmates could not absorb normal fare, particularly if it was introduced suddenly.

Many more survivors, liberated by the U.S. and British forces, became gravely ill when offered unsuitable food. Though the liberators had kind intentions, their generosity was misguided. The starvelings who gorged on chocolate or bacon caused themselves great damage because their ravaged bodies could not absorb a normal diet. Many perished before the Allied forces learned what the Russians knew all along, namely, that the effects of severe and protracted starvation could only be slowly ameliorated by easily digestible foods in gradually increasing amounts. Many long-term inmates had up to 25 percent of their digestive systems atrophied and their ability to process food had to be rebuilt with caution. The Russians had had their own tragic experiences with starvation during the long siege of Leningrad (now St. Petersburg).

Once within the camp I began to feel tired, almost at the end of my tether. But I had to push on. I scanned the new look of the camp and I set out to find Arthur. He was in the hospital, flooded with work, the last place where conditions were still out of control. Patients were packed everywhere; floors were covered with dead and dying from wall to wall. Many did not even have beds, mattresses or even straw to sleep on. Here death still ruled supreme, only reluctantly yielding ground.

Arthur's injury had improved greatly and he planned to leave soon. He was obviously happy to see me but the last weeks left an indelible mark on his appearance. He was all too slim, almost haggard, tired and drained. He and a handful of his helpers attempted to bring some order to the chaos, doing work others would not touch with a barge pole.

Arthur was telling me about the rules implemented by the Red Army, all beneficial for the recovering inmates in these conditions. He brought me a sample of the food distributed to the ex-inmates. The sight of it was not appealing for it was bluish cereal with no salt or sugar added. It tasted like overcooked barley porridge, with some added potato pieces. To me it tasted revolting because I was no longer ravenously hungry and I had already tasted normal food in Prague; no longer would I voraciously gulp down anything just to still the pangs of hunger.

Arthur reiterated what I had already noticed: that the Russians were conquering the epidemics. Though many still perished, the piles of bodies were cremated, the many Musselmen who pulled through began to regain human shape, and even the ubiquitous terezinka (dysentery) was nearly wiped out. All in all, the Red Army did an excellent job in taking charge of the situation in challenging circumstances.

As we discussed all the changes in the camp as well as our future plans, I fell ill once more. The fever crept up, and I lay on a bunk soaked in sweat and totally miserable. There was still no medication at hand.

The second day after my return, my condition deteriorated greatly. I ran a high temperature, sweated profusely and generally felt sicker than during earlier episodes. Arthur found a space for me in the yard, for it was a glorious, sunny day and our little attic was stuffy and dark.

I had plenty of company—most were much worse off than I was. Many patients were placed outside the overcrowded hospital. Not that I cared for company, I was drifting in and out of sleep, never quite certain what was a dream and what was reality. My restless, feverish state blurred my awareness. It took several days for my health to improve and for Arthur and I to engage in a serious debate about our future.

First, I shared with Arthur my desire to study, to fill in the enormous gaps caused by the fact that the Nazis had expelled me from school at the tender age of 13. I was even short of the compulsory minimum and I wanted to enroll in university and study medicine. While I spoke, I noticed that Arthur's smile vanished, his face disclosing a palpable surprise, eventually changing to unvarnished annoyance.

It is perhaps characteristic of the times that we had never discussed our future hopes or expectations. I certainly never thought in terms of our long-term future and Arthur, who ardently believed in our survival, never pressed the matter. Now it was a burning issue. In camp, all our strength and abilities were aimed at surviving in that moment, and, with some luck, perhaps to the next day. To find food, to stay out of harm's way, to keep body and soul together—these were the overriding considerations, not plans for some nebulous, uncertain future.

Now to my surprise I realized that we had dramatically different expectations. Arthur wished for a settled life and he hoped that I would find fulfillment as a housewife. He realized the dire need for two incomes but he hoped that my work would not demand educational or emotional investment. Though taken by surprise and startled by our first serious impasse, unhappy about having to hurt him, I knew that I could not do as he wished. I knew I had to try, perhaps in vain, but I had to give it my best. I wanted to fill the gaps in my knowledge and I burned with desire to develop and advance myself. Perhaps I was also mindful of the hopes and wishes of my parents. I felt very strongly that they had experienced so much sorrow and suffering in their last years, I certainly would not let them down, even posthumously. I would fulfill the dreams and trust they had invested in me. In addition, I had a genuine thirst for knowledge, insatiate for a long time. I had so many questions and I expected to find my answers in books and regular school attendance. I always associated happiness in life with a never-ending search for knowledge.

It was this June day which brought the first serious rift in our loving and passionate relationship. Neither of us said much but we both knew that something quite serious had disrupted our previous harmony. I felt hurt by his lack of support and understanding. I was startled by his reaction. Arthur made me feel as if I had let him down, as if I had shattered his expectations or broken an important promise. The first signs of tension were evident, caused by our age difference and Arthur's conservative outlook on a woman's role in the family. His long years of bachelorhood were behind him, and while he enjoyed his single life during his university years, followed by two years of service in the army, he was ready to settle down. With freedom now giving him a new lease on life, he fervently hoped to build a warm, loving home for his wife and himself. I was genuinely sorry to see how crestfallen he was, how shocked and deeply saddened by our deadlock. I thought that it would be best to postpone any drastic decisions. It would be tough to reintegrate and adapt to normal life, and we should not be precipitous in such a time of pressing changes. Perhaps our relationship was strong enough to help us bridge our discrepancies. However, if we could not make a go of it, we would have to part. The thought alone was very painful, and I decided not to pursue it for the moment.

Before leaving, I broached my inability to move into the comfortable apartment of my family. Here Arthur understood immediately; some things were logical to those who shared the Holocaust. Few, if any, explanations were necessary.

The next morning we agreed that Arthur would return to Prague and join me in my little dwelling as soon as his health and work commitment would allow; we would discuss our future from there. In the meantime I wanted to join the high school class that I had left in 1939; in 1945 my schoolmates were preparing for their final exams, the senior matriculation. It seemed preposterous to attempt it: I had been out of any conventional educational system for six long years. Although Father taught us high school subjects till our deportation, that was halted once we became prisoners. All that happened before our deportation seemed unreal, as if in another life. I felt almost like an impostor trying to play the role of a student.

The principal of the girls' school received me in his office where he listened to my request to enroll in the senior class which I belonged to only by virtue of my age and onetime attendance. As I spoke I noticed that his eyes glistened, perhaps with tears or then again it could have been just the rays of the late afternoon sun piercing into his office. The school was in summer recess; the students were preparing for the delayed matriculation on their own. But he had a suggestion for me: he and all the teachers would join forces and help me bridge the educational gap from my long hiatus.

And he was as good as his word. They all stepped up to the plate and did their absolute best to upgrade my knowledge. During the few short weeks left, they invested their private time—rewarded only by my gratitude for their noble endeavor. They all did their utmost to prepare me but it was an impossible task. Then came the day of the exams, and under normal circumstances I would have never passed, but the teachers, most of whom knew my sister and me from better days, were shocked and overwhelmed by the extent of the Jewish tragedy and bent over backwards to help me out. The questions addressed to me were easy, way below the level of the final high school year. It was my good fortune that the exams were oral, for when my answers were not forthcoming, the examiner rephrased the question, reducing it to an even easier level. While that went on the faculty remained serious, keeping poker-faced, trying not to make me feel inadequate. I passed the senior matriculation, and I have always perceived it as a gift from my old school, an attempt to offset the great wrong perpetrated on Jewish students.

Before the ink on my matriculation certificate had a chance to dry, I enrolled at the reopened Charles University as a first-year medical student. The classes started in October and were transferred to a large auditorium, one normally used for concerts or rallies. The university reopened its doors to a record number of students; the first-year medical class alone had 500 eager candidates. For six long years nobody had been able to study and there was a dire shortage—never before experienced in the Czech lands—of university-educated professionals. The government counted on a high attrition rate and, sure enough, within the first year, 50 percent of the students had dropped out.

Before my classes began, I suffered a few more febrile attacks. The physicians decided that I needed a stint in a spa to accelerate my recovery. The government provided this treatment free of charge to all liberated inmates of the concentration camps as long as prescribed by attending physicians. I was lucky, for I was assigned to Carlsbad, one of the most beautiful places on earth. The spa is situated in a valley, surrounded by pine forests that exude an exquisite fragrance. Once it had been the meeting place of the world's elite. In prewar days Eva and I joined Mother on occasion in Carlsbad, where she spent time enjoying the curative qualities of the spring waters. In 1945 it was a different place altogether. Postwar Carlsbad was occupied by the Russian army. The best hotels were reserved for officers, the lesser ones for the rank and file, and the least desirable ones were left for the victims of Nazi terror. The health officials provided me with a warrant for a three week stay in the spa.

In the meantime Arthur had returned to Prague and, to my surprise, reneged on his promise to join me in my dwelling. Instead, he moved into the flat where he lived prior to his deportation. While his apartment was not luxurious, it was certainly more spacious than the one I lived in. In reality it was an artist's studio under the roof of a high-rise, with slanting ceilings, a tiny kitchen, two small bedrooms and facilities. The building was not equipped with an elevator but Arthur was young and the five flights of stairs did not present a problem. His resolve to go his separate way signaled an obvious and deep rift in our relationship. He visited often but he never tried to move in with me.

He wanted me to give up my place and come to live with him. The apartment question was only a symbolic obstacle between us: if I had moved in with him that would have meant that I had accepted his terms and would give up my ambition to study. He wanted our marriage to be structured along his wishes. Any alternative, even if feasible, would have been a source of tension, a permanent battlefield between the two of us. I had little predilection for a festering conflict. Just before my departure to the spa Arthur decided to exercise his right as a survivor and also apply for a recovery stint in Carlsbad. In the eye of the law we were still married; the law that was about to annul all camp marriages was just prepared and would be soon placed on the books. The Czech government alleged that most marriages sealed in concentration camps were entered into for the wrong reasons, and there was little sense in perpetuating matrimonies under duress or coercion. The law alleged that the rabbis officiating in the camps were not state accredited and thus not legally authorized to join couples in matrimony.

Arthur and I left together for Carlsbad and we spent three lovely weeks together which ended when I had to return to Prague to begin my studies. While we had a great time there, the unresolved impasse burdened our relationship. We no longer fought over it. We would rehash it only on rare occasions, but when we did, Arthur always became angry, stressing repeatedly the difficulties I would face as a student, living on the low orphan's pension paid by the government. I could not understand his deep disaffection and anger triggered by my ambition to learn and pursue my interests. I was confident that I could fulfill the obligations of a housewife and study at the same time. While we loved each other deeply, shared many interests and activities, we began to feel the invisible barrier erected by our basic misunderstanding. Had we not worried about our inability to bridge our differences we would have had a whale of a time. As we parted we were no closer to a solution than when we first got there.

Arthur decided to stay for few more days at the spa so I returned home alone and began a new life as a student. I walked to the lectures daily, saving the little money I had for food instead of spending it on streetcar tickets. I believed that I ate well, only my fare did not include meat, butter or eggs because these foodstuff were hard to come by. You could buy them on the black market if you could afford to pay prices that were through the roof. As I had problems with the absorption of dairy products, my diet consisted mainly of coffee, rolls or bread, except on two Sundays a month when I was the guest of the Vrzaks where I had a standing invitation. I enjoyed two wonderful, rich and tasty meals a month. Mrs. Vrzak often commented about my changeover, from a picky eater as a child into a voracious one, a person who gulped down all what was on the plate in record time. On many occasions Mrs. Vrzak would pack me a doggie bag and I would gratefully take it with me.

The Czechoslovak government granted me an orphan's pension; I qualified because of my father's status as a government employee. Although I was already 19, I was entitled to the pension for as long as I continued my studies. The Finance Ministry reopened my father's file, promising to repay lost wages once the courts had gone through the motions and declared me the sole heir of my family. That promised to be an impressive sum but bureaucracy everywhere moves at the speed of a limping turtle and the Czechoslovak variety was no different. Until then, I had to subsist on the orphan's pension and that was a tall order. Few had an idea how precarious and difficult it was to manage on this tiny stipend.

My classes were wonderful. I enjoyed the lectures in anatomy, histology and physiology—all easy and interesting, but I ran into difficulties in chemistry and physics, both courses based on material taught in high school. There were few textbooks available and, though I had to forgo a meal or two, I bought elementary texts, only to find out that without an explanation the material did not make much sense to me. I could not afford private tutoring and, for the time being, I was unable to resolve my problems in chemistry and physics. I therefore petitioned the faculty for postponement, and my request was granted. Every now and then, less frequently if not less severely, I suffered from recurring bouts of fever but the intervals between attacks were getting longer so that at times I was genuinely surprised when I experienced yet another relapse.

Unsure of my abilities to pursue my dream, I was trying to decide what to do. I got into the habit of taking long walks through Prague, carefully avoiding the streets and corners where once my uncles, aunts, cousins and friends used to live. I did not mind that I shivered in my threadbare coat, one I received from State's social welfare. My mind was focused on my dwindling hope for some relative to come back. No one had showed up so far, and I was running out of steam and hope that anyone survived the war. I felt desperately unhappy, lonely, robbed of my family and youth.

The first postwar year was the unhappiest time in my recovery. My hopes that any of my relatives survived began to fade. I sank into a leaden sadness. Although I tried to find reasons for optimism, I soon understood that the complete ruination of my family was a shock that I might never fully recover from. Then I feared that the problem was mine alone. I questioned my ability to adjust and integrate into society. I was terribly lonely and felt so even while among friends. While my one-time Gentile acquaintances debated their romances, the balls and parties they planned or attended, the hardship of buying dresses and accessories due to post-war shortages, I was gathering information about extermination camps and accumulating a long, hopeless list of murdered relatives.

In later years I found out that most survivors felt the same alienation. The highest number of survivors' suicides occurred during the years right after liberation following our return home that no longer provided comfort and solace. Self-conscious and disconsolate, I did not dare talk to anyone about what I thought of as my private, individual emotional malaise. I feared I would be perceived as weird. Surely it was not a normal reaction to an almost miraculous rescue from the clutches of death? Everything surrounding me tried to convince me that I should be happy, overjoyed and able to cope, not to indulge in my crushing sorrow.

Only 19 years old, I did not comprehend that this was the first time that survivors could pause and think about what had happened to us. I did not realize that I first had to come to terms with being an orphan, adjust to harsh realities and only then embark upon building a new future. The otherwise kind and helpful Czech social agencies had no emotional assistance in place; our trauma was unprecedented and the only help at hand was for our assorted physical illnesses. Most of the medical profession did not concern themselves with short- or long-term emotional traumas and so we had to cope on our own, any which way we could. To be fair to the medical authorities there was no precedent for such events. How do you treat people who lived for years in continuous shock? Perhaps the final shock was added after liberation.

While we were imprisoned in those infamous concentration camps our tormentors took care that we had no minute for ourselves and so we never mourned or really absorbed our losses. The privation and dangers of the camps never allowed us to dwell or deal with our emotional pain; it was after the liberation that we had to confront the full impact of what had happened to us. For the first time we had the luxury of free time and we could no longer ignore our feelings. All of a sudden our wounds, covered with thin layers of scar tissue, opened and began to bleed.

Prague, the city I once loved so much, seemed to be a huge cemetery: on every corner I saw a shadowy ghost of a relative or a friend who had not returned. The few who came back reported similar, horrific experiences, and slowly it became evident that almost the entire Czech Jewry had been wiped out. How could it have happened? Why were we so tragically afflicted? Where was our guilt? Why did the world at large permit such a horrendous crime to be perpetrated? Why were there no nations to open their hearts and gates to the Jews to save at least a few? Why were we hated throughout history and persecuted in so many countries in the world? All these questions racking my mind demanded answers but none were readily found.

Most of the Czech Jewish survivors in the early stages of attempted reintegration decided that we had suffered enough. For many of us, we had to ensure that "never again" was more than just words. We wanted total assimilation, submersion into the majority, leaving the fold and by doing so we would extinguish our differences. Never again would we be scapegoats to be slaughtered. Never again would we be called Jews.

14

How Did It Happen
and How to Go on from Here?

Most of my co-religionists made up their minds to leave the Jewish community. As it was, even before the war, Czech Jews felt only lukewarmly affiliated with the community and most belonged to synagogues that followed the reformed version of the Jewish faith. A minority of Jewish families preferred a more conservative way of worship and even fewer were orthodox.

That was then. Now most of us grappled for answers but it was an uphill battle. Time and again the debate revolved around the burning questions: if God existed, would He have allowed evil to be perpetrated on such a scale? Would He not have heard the cries of innocent men, women and children suffocated by Zyklon B? Would He not have smitten the perpetrators before they murdered six million blameless victims? I did not find answers to any of our questions but I was firmly determined to find out all about the reasons for the 2000-year-old hatred which had culminated in the Holocaust.

I remembered my father's regrets about his mistaken course of assimilation. In the camp, towards the end of his life, Father came to realize that assimilation was a pipe dream. His final conclusion was that the tragic, persecuted Jew could only find refuge from his trials and tribulations in his own land where he would be master of his own destiny. Dad said repeatedly that the host nations we dwelt in abandoned us, they never really perceived us as their own and now we had to change the course of two millennia of history. Though he felt that he would not be around to make these changes, he did not hesitate to voice his support for Zionism, the establishment of a Jewish homeland, as the solution of our unwanted diaspora. I did not know much about Zionism but I decided to find out. I would do my homework thoroughly before I came to any conclusions. I wished to base my future on a rational foundation, unaffected by my visceral attachment to the Jewish nation. Neither did I want my present pain and trauma to decide my future.

Until about the beginning of 1946, I still nourished a flicker of hope that some of my relatives—perhaps only one of them—might come back. But slowly the sinking feeling of doom began to seep in. I could delude myself no longer. The majority of those who had survived the genocide had returned by now; not one of my family members were among them. I sank into a disconsolate depression. Soon thereafter I found out how they had died.

The Jewish community of Prague notified me about the fate of my mother's three brothers who were included in the infamous transport labeled AAH (Attentat Auf Heydrich) along with their families. The reasons for this transport have to do with events of May 1942, when the bloody German "protector" Reinhardt Heydrich was assassinated by the Czech resistance. The assassination, which almost failed, was planned by the government in exile and executed by two brave volunteers who parachuted into Czech lands. The twosome, both brilliant men, volunteered for this suicide mission to rid the Czechs of the rule by the vicious Nazi official Reinhardt Heydrich. Jan Kubiš and Jozef Gabčík were selected by the president-in-exile to carry out Operation Anthropoid. They were dropped in the dead of night into the Czech countryside. All went according to plan and they made their way to Prague. On the pre-arranged day (May 27, 1942), the two men positioned themselves on a corner in Prague where Heydrich's limousine would pass by.

Heydrich was known to be rigid man who never deviated from his route to work. He took the same road day after day as he was driven from the castle in Panenske Brezany where he lived in great luxury along with his family. He was always punctual. He was only vulnerable when his limousine had to slow down around one particular corner, nearly coming to a standstill. Gabčík, an expert sharpshooter, positioned himself on the sidewalk, appearing to be waiting for a streetcar; on the opposite side stood Kubiš, the back-up man. Both men strolled casually back and forth waiting for their target to arrive. Right on time, as expected, the limousine reached the corner and at this moment, Gabčík was supposed to shoot the protector almost point blank. Gabčík aimed his revolver and pulled the trigger but nothing happened. The gun jammed. He tried again with the same result. Meanwhile Heydrich looked in disbelief at the young man who aimed a gun at him and pulled the trigger in vain. The chauffeur grasped the danger of the assassination attempt and suggested speeding off, but was overruled by Heydrich, who angrily reached for his own gun.

While this played itself out, Kubiš realized that something went awry, and he needed to step in to complete their mission. As pre-planned he aimed at the car and tossed a grenade that exploded in the rear of the vehicle. It wounded the protector, but he continued to stand upright, aiming his gun at Gabčík who now was trying to escape. The driver again suggested a speedy retreat, only to be upbraided by Heydrich. Though bleeding, and in pain, he decided to pursue the fleeing Gabčík and ordered the driver to follow the other man. This was a fatal mistake on the part of Heydrich. He stepped out of the car and collapsed on the pavement. His driver unsuccessfully chased Gabčík who vanished, mingling with the early morning crowd of pedestrians. Both men reached the first safe house in the heart of Prague, out of harm's way for the time being. Heydrich lay on the pavement, bleeding profusely. He was taken to Bulovka, the nearby hospital, where the doctors tried to stabilize him and treat his serious injuries.

When informed of the assassination attempt, Hitler flew into one of his rages. He forbade the Czech doctors to operate and dispatched his own surgical team. The delay in surgery was not to the patient's advantage but all the Czech physicians were allowed to do was to stabilize the gravely wounded protector. When the German medical team arrived they performed an emergency splenectomy and Heydrich seemed to be recovering.

Although Heydrich experienced improvement in the first two days, complications set in on the third day. A massive infection began to threaten the life of the patient. His wounds were infected by the horsehair stuffing of the backseat that had been propelled into his abdomen by the explosion that ripped the seats open. For three days Heydrich laid in agony, tossing between life and death, ordering a priest to kneel at his bedside, praying and offering spiritual succor. But Heydrich was beyond consolation; he convulsed with pain and fear of retribution. A religious and devout Catholic, he dreaded the afterlife where he would have to answer for his crimes. Ironically, the Czech nation prayed for his recovery, fearing the ramifications for assassination of one of Hitler's favorite cronies. Few doubted the severity of the punishments that would surely follow his death. But there was to be no reprieve for Heydrich. He died, conscious to the end. His body was flown to Berlin for a state funeral.

The reprisals began right after his interment. The Nazis staged searches and waves of arrests followed throughout Bohemia and Moravia. The dragnets continued day and night. Countless people were taken into custody; many were shot without a trial. Two villages, Lidice and Lezaky, were totally obliterated. Men were shot, women sent to a concentration camp in Ravensbruck, and children put up for adoption. In addition, 1,000 Prague Jews were transported, destined for instant execution. My mother's three brothers and their families were included in this group.

Kubiš and Gabčík had reached the safe houses and remained there in hiding, hoping to wait out the storm. The infuriated Nazis, humiliated by their inability to catch the culprits, posted a monetary reward for anyone who would assist the Germans in apprehending the assassins. They offered the impressive amount of 1,000,000 Czech crowns for the Judas Iscariot of the Nazi era. Karel Čurda, a member of the inner circle of the conspiracy, swallowed the bait and led the Germans to the basement of a small church in the heart of Prague.

During the ensuing shootout both men fought valiantly till the penultimate bullet, keeping the very last for one another. The Nazis had hoped to shoot the two men in their hiding place but later decided to flood the basement of the church and drown them. They filled the basement with water while Kubiš and Gabčík continued to shoot at the Germans who had the church encircled. When the water reached their mouths, they hugged each other and used the last bullet on the other man. The Germans waited until complete silence in the church indicated that the two men were no longer alive. Only then they pulled the two bodies out. They left them on display on the street for some time. The sight of the corpses was to serve as a deterrent to those who would stand up to the Germans' brutality. Čurda collected his money, but right after the liberation in 1945, he was the first man sent to the gallows for high treason.

In the aftermath of the bloody protector's assassination in Prague, my mother's family were victims of Nazi reprisals. They were among the one thousand Prague Jews rounded up for the AAH transport and deported to Poland. This was only one of the punitive measures that followed the assassination. Much later I learned that they were executed at Ujazdow, a village in Poland. The train packed with these unfortunate hostages traveled for a couple of days without food, water or sanitation. The train came to halt at Ujazdow, where those who survived the journey were ordered out of the box cars. They were marched to a nearby field. There the SS, aided by the Einsatzgruppen (paramilitary units of Polish and Ukrainian volunteers), forced the men, women and child prisoners to dig trenches. When the trenches were deemed long and deep enough, the victims were ordered to undress, fold their belongings and move to the edge of the trench. Standing above their own graves, they were mowed down by the machine gun fire on the order of the SS. The bodies fell into the open trenches. Wave after wave of the hostages was marched to the edge of the trench and there they met the same end.

My tragic relatives! This, then, was the fate of those who had shared with us so many past highlights and joyous moments of our family. Those who were murdered at Ujazdow were innocent even of the slightest participation in the assassination of Heydrich. These were some of the members of our family I had hoped to find and reconnect with. Now I was told that they had been slaughtered at the whim of the odious Germans. At first I refused to believe it. Why my relatives and why all of them? It boggled the mind and I could not take it in. Next I wanted to suppress the information and with it the sadness. I resolved to live in denial; perhaps it was only a horrible rumor that would prove incorrect with time?

Eventually the day came when I realized that I could not hide my head in the sand. I had to come to terms with the cruel reality. It was extremely difficult for me to face and accept the brutal facts and indeed it was an arduous process. Slowly the dread of their final hours began to sink in. I shuddered during the days but the nights were far worse. My sleep became tormented by nightmares, all revolving around their last moments on earth. I would wake up, drenched in sweat, following what I perceived to be a machine-gun blast. I would lie, wide awake, recognizing the faces of my uncles and aunts, imagining them digging their graves. I would discern the handsome, mischievous face of my cousin Viktor, two years my junior, and right next to him the youngest of our family, sweet, little Hanna, just ten years old when massacred at Ujazdow. I would see her large brown eyes, her lovely face framed with golden locks, her ever-present smile radiating the trust of an innocent child.

Though I was wide awake, my nightmare continued, sharply taking an even uglier turn. I look at them as they shiver, trying to support one another, realizing their imminent doom. During their last moments on this earth, did they panic? Were they resigned to die by that time? Did they pray for fast deliverance? Did they retain a flicker of hope, or did they pretend for the children's sake? I could not stop these torturous mental images any more than I could stop breathing. Time and again these vivid visions kept unfolding.

In the final act of these nightmares, I swear I could hear the ear-shattering blast of the SS man's gunfire that wiped out my relatives. The nights would drag on as I visualized their faces in their last moments on Earth—contorted with pain, eyes bulging, and then spattered with blood. Was their last thought a question: why? I wondered if they died instantly or if they were injured and lingered for some time in agonizing pain. As if that were not horrible enough, I cannot but envision Viktor, the companion of our childhood games, with his face covered with blood as he lies next to Hanna. Hanna's face still has a trace of a smile, only now her golden locks are caked with blood, creating a bizarre, obscene contrast.

All eight of them (Uncle Adolf and his wife Irma, Uncle Alfred and his wife, also called Irma, and their son Viktor, and Uncle Oskar, Aunt Miriam and their daughter Hanna) perished during this bloody massacre. They have followed me ever since, through my days and, worse, through my nights. I do not know if their execution was anything like my haunted vision. But these are the images conjured by my tortured imagination which are etched into my mind. Whenever the last hours of their lives come back to me, usually late at night, I no longer try to suppress the images in order to sleep. Now I accept that it is all but impossible to will my ghosts into oblivion: they will stay with me. I spend the rest of the night remembering and imagining their last journey. There are a few convictions that sustain me, and the most important one is that nobody has the right to forget or forgive their innocent martyrdom!

Still reeling from the official notification of the demise of the entire Taussig family, I was hit by information about the fate of my closest relatives on my father's side. Both my father's sisters and their families were deported from Prague during the summer of 1942. Their road was different from my mother's family but equally disastrous. The two families were deported in two different transports, both within a short time.

Both went from Prague, via Theresienstadt, to Maly Trostinec, an extermination camp in Belarus. Even in 1945, the Jewish community had only scant knowledge what had happened in this death camp. I do not know if my relatives were alive when the trains reached Maly Trostinec because the journey lasted several days and many perished in the tightly packed cattle cars without food, water or sanitation. I was informed that those who survived the journey were quickly packed into large vans which were in reality mobile gas chambers. The large lorries had the exhaust pipe rerouted into the passengers' cabin thus discharging carbon monoxide into the tightly shut space. The time needed to suffocate the prisoners was roughly the same time required to reach a nearby forest, Blahovstina, where the bodies were unloaded and cremated in large pits dug by Russian prisoners of war.

Somewhere in Belarus are the ashes of my family—both sisters of my father with their families and my married cousin Oskar, his wife Ida and son Jiri. Oskar and his family were the cousins who, unbeknownst to us, shared our deportation, also members of the AU transport from Prague. We too were supposed to continue the journey to Maly Trostinec. We would have been gassed there if not for Mr. Bleha and Dr. Tarjan.

The terrible end of the other half of our family creates another nightmare for me. I cannot help but imagine them choking, retching, fighting for air during their slow, agonizing death inside the vans. It is my misfortune that I have to relive the horrors of Maly Trostinec and Ujazdow time and time again.

Much later I learned more about Maly Trostinec. I made contact with the only known survivor of this notorious place. He shared with me the incredible details of this camp that was hidden from the world's attention. The sole survivor was then a young and strong man who, against all odds, succeeded in escaping, hiding, and fighting his way to a nearby Russian partisans' camp and joined the battle against the Nazis.

It was a sheer coincidence that I connected with Mr. Hanus Munz, the only man who returned from Maly Trostinec. A friendly clerk of the Jewish community of Prague replied to my repeated queries looking for details of Maly Trostinec. It was 1993, the oppressive Communist system had been toppled, and I felt that perhaps some new information might become available. I did not nurse many hopes, but I thought that when the Communist repression ended, I should make another effort. The Communist regime persisted in denying the uniqueness of the Jewish tragedy. As far as the Red dictators were concerned, the murdered Jews were only one group oppressed by the German fascists.

To my surprise, the letter from Prague contained the address of the one man who knew all about Maly Trostinec. He alone was able to tell me the truth about the camp. I knew he must be getting on in age—we were all old in 1993. I was deeply touched when I held his reply letter in my hand. Although his writing revealed the shaky hand of an old man, his mind and recall were formidable.

Mr. Munz explained in his letter that Maly Trostinec was in prewar days a "sovchoz," an agricultural settlement administered by the Communist government. In was located in Belarus and the nearest large city was Minsk. As the Russian army retreated and the Germans occupied Belarus they chose Maly Trostinec as a site for a concentration camp.

In 1942, when the first Jewish transports from Austria and the Czech lands arrived, there was little left from the fierce fighting. All that was left were a few barns and some dilapidated buildings. Eventually some barracks were added and furnished with a few bunks. Mr. Munz continued in his description of the place, which had ultimately some infrastructure in place. He singled out starvation as one of the most common causes of death and suffering there. The Nazis allowed only an insignificant number of inmates to stay alive and these were handpicked to create the infrastructure of the camp. The rest—the vast majority of the newly arrived—were immediately gassed. Maly Trostinec was guarded by Lithuanian volunteers but it was under the jurisdiction of the Gestapo in Minsk. The German commandery in Minsk was interested exclusively in the confiscation of gold, jewelry and furs.

Though Mr. Munz downplayed the extraordinary achievement of his escape, I know what it entailed to succeed in a flight from a German concentration camp. When he wrote his reply to me in 1993, he was 83 years old. He reflected on events which had occurred when he was a young man of 33 years of age. His letter showed understatement, modesty and even self-deprecation, the qualities of a real hero. After 1943, the time of his escape, he joined the partisans and fought along with units of the Soviet Union against the Nazis. His heroic escape added yet another glorious chapter of Jewish resistance and bravery during the years of Nazi horror. It took an exceptional man to accomplish a feat of such daring. Some of his information was unique and revealing. For example, the camp existed until June 1944 when the last inmates were herded into a barn which was set ablaze. There were no known escapees from the fiery inferno.

With respect to my more distant family members my search had a similar disastrous outcome. One and all died in different camps, mostly under gruesome conditions. With time I filled in the missing pieces of information and completed the tragic mosaic of what was once my family.

Back then in 1945, reeling from all this disastrous news, I feared that I might succumb to depression. But more powerful than my own despair was the feeling of having a debt to those who had lost their lives. I had to live up to my parents' expectations and the values they had instilled in me. Another obligation of mine was to find Mr. Bleha, to thank him and also find out more about his wartime trials and tribulations.

That proved to be another formidable challenge. In 1945, Theresienstadt was still inhabited by the inmates who were quarantined because of the typhus epidemic. The Gentile population had not been allowed to return yet, and nowhere could I find information about Mr. Bleha's whereabouts. He was not in nearby localities where most of the evicted citizens of Theresienstadt found haven. Finally, a distant relative of his shared with me, somewhat embarrassed and still fearful, that Josef Bleha had been denounced and arrested by the Germans. His was accused of helping Jews which was a major offense by the Nazi yardstick. He was imprisoned in the notorious Small Fortress jail, from which few were released alive. All my letters to authorities remained unanswered; I could not find any more detailed information about Mr. Bleha's fate. The officials offered little enthusiasm or cooperation for my search.

I never gave up in my attempts to find the man to whom I owe my life. Periodically I wrote to pertinent administrative offices, all without success. The Red Cross (Czech and International) was also of little assistance. Unbelievably, it took me until 1991 to find out that Mr. Bleha had not survived his imprisonment in the Small Fortress jail; according to Nazi rules a man who assisted Jews was doomed to the worst of deaths.

I accumulated evidence to demonstrate how Mr. Bleha has helped my family. The Yad Vashem organization awarded Josef Bleha the noble title "the Righteous Among the Nations" in 1994. This lofty honor came late but he will be forever remembered as one of the few who sacrificed his life to help a friend in need. Today his name is entered in the annals among the illustrious individuals who proved their qualities under the most challenging circumstances. The government of Israel, recognizing the excellence of their character and their moral fiber, placed these individuals in a class of special distinction. They are the tiny group of moral heroes who performed feats few others were willing to. Mr. Josef Bleha's number is 7176 on this unique honor roll.

The carob tree was chosen to line the road leading to the hall commemorating "the Righteous Among the Nations." It has the unique quality of being able to withstand fire. The carob tree and those named "the Righteous Among Nations" are in a special category of one.

In the first postwar year, the only social contact which seemed to flow spontaneously and without pain was the occasional meeting with Arthur. When he dropped by, we would chat, share a meal or go for a walk. We no longer fought over my ambition to study, the one divisive issue of our relationship. When our marriage was dissolved by the Czech authorities, we were again single, unattached and free individuals.

Arthur's integration into normality progressed much smoother than mine. The biggest difference (by far) was that his family, as if by a miracle, survived the war, and they became reunited in their entirety. Arthur was also more successful professionally. He was offered a position in the public relations department of the Institute for Chemical and Pharmaceutical Corporation and promised a transfer to its research branch. For the time being he was assigned to north Bohemia and, therefore, his duties took him out of Prague sometimes for an entire week. He would return to the capital on weekends and deliver his reports on Mondays, just before leaving for yet another stint to the region he was responsible for. The main objective of his provisional work assignment was the popularization of products marketed by the company. The long years of war had not only stunted the production of pharmaceuticals but also crippled the dissemination of information to practitioners in remote regions of the republic.

Arthur liked his position. He enjoyed an easy rapport with people; he liked mobility and the change of scenery, all of which were part of his working day. He looked forward to his eventual transfer to the research department and so, by and large, he was pleased with his reintegration. He still lived alone in the former apartment of his family but his younger brother was to join him once he was discharged from the army.

I had no comparable news to share with him. I had not worked hard enough to unravel my twin problems of physics and chemistry in recent weeks, for I was reeling from the double shock of the total annihilation of all my relatives. But I insinuated to Arthur that basic sciences were very complex, hoping that he might volunteer to help. He must have been proficient in both, for they were an integral part of the pharmaceutical course, but no offer of help was forthcoming. Just the opposite, he repeated his by now hackneyed comment that my struggle to study was not worthwhile and that I should rethink the course I had embarked upon. He proposed to renew our links and invest our energies into building a joint destiny. Almost as an afterthought he added that I should not reject his offer offhand. He would be back for a friendly chat, just touching base. I was familiar with his reasoning, but I was not so desperate as to give up on my studies. I returned to my scholastic endeavors, haunted by my twin nemeses.

Two classmates befriended me and offered to assist me in decoding some of the riddles of the two science subjects. As we began to unravel the mysteries of physics, I discovered early on that they had different goals in mind. I remained alone again with no potential tutor in sight. Later, I made efforts to expand my circle of friends and, though I never had problems socializing in the past, I could not find any common ground with my post-war acquaintances. The girls my age worried about boyfriends and fashions, and they giggled and chatted about matters which seemed trivial. Although I wanted badly to partake in these interests, I felt old, drained, misplaced and warped by the past six years. Finally, I accepted that I was different and gave up my efforts to emulate them.

It was no coincidence that, following the war's end, most of the survivors married early on, and almost none intermarried, though a greater part of them renounced their Jewishness for the safe haven of belonging to a national majority. In spite of that we were more comfortable in the company of fellow Jews, most of whom shared our tormented past. To be in the presence of someone who was there and knew it all was reassuring and much easier. Such company provided the comfort of shared experiences; there was no need to explain anything. We formed some strange brotherhood of ex-inmates who understood all and whose presence offered relaxing comfort. We remained in many aspects different for we were molded by such outlandish experiences that most could not begin to understand. For many years we felt like members of a strange, distinct society, set apart by our tragic past. Perhaps this kindred feeling contributed to the permanency of those marriages. There were few divorces between the survivors who joined their lives after the war. Perhaps we were not so exceptionally compatible but we were bound by the powerful ties of our past that we believed no one could share or grasp.

15

On the Road to Recovery

Gradually the miserable winter gave way to milder weather and a beautiful spring, the season that brings out the best of Prague's melancholic beauty. The many parks and gardens revive their unique beauty, redolent with the intoxicating fragrance of the many budding blossoms. It tended to lift the spirits of all, and it began to work wonders for me. Almost daily I would set out for walks through the parks, pondering my future.

Surrounded by all that loveliness I felt better; the spring took on a symbolic meaning of renewal. The splendor of nature against the background of Prague's architectural marvels offered a sense of continuation. Somehow, I began to take in nature's endurance, although I still frequently felt devastated since becoming aware of the annihilation of my entire family.

I made up my mind to try one more time to find a solution to the two subjects (chemistry and physics), the sword of Damocles hanging over my head, thwarting my dream of academic pursuit. In spite of my best efforts I fell short of expectations. Gradually I reached the conclusion that I had little chance of success. One additional complication was the bouts of fever that still occasionally plagued me, draining whatever strength I had regained.

I consulted a friendly physician who became quite alarmed in light of my medical history. He sent me hurriedly for an X-ray examination. There were shadowy spots on my lungs which seemed far from healing. He thought I would be best served if I were to enter either a sanatorium or perhaps try to take vacations. The health authority dispatched me to a place beneficial for treatment of lung disorders. I was to stay in Cesky Dub for as long as it took to ascertain that the illness was either healing or at least showed calcification of the spots. As I was about to leave, Arthur paid me a visit. I explained to him that the as-yet undiagnosed lung ailment called for rest and treatment in Cesky Dub. I was genuinely surprised when, two days later, Arthur showed up there. He decided to spend his vacation with me, though it was not at all certain if my illness was contagious.

We had a beautiful time together, far from the pressures of city life and a need to come to decisions. We went for long walks, afternoon swims and, in the evenings, we danced to the cheerful tunes played by the orchestra at the resort. My strength and sense of well-being returned quickly. I began to feel better for I had three square meals a day to help me in my recovery. I realized that my Prague diet of bread and coffee left a lot to be desired. I scrimped on my meal expenses, bringing them down to the bare minimum just to bridge the times of financial hardship until the Finance Ministry reimbursed me for Dad's unpaid wages. Only then would I be able to afford a private tutor who could help me to make up for the missed years of high school. It went without saying that I would also be able to upgrade my living standards. But evidently my health was not sturdy enough to allow me to get by on a substandard diet in the meantime.

My markedly improved well-being, along with the picturesque loveliness of the countryside, slowly brought back some of the romance into our much-shaken relationship. We leisurely talked about the future, hinting that we would each make concessions to smooth over our acrimonious split, but without making any real commitment. As always Arthur tried to persuade me to give up my ambition to study and instead work on our once loving relationship. He made it plain time and again that it was his belief that we could be happy together. And perhaps if we had a child of our own, I would find satisfaction and joyful bliss. Gradually he swayed my already undermined self-esteem. As it was, I had serious doubts that I could conquer my complex academic problems. I became convinced that I was doomed to fail; I sorely mistrusted my ability to achieve my goals.

I decided to temporarily interrupt my academic pursuits until I had recovered my father's lost earnings that would enable me to hire a private tutor to assist me. I talked myself into believing that I was not quitting, only delaying for more propitious circumstances. It was a conclusion so out of my character that I later wondered what happened then to my fighting spirit. Why did I quit before I was really defeated? Was I that tired or ill or did I lose all my self-esteem? I honestly don't know; perhaps it was combination of all these elements.

Arthur was delighted with my change of heart. He even agreed to my hypothetical future project to retain a tutor who would help me to bridge over the lost years. He knew well enough that I was hurting badly; he did not want me to feel defeated. He was sensitive enough to know that it would be a bad start if he were to gloat over my decision. I was left with a face-saving formula for a nebulous academic future neither of us really believed in. While I never understood Arthur's inability to accept my aspirations for an independent career, I never questioned his love for me. He could not empathize with my desire to have my own professional career but he always wished the best for me. Though we both loved each other, in certain aspects we lacked common understanding. Strange what attracts and keeps people together!

Now we began to forge our future in all seriousness. The major concern was my shaky health and then there was the great enigma of whether or not we had a future in Europe. All Czechoslovaks were worried because of the deteriorating political situation around us. In the first free elections (in May 1946), the Communists won an impressive 38 percent of the popular vote. As a result, most of the key ministries (premier, interior, information, agriculture and finance) of the new government were controlled by the Communists. From the beginning, however, collaboration between the Communists and the non–Communists was troubled and difficult. The threats to the Czech democracy were evident as the Communists turned out to be puppets of the Moscow regime, maneuvered by their manipulative puppeteers. Building a new life in Europe didn't seem wise, especially when Arthur and his family received an immigration permit to the United States. But in the summer of 1946, we shelved all these concerns there in Cesky Dub, and Arthur embarked on plans for our wedding.

We agreed that I should move into his larger apartment. Faithful to his decisive disposition he set all our projects into motion quickly and, as soon as we returned from our summer holidays, I moved in with him. The date of our second wedding was set for October 1, 1946, and we opted for a civil ceremony which took place in the Clam-Gallas Castle, the official site of civilian, state-sponsored marital ceremonies.

My task was to find some proper attire for the wedding but it was not an easy one. Many of the better-quality items were sold on the black market at exorbitant prices, out of the reach of my budget. Following a futile search, I settled for coordinates that once belonged to my mother. I liked my outfit; I almost felt as if part of Mother was there with me. The only accessories I found were black, not my favorite color, but matched my suit well.

The civil marriage ceremony in Prague of 1946 was a short affair: the clerk had a standardized speech and a phonograph played the wedding march. It all reminded me of an assembly line production. During the somewhat impersonal speech and the accompaniment by the scratching sounds of the old, overused phonograph, I remembered longingly the pure melodic tones of Hambro's violin. In compliance with the law, we provided two witnesses, both of whom were Arthur's colleagues from his workplace. Arthur's family were also present and even a few friends came to honor the occasion. My groom brought me a bouquet of white carnations and an elegant gold ring.

All in all, the marriage ceremony was dignified, simple and meaningful. This was an entirely different wedding from our first, only the ceremony under the torn canopy in Theresienstadt felt more spiritual and reverential, appropriate to celebrate the dignity of the union. For a reception, we had a family lunch in a local restaurant on our shoestring budget, hampered by stringent food rationing.

During the second postwar year, we were required to pay for the contents of our apartments. The payment for our place was steep. Nolens volens, I had to take a job if only to offset the high cost for the furniture. The government demanded the payments, never showing sympathy or consideration for the returning survivors of the Holocaust.

Vera and Arthur's postwar wedding in Prague, 1946.

My first workplace after the war was with an organization called the Association of the Liberated Prisoners. I was manning the desk and was initially quite happy working there. But before long the executives of the organization decided that their main responsibility was to the prisoners who had been jailed for political activities (mainly Communists) rather than those prisoners who were jailed because of their Jewish roots. This policy was entrenched into the statutes of the organization. I was genuinely shocked and resigned my position on the spot, right then and there. This discriminatory practice of this organization persisted and they never deviated from this infamous anti–Semitic stance.

Shortly thereafter I found a new job. It was another administrative position, this time in the office of the Jewish community of Prague. I was hired as a secretary to the director, Ing Frisher. I was surprised that as a newcomer without special skill or experience I was chosen for this rather well-paid job. Soon I had the answer. My boss was loathed and no one

Vera and Arthur's postwar wedding, 1946.

wanted to work for him. There were some strings attached, though. I had to master typing, for the bulk of my duties would entail taking dictation and typing letters. I had already learned shorthand, for I needed it to take notes during university lectures. In those days, one had to write as the lecturer spoke; there were no handouts or printed abstracts available.

All these duties filled my day to the hilt for I also had to take care of our household which was by no means a simple task. We had no refrigerators, washing machines, vacuum cleaners or mixers—everything had to be done by hand and from scratch. Shopping was yet another chore which occupied a disproportionate amount of time: everything remained rationed and could not always be found on the stores' shelves. I had to try several shops before I assembled the minimum needed for the day. The concept of supermarkets was then unknown; each store handled only one type of merchandise (i.e., dairy products, baked goods) and sold only a restricted number of items, even in its own specialty. Our home on Horni Stromky Street did not have an elevator and our apartment was on the fifth floor, right under the roof. I had to carry all our shopping up the five double-tiered staircases. I certainly felt very tired and unwell. I attributed my indisposition to my strenuous life and lack of rest and recreation.

The specialist in lung diseases was pleased with my progress, mainly because the threatening spots on my lungs were scarring, healed by calcification, and some had all but vanished. He discharged me from his care and advised me to seek out an obstetrician who could treat the hormonal imbalance, the last lingering disorder from my years of imprisonment. The almost chronic night blindness disappeared as did the ugly brownish spots of pellagra. The last ailment was to be treated by an obstetrician. I turned to Dr. Klein, the man I knew so well from our shared imprisonment. I became his patient, and he was confident that nature would stabilize the last effects of my lengthy privation.

I visited Dr. Klein, sometimes as a patient, sometimes as a friend. He encouraged me to drop by, for his office was on my way home from work. He was a kind and accessible friend and he remained so for a long time after our liberation. Though I had returned from vacation not so long ago, my health was again quickly worsening. I therefore visited Dr. Klein and, following my check-up, he seemed more pleased than worried. Normally he was not a talkative man but on this occasion he spoke at some length. At first he told me that I was pregnant, roughly three months along, and that he wanted to deliver my baby. There was a hint of undue urgency in his voice. His next sentence explained his insistence. He added that birth of Jewish children would vindicate his work in the camp and breathe new life into the decimated numbers of the Jewish nation. However, Dr. Klein was concerned if my health was up to the challenge of a pregnancy. He would have preferred me waiting longer. "Well, tell me, Vera, why do you have to hurry with everything? You have all your life in front of you." Still, he was happy for me and he promised to look after me like a hawk. And that he did, with all his knowledge, energies and conscientious concern.

I recall that I was astonished by his emotional outpouring, so unusual for this cool, controlled intellectual. But times were hard for him; he may have been battling the memories of the many abortions he had had to perform. Even though he had done them to save the lives of the many pregnant women, he might have been haunted by his own nightmares. After my initial surprise, I felt happy—very happy indeed. Suddenly I wondered why I had never thought of having a child, one I could love and protect, pamper and raise. I dismissed the fact that I was only 20 years old, did not have any relatives to help or advise me and that we had next to no financial security. That was the first time I pushed my dream of an academic career into the background and I had no regrets contemplating the loss of my job because I did not enjoy what I was doing anyway. I rushed home to share the news with my husband. He was pleased but also worried about our precarious financial position. My enthusiasm must have been contagious, for soon he joined me in forging our plans for the great change in our near future. I realized that I was happy—an emotion I had almost forgotten existed. It was not an euphoric happiness but a feeling that little else mattered but the baby I was carrying.

I continued working throughout my pregnancy which was by no means an easy one. I felt unwell and tired. If not for the warm feeling of anticipation, I would probably have been miserable. I have always suffered from headaches, and my pregnancy exacerbated this condition so that I hardly experienced a day without one. I could not take any painkillers: Dr. Klein was adamant that I stay away from all medication, alcohol and cigarettes. He felt that the odds were stacked against me anyway, for he feared the consequences of the protracted malnutrition of my very recent past.

I carried out all his recommendations religiously. From the moment I became aware of my pregnancy, I tried to avoid all the melancholic thoughts and memories that used to follow me like shadows. I stopped analyzing the roots of the Jewish tragedy; I set aside all my doubts about our future. I desperately wanted to generate a happy frame of mind so that my baby could take it in, perhaps by osmosis. Certainly Dr. Klein always stressed the need for a happy, relaxed, unburdened mental disposition. I adhered to a healthy lifestyle and followed as good a diet as the chronic shortages allowed me to. Dr. Klein insisted on proper rest and sufficient sleep. In any case I dragged myself through my days at the office, and when I was done with my household chores, I was so tired that I usually dropped off to sleep. My energy level was so depleted that I barely managed the essentials. It was a cold, tough winter and I was not much fun to be with.

Arthur, on the other hand, seemed to burst with energy—his recovery was amazing. He was not, as I discovered, a man whose idea of an enjoyable evening was to read or listen to music. He felt that all those years of deprivation and confinement had to be compensated for. He wanted to see friends, go to movies, dance or some other activity denied to us for such a long time. While I delighted in all those activities as well, I did not need to be on the go at all times, and during my pregnancy I had little energy left to partake in extracurricular activities.

My employment terminated in mid–May, about a month before my projected delivery. My boss bid me goodbye; we both knew that we would not miss each other. I began a much happier phase of my life by shopping and preparing for our baby. I could only afford to purchase secondhand items but I chose very carefully because I wanted only the best for my child. I bought a nice bed, a play pen and a whitish baby carriage made out of wicker. Most of them looked almost new but the pride of my acquisitions was the baby carriage. It was an old fashioned, large carriage, obviously lovingly handled by the original owner; it still displayed traces of its fine craftsmanship.

I had no maternity wardrobe. I got ahold of a loose brown frock, one I hardly needed anyway. To the great concern of Dr. Klein I was not putting on weight. In last trimester he insisted on my seeing him twice a month.

My appointment fell on May 17, coinciding with my 21st birthday, by far the happiest in a long time. Dr. Klein extended his congratulations: in Czechoslovakia when one reaches their 21st birthday, it is the age of independence and voting privileges. However, these were bestowed upon me by the courts at the age of 19 when I returned from the camp. Czech legislators recognized that survivors did not need legal guardians and granted us these legal privileges when we returned.

A few days later, for the same occasion, we were invited to my mother-in-law's place. Right after a light supper, Arthur and I got up to dance, when all of a sudden I felt a sharp cramp, which I attributed to the quickly ingested supper. After all, I had another three weeks left before the arrival of my child, no reason to worry. But the pains kept on coming, and I automatically glanced at my watch. The pains were coming at regular intervals. Soon Arthur caught on and we decided to call Dr. Klein, describing my symptoms to him. Dr. Klein ordered my immediate transfer to the Boruvka Clinic where he had admission privileges.

Once we reached the clinic matters took a quick turn. I was admitted and Dr. Klein advised Arthur to go home, keep in touch by phone and not expect news for a long time. In those days, no husband was allowed into the delivery room where only authorized personnel were present. Not only did we lack the comforting presence of our husbands but also all deliveries were unaided by painkillers or anesthesia of any kind with the exception of Caesarean sections, which were performed under general anesthesia.

That night Dr. Klein never left my side. He offered his arm for comfort, telling me that if I squeezed it hard enough during my pains, it might help. He talked to me for the better part of the time, explaining that the protracted, tedious delivery was due to my still run-down condition and, worse yet, my baby was in the position known as breech: my baby had decided that the normal entry into this world, namely head first, was not the right one and instead had chosen his other end. Was it ominous of what he thought or was it his assessment of this world? At the time, though, I was not in the mood for jokes. Finally, in the early morning hours, my son was born. Dr. Klein, who announced the arrival of my boy, looked tired but happy. As he congratulated me, he added that this baby would usher in a new and better chapter in my life.

For me what followed was an hour of absolute happiness. A nurse handed me a bundle, giving me a chance to kiss my baby. As I looked at my son I was convinced that he was perfectly lovely. I thought that there had never been a more gorgeous newborn anywhere: his pink cheeks, ten fingers and toes, the adorable cowlick on his flawless head.

When I kissed my baby's cheeks for the first time, the bells of all the cathedrals and churches of Prague began to toll, honoring the May 28 state holiday, for it was the birthday of the incumbent president, Edvard Beneš. Dr. Klein and I exchanged comments about the welcoming sounds which marked special events in the life of the nation. I interpreted the ancient, festive, and majestic tolling as a good omen for my son. Previously I had always felt a slight contempt for the much extolled and glorified miracle of birth. All the mushy and mawkish exaltation sounded phony to me. Suddenly I agreed with all those clichés. I was humbled by the momentous nature of the miraculous event; it was a feeling of indescribable bliss.

Vera with her sons, David (right) and Michael, circa 1956.

Dr. Klein was right: May 28 commenced a new and better era. In spite of all the hardships, three different emigrations, political upheavals, health problems, financial and professional difficulties, all the perplexities of our complex lives, straddled over three continents and at least as many political systems, my outlook on life never sank to the depths of despair as it often did in the first postwar year. I always drew hope, joy and strength from my sons, who to me were the answer to all my dreams and hopes. Indeed I was fortunate and blessed; I never could have hoped to have such wonderful sons as my two boys.

With the day shift arriving at the clinic, I was transferred to my room. Filled with proud anticipation, I awaited Arthur's arrival. At ten o'clock sharp, Arthur stood at the door but instead of rushing forward, happy and delighted, he remained thunderstruck. The bouquet of red carnations dropped out of his hands and it took him a few seconds to regain his composure. Moments later I understood his shock, for he handed me a mirror, and I saw that my complexion had changed to blue, burnt sienna and black hues. Dr. Klein dropped by as well and he explained to me that the change was transient, caused by capillary trauma. Then, smiling gently, he rolled up his sleeve, displaying a hematoma that reached up to his elbow, the result of all my squeezing.

While I was expecting we never pondered a name for our child. Perhaps I was fearful not to insult Fate by taking his or her arrival for granted. Somehow in the back in my mind was the fear planted there during the war years that capricious destiny has mind of her own. Now that our son was here we had to make the momentous decision. Arthur and I decided to name our son Peter Edward. We liked the name Peter and the middle name was to mark the coincidence of the birthdays of our boy and the then-incumbent Czechoslovak president. His Hebrew name was to be David, in honor of Arthur's grandfather. I racked my brain for the Hebrew name of my father but could not remember it. Perhaps I never knew it. Was it possible that he did not have one? It pained me then that I could not recall a single Hebrew name of my lost relatives. How far did our futile attempts to assimilate and gain entry into the mainstream get us? How much of our traditions, values and identity had we lost, gaining little or nothing? Did not all those we tried to please and emulate leave us high and dry?

I had no quarrel with the name of my son but I knew that we had to come to terms with another decision that frightened me, to say the least. Arthur took for granted that, on the eighth day after the baby's birth, he would be circumcised, a religious rite that would mark David's entry into the covenant. However, the pending "brith milah" threw me into emotional panic. It was May 1947; we had just survived the Holocaust and I recalled that the Nazis had used the physical distinction of circumcision during their dragnets and mass arrests to identify Jews. I could not help but agonize over a possible recurrence of history and my child's vulnerability. I consented to a brith milah in deference to tradition and my husband's fervent wish. But even today I remember the sheer terror that burdened my decision. Did I do the right thing? Did our decision to have him circumcised expose him to danger? By that time I gradually reached the conclusion that I would not join my friends who had denounced their past and rejected all religious affiliation. I would remain a faithful Jew and worked towards a deeper understanding of my religion.

The first few months of my baby's life were not easy, more so for me than for him. David slept mostly during the day while crying the better part of the night. I tried many remedies, including those recommended by old wives' tales aimed at alleviating his painful colic, all to no avail. I became worried that he was unwell, that I was doing something wrong, and that, in the end, I might lose him too. My only guidance was a book for young mothers and the pediatrician, whose office I visited religiously.

The pediatrician, Professor Epstein, was a survivor of Auschwitz, where he had seen his family perish. His only saving grace in the eyes of the Nazis was the fact that they needed a physician, and so they installed him as the physician-in-chief of the gypsy camp. God knows why he emerged from there with a somewhat tarnished reputation. Prior the Nazi persecution, Professor Epstein stood at the helm of the preeminent children's clinic in Prague and enjoyed international renown. There were many of us, the postwar young mothers, who placed their trust in Professor Epstein, for we had no grandmothers or other senior relatives who could guide us or offer help. We had all just recently escaped the clutches of death and now, overwrought and anxious, we were attempting to learn the skills of motherhood.

Most of the survivors chose to start families very early on. Perhaps we regained confidence in life and its glory, or maybe we sought to escape our nightmares? We certainly pined for families of our own and most likely it was a combination of several reasons. So, within the first few years, many of us had babies though none had stable homes or financial security. We had no extended family for our children but we were devoted to our new role with great eagerness. We were unsure of our deftness and competence in giving the best care to our offspring; riddled with uncertainties, we flocked to our great guru, Professor Epstein, a man in whom we invested our trust to enlighten us about maternal skills.

In retrospect I realize that it was a poor choice. While he was probably a formidable physician, he was also a stern, unapproachable man who had the manners of a German professor—more military than medical. Professor Epstein was in reality a tragic figure, another victim of Nazi madness, one who remained engulfed in the pain of the loss of his family. He was a man in his fifties, too young to give up on life and too old to start a new one. As a result, he was bitter and harsh. Though he treated most of the young mothers with contempt, he cared for and was fond of the babies. We were afraid of him but we believed that he was the best expert in pediatrics. And only the best was good enough for our newborns.

According to the prevalent theory then, an infant had to be fed at regular intervals, the length of which was determined by its weight and, without exception, no allowance was permitted for feeding outside the appointed times. We did not dare violate Professor Epstein's recommendations for fear of harming the babies. This method caused unneeded hardship to mother and child alike.

All the regular demands of motherhood—aggravated by the postwar shortages of food and clothing and the total absence of household appliances—were compounded by the orders of my exacting pediatrician; his recommendations absorbed my days, evenings and, at times, part of the night as well. However, all this hard work was well compensated by one toothless smile of my child.

In spite of our hardships, the better part of 1947 was a delightful and happy time. My friend Lilly (whose son was the same age as mine) and I would go to parks or a nearby cemetery, where our babies played. According to Professor Epstein, these daily outings were compulsory, an essential part of healthy child-rearing. Lilly and I therefore walked for hours, pushing our baby buggies in good or bad weather, in rain or sunshine, in snow or thaw. We did not miss a day for we were such conscientious mothers! The kids seemed happy, protected from the cold, swathed in their fur sacks and warm clothing. Only we froze, for neither of us had much in the way of a winter wardrobe yet. Nevertheless, we kept on walking.

At the best of times I was a poor sleeper, but in the course of my boy's early months, I hardly slept at all. I learned to anticipate the signs of his discomfort and somehow, like the neurotic professor, I waited for the first whining sounds. In between I read and read some more. I was determined to find out why we Jews were cursed, why the world at large had been so indifferent to our suffering, and the reasons for the two millennia of hate and persecution. The more I read, the less I understood. As a result I decided to approach my quest systematically, setting forth from the outset of recorded times. That was a tall order, but the Prague libraries were well stocked, unaffected by the war's air raids. It was my good fortune that an elderly, friendly librarian became impressed by my enthusiasm and helped me choose the right books. The more I read, the more curious I became, and so I filled my evenings with my search for answers. No matter how much I read, though, I did not find what I was looking for. The roots of our suffering remained obscure to me but I enjoyed learning history.

Arthur watched my obsessive interest with some amusement. He was not tormented by our past tragedies; he found his answers in his religious convictions which enabled him to find his equilibrium. It was not as simple for me: I could not find peace of mind until I understood. Besides, Arthur was never a bookworm. His idea of fun was sports, socializing and dancing—things I could not share with him in my days of young motherhood. On occasion, Arthur would stay at home, but he would quickly become restless and ill-humored. Clearly, he needed all his activities just as much as I coveted my reading.

Our boy developed well; he was a beautiful child indeed, though never on the hefty side. He walked and talked very early on. He welcomed me every morning with a radiant smile; I looked forward to his rising and our greetings. Slowly his sleeping habits improved. Then he sat up, began to crawl and became curious about the place, no longer willing to stay in the play pen or his buggy. Our daily strolls with Lilly deepened our friendship which blossomed into a warm and supportive relationship. Even though our connection was to be severed soon enough, we formed a lasting bond during the first years as inexperienced mothers, exceeding many subsequent friendships of much longer duration. Gradually my sorrow began to recede, for I basked in the warmth and glow of love for my boy. His hugs and kisses began to erase the pain and bitter memories.

I imagine that today, affected by the many changes advanced by the women's liberation movement, few young women would consider themselves satisfied with motherhood accompanied by a host of economic hardships and an almost uninvolved husband. The custom then called for the man not to take an active part in the rearing of children in their infant phase. Traditional Czech society believed in the near exclusion of any paternal role in the early stages of a baby's life. The father would begin to take an active interest in his child sometime when it reached the stage of a toddler. Until then, it was proper to restrict all the nurturing care to the mother. The nursery was her domain. We hardly ever questioned the wisdom of this accepted practice.

In our case, Arthur could not, had he wanted to, help me care of our baby because his work removed him from Prague for most of the week. I often thought that this position was tailored to his needs: he liked mobility; he loathed an eight-hour day enclosed in one place; he had excellent rapport with people of all walks of life; and he was unencumbered by superiors, for whom he rarely had any use. I did not see a great deal of him and it bothered me, but I hoped to be able to join him later when my child was a little older. I wished that we could have shared more time and hobbies, but that had to be put on hold, for Arthur was neither an avid reader nor did he enjoy debating or dissecting an issue. To continue living in harmony we had to learn to accommodate our different temperaments and priorities. We did not try to force our own predilections on the other; we agreed to follow our interests without encroaching on the interests of the other.

In 1947 I was awarded the final and generous settlement by the Finance Ministry. It entailed a great many meetings and I signed countless documents needed for the reimbursement of the deferred wages and pensions, imperative to close my father's file. The official death certificates had to be issued; I had to surmount mountains of red tape. And there were many like me. We all had to wait, fill out stacks of questionnaires demanding information we could not always provide. It was relatively simple as far as my parents, sister and grandmother were concerned because they all died in

Theresienstadt. It was far more complicated for the rest of my family. I had only approximate dates and localities where they were murdered. A lot had to be improvised to satisfy the bureaucrats and their never-ending need to fill out forms.

My next self-assigned task was more arduous. I initiated the claim to the properties of my uncles and that presaged another legal labyrinth. I was driven by my desire to better our financial situation and, slowly, my aspirations began to pay off. I still hoped to return to my studies. Backed up by some financial reserve, with hope for additional restitution of my extended family's assets, I set a target date for my return to university. I projected it for the fall of 1949, preceded by a summer of private studies to overcome the gaps in basic sciences. While my personal situation was slowly improving, the same could not be said for the economy and the political climate of our country.

The economy was stagnant. It could not take off because although the country was officially free and independent, it was so only on paper. No measure could have been taken without approval of Big Brother in the east. The recovery was hampered by the iron-fisted rule of the Soviet Union. Czechoslovakia was not allowed to develop on its own initiative; it had to heed orders coming from the Soviet Union that were imposed by proxy. Czechoslovakia, for example, was not allowed to join the Marshall Plan and that was a major setback for the struggling economy. Tragically, the fate of our country, though nominally independent, had been determined at the Yalta and Teheran conferences where the Allies had decided that Czechoslovakia was one of the countries that would belong to the Soviet sphere of interest.

One more time the Czechs were destined to comply with the judgment of powerful nations without being consulted about the resolutions which affected them. History had repeated itself. The small republic had been sacrificed in 1938 on the altar of appeasement to Hitler. In 1944 Roosevelt and Churchill offered Stalin a virtual blank check with one weak non-committal promise from the Soviet dictator: he would grant free elections to the Czechoslovaks. Few paid credence to Big Brother's promise.

Economic stagnation was accompanied by political gridlock between Communists and non–Communists. In accordance with the Czech constitution, new elections were to be called in 1948, and it was a foregone conclusion that the Communist Party would not retain its strength. Most people were deeply disenchanted by its heavy-handed approach, including a systematic ideological indoctrination in factories and other working places and the formation of a "workers militia." We watched the unfolding scenario with grave concern. Were we observing a return to another police state, the red dictatorship replacing the just defeated brown one? To us it appeared like a replay of an already familiar Dantesque script, an ascent of the forces of evil winning the contest for power against the feeble, fledgling republic. We were petrified by the emerging nightmare and could do absolutely nothing to counter it.

16

Takeover by the Red Dictatorship

The much-dreaded coup d'état shattered the weak Czechoslovak democracy in February 1948. Few were genuinely surprised. Indeed, before the coup, Prague was filled with rumors and sinister predictions—most people were deeply worried about another impending cataclysm.

The script for the upheaval was neither subtle nor ingenious. It was a heavy-handed take-over concocted by the Soviets. In spite of the crude coercion there was no lack of opportunists who jumped on the bandwagon, hoping to rise to the top with the newly-emerging power. The next election was about to reduce the Communists to, at best, an opposition party. This was unacceptable to the Russians who decided to precede the elections with a forcible take-over.

This coup d'état was not spontaneous. Since 1945, the Czech Communists knew that they would have to maintain and hold on to power by force. They had prepared for it, guided and supervised by the Soviets who were the experts in subversive manipulations. Once they took power, the Communists began to enforce systematic political and ideological indoctrination in factories, offices and workplaces of all sorts. People were exposed to never-ending harangues which were tantamount to brainwashing. All this reached its noisy peak in 1948 when threats were added to lessons in ideology. The Communists did not rely solely on the power of words; they had more faith in the power which comes forth from the muzzle of a gun. They soon established a worker's militia. These paramilitary units received arms, supposedly for an insurrection or other political upheaval. Much-needed production work took a backseat to political maneuvers, all deftly orchestrated by the Soviet commissars.

Government officials bungled their responses to the Communist provocations. But it did not matter, for they never had a chance! The Czech government looked like a bunch of schlemiels, botching their pathetic attempts to stave off the indomitable leftists. The Soviet emissary, Valerian Zorin, who had been dispatched to Prague to orchestrate the coup, had an easy task. Disheartened, we watched the scenario unfold. Firstly, the Communists provoked a constitutional crisis by appointing (contradictory to the law) some Communists as high police commissioners. They refused to bow to pressure and reverse the illegal appointment of their nominees, thereby creating the constitutional crisis they hoped for.

In protest, the democratic representatives resigned, expecting to bring down the government—a move that was supposed to result in immediate elections. Elections, however, were not what the Communists desired. They wished to bypass the legal process by massive threats of violence. President Beneš, then an old and sick man, agonized over the hopeless dilemma, and, fearing bloodshed, he accepted the resignations. This was a signal for militia units, bussed in large numbers to Prague, to begin their marches, with guns poised. Their endless procession roamed through the streets of Prague, menacing and noisy; they were dressed in red bandanas and scarves, shouting their slogans, professing eternal loyalty to the Soviet Union. Beneš wavered, and then, terrified of a potential fratricide, he capitulated entirely.

After the coup our search for a sanctuary began in earnest. Very soon we discovered that we were out of luck, there was nowhere to go. The Communists suspended all exit permits; it seemed that one more time the trap had snapped shut.

We were filled with dark foreboding. We nursed some vague hope that the Czech variant of the red dictatorship would become more humane. That proved to be another pipe dream. How could it be different when the winds of power blew from Moscow? In some ways it was even worse because the Czechs often tried to outdo the masters. We could only think about the bitter irony of fate. In the early days of our liberation, we wanted to remain in the country we loved and perceived as our home, but following the coup we began to look abroad for a potential haven. There was, however, no escape: all the routes were closed and all exit visas were cancelled and no new ones were issued. The word "emigration" alone, although on everyone's mind, was not uttered for fear of being accused of treason or hostility to the state.

The new Communist government introduced changes that rapidly altered the fabric of our lives. It began by installing a trustee, a member of the Communist Party in every apartment house, whose task it became to supervise the other tenants. He was a man who was authorized to enter anyone's apartment at will, inspect reading material for signs of loyalty or lack of it. He could scrutinize whatever he deemed suspicious or subversive to the new order.

In our apartment house, the deep waters of local Communists churned up an appointee who fit the bill of an ideal Communist trustee:

Mr. Vaclav Mrazek, a former factory worker. We were one of the first families he singled out for a visit. As he slowly walked from one place to another he began to issue many orders. His disdain was directed at our books and he ordered that many be removed. Most were not even political but Mrazek became paranoid for they were written by authors he knew nothing about or because the sound of their names was neither Czech nor Russian. For a man like Mrazek, everything connected either to the democratic past or to the Western world was suspicious and potentially dangerous. He instructed me to remove the pictures of the two past presidents of the republic, Masaryk and Beneš, from the walls. He indicated wryly that he would come back to check up on us. We did as we were told; we knew better than to contest an emissary of a police state, no matter how much contempt we felt for the primitive, nearly illiterate emissary.

The mood of the land changed. Everybody suspected the other of some nefarious deeds or connections. The implied threats spread fear and anxiety. People froze emotionally and, in turn, other developments were affected. All life's joy and free expression vanished. Folks became guarded, turning inwards, to their homes and closest ones, but ultimately, there, too, the fabric of familial trust broke down. Parents began to fear their children because the youngsters were tutored and encouraged by their teachers to report on their elders about any actions that were unfriendly to the state. They were enticed by the promise of better grades and other scholastic advantages. With time, the same tactics poisoned many a marriage, where husband and wife would denounce one another, attracted by promised privileges.

In quick succession new laws were passed nationalizing all properties with the exception of the smallest dwellings in the countryside. All factories and businesses were expropriated and taken over by the state. The legitimate owners were kicked out and replaced by state-appointed officials. Capitalists became the most persecuted class of citizens. To be called a capitalist or bourgeois was the worst of insults. Such people were relegated to life on the margins. Never before have people tried to appear as dispossessed as after the Communist takeover. Everybody whose roots were not steeped in the working class tried to rework the family history and come up with an ancestor who had toiled in the mines or factories or at least was a farm hand. Being from a wealthy family line was the worst possible liability, resulting in ruthless discrimination; often such people would find themselves in a menial job or factory assignment; children would be automatically deprived of any higher education. To be a descendant of the much-hated bourgeoisie made the next generation suspected enemies of the state, marked with the sign of Cain.

We removed the pictures from our walls; we got rid of the offending books and conceded to every order issued by Mr. Mrazek, the party confidant supervising our building. He and many like him rose overnight from the obscurity of a lowly factory worker to a powerful and threatening figure whose favors had to be curried. While we feared Mr. Mrazek and his heavy-handed approach, we knew that he was just a tiny cog in a huge menacing machine. All he was authorized to do was to watch and listen to the tenants and report his observations for future use to his superiors. They sifted through the information, used some and put aside the rest. All potentially compromising material was stored for some future eventuality. The party opened a dossier on every citizen, filing information that could be fished out and used for blackmail or denunciation.

Matters were even complicated on the fifth floor of our otherwise unassuming high-rise apartment building. The fifth floor consisted of four identical units, none suited for a family. All our neighbors were childless couples. One was the already mentioned notorious Mr. Mrazek, and another unit was occupied for many years by a middle-aged couple, always friendly, chatty and smiling. The fourth unit was inhabited by an enigmatic pair who moved in following the war's end and became a source of much speculation. The Mrazeks were the only ones who held politically identifiable views; the rest of us never shared our views or affiliations with anybody. But the one couple, the latest arrival, stuck out like a sore thumb because of their peculiar lifestyle.

To be fair, Anna seemed ordinary enough. She was not employed which was strange but it could be explained away because she only had a smidgen of Czech. She and her husband had arrived in Prague only recently. She was of Hungarian extraction, rather plump, a pleasant-looking woman, somewhere in her mid-thirties. She seemed lonely yet hesitant to establish closer contacts. Quite like Anna, I spent my days at home, and I invited her for a chat and a cup of coffee many times. She would gladly accept, come in for awhile, but the moment the conversation took on a personal or serious turn, she would rise and leave almost abruptly. She seemed happy to chat about all kinds of trivia but became much alarmed by personal questions. Even topics as banal as preferences in reading, plays or music threw her off balance. Her strange reactions, attempts to socialize but at the same time remain aloof, gave rise to much speculation about such peculiar, uncommon shyness.

Anna talked a lot but told little. She mentioned that her husband had spent the war years in Russia where he became commander-in-chief of the Czechoslovak parachutist units. He hailed from Sudeten, the northern part of Bohemia, a region inhabited mainly by German nationals before the war. I speculated that her husband, since he was not a Jew, must have fled to the USSR during the Nazi occupation because of his political affiliation with the Communist party. The Nazis' persecution of the Communists was almost as brutal as their wrongs against the Jews. Many Communists fled to the Soviet Union and returned only after the war as heroes. Most were awarded prominent governmental appointments. I speculated that our neighbor was probably a high-ranking Communist or potentially a mole.

Europe during the Cold War was full of strange, secretive individuals, some working for both sides of the divide; others engaged in shoddy political or business deals. Our neighbor was a tall, gaunt man with a sallow complexion, deep-set eyes and a cool, uninviting facial expression. He never engaged anyone in conversation and he never smiled. He hardly replied to a casual hello, seemingly always in a hurry on some urgent business.

Few if any tried to approach him; we all felt his disapproval. His cold glance discouraged any attempt to socialize. I, for one, always shuddered when I met him because he reminded me of the SS men of late. Even the long black leather coat bore a resemblance to the Nazis' preferred dress code. If and when I ran into Augustine Schramm, I hugged my baby tightly and rushed away as fast as possible; I attempted to be civil enough to conceal my discomfort.

I concluded that he was perhaps assigned to some special or important project for he was picked up daily by a chauffeur-driven limousine but never at the same time or place. In the early postwar days cars were not a common sight in Prague. It was the privilege of members of the cabinet and a few handpicked party apparatchiks. The automobile that daily arrived to pick up Schramm would wait at different corners, hardly ever in front of the house. Little escaped the attention of those in a quiet apartment building; we noted, for example, the peculiar times he returned home—mostly in the early hours of the morning, yet he did not come across as a drunkard or a playboy. I never broached these topics with Anna; I knew better than that. I recognized this was taboo territory. She only shared with me her maiden name of Bembritz and her homesickness for her native Hungary. She pinned her hopes on their projected move to a larger, better apartment, scheduled right after the Easter holidays of 1948. She refused to tell me her new prospective address. I hoped that she would find more happiness in her future flat, and I wished for nicer, more cordial neighbors.

On Wednesday, March 10, 1948, the entire Czechoslovak nation heard a shocking radio broadcast, announcing the tragic death of the popular and loved Jan Masaryk, the incumbent minister of foreign affairs. His official cause of death was suicide by jumping out of his bathroom window. Jan, as he was affectionately called, was the son of the first president of the republic, the revered president liberator, Thomas Masaryk. Masaryk senior commanded much respect as a statesman, writer, philosopher and ardent humanist, and his son enjoyed enormous popularity among the entire nation. He was a charming, witty, warm-hearted man with whom people could identify and connect. Jan loved to stroll through the streets of Prague at any time of the day or night and talk to people from all walks of life about their problems. He cared little if the man was a prominent personality or a street cleaner. Though he was an accomplished piano player, he spent most of his professional life in public and diplomatic service.

In spite of the Masaryks' traditional adherence to the Socialist Democratic Party, Jan did not affiliate himself with any political organization. Aware of his liberal leanings, many were genuinely surprised that he opted to continue in his official capacity as foreign minister after the Communist coup. It was common knowledge that he entertained many contacts and friendships in the west and would not have had problems escaping the country as it descended into darkness. Some speculated that he remained behind the Iron Curtain to support the ailing Beneš, once a devoted follower of his father. Many doubted the news that March morning from the onset for defenestration was the least likely option for a man like Jan. In the past he had been candid enough about his dread of pain and injuries. Why would a tall, hefty man decide to jump from a small, hard-to-access bathroom window? It had such a narrow frame that his body had to be squeezed forcibly through it. Why would he want to fall into the courtyard of Cernin Castle, which was both the Foreign Ministry as well as his residence? All those questions, of course, remained unanswered. Naturally there were hushed accusations that he was murdered by the Communists who never really trusted Jan.

Thousands paid their last respects, passing by his open coffin at Cernin Castle where the body laid in state. Everyone noticed the small bunch of snow drops placed behind his right ear. What a peculiar site for flowers! Were they there to cover the hole where the bullet entered, that the embalmer had not camouflaged well enough?

There was no end to the speculation, particularly when medical information became public. Jan's personal physician acknowledged that he had issued a prescription for sleeping pills to alleviate Masaryk's insomnia. If Jan had really wanted to die, would he not have chosen to overdose instead of the melodramatic showiness of jumping out of a window that was so out of sync with his character? The rumors did not quiet down. A short time later, the police pathologist who performed the autopsy was found dead. The official report stated that the doctor had committed suicide by injecting himself with benzene. All who were around Jan or the castle on that March night began to disappear under mysterious circumstances: his butler, the guards at the gates, his valet and others. The air was filled with uneasy conjectures.

Weeks passed, and with the arrival of spring, Arthur told me of his plan to attend an all-night party at his tennis club. As usual, I could not find a baby-sitter and he decided to go alone. The party took place on the eve of a statutory holiday. On that morning I got up early when David woke up and demanded his breakfast. All around me was perfect silence. Obviously my neighbors enjoyed the chance to sleep in. Suddenly the perfect stillness was interrupted by the Schramms' doorbell ringing. The bell was answered as always on Sundays and holidays by Augustyn. Anna boasted of his affection for her because he allowed her to sleep in. While stirring the cream of wheat, I wondered why there was such an early caller at our neighbors'. Right after the door opened, I heard a voice breaking the perfect silence. The men clearly said in a fast, almost hurried voice: "This is from Jan." These four words were followed by two or three staccato echoes resembling firecrackers or gunshots. I then heard a heavy thud as some weighty object hit the ground.

For a second or two I was undecided what to do. What had happened and what should I do? Then the thought occurred to me that poor Anna might need help; she was in no position to ask the angry visitor what he wanted from her husband. I could imagine how bewildered she would be. I opened the door, all but forgetting that I wore only a short nightgown. I scanned the empty hallway, and then I noticed at the turn of the staircase a young man who jumped two to three stairs at a time. The building did not have an elevator and most of us, when in a hurry, took a few stairs at a time, only this handsome young man used a strange technique: he jumped with both his hands thrust deeply into the pockets of his beige raincoat. He seemed startled by the noise of my door opening. He turned his head quickly, looked at me briefly and then placed his forefinger over his lips in the universal sign requesting silence. There was something imploring in his eyes, an urgent request that seemed sincere and I nodded in consent.

All this happened in a second or two. The young man continued his hasty jumps down the stairs. After that I turned to the half-opened door of the Schramms' flat where I saw, to my horror, the half-slumped, bleeding body of our enigmatic neighbor. He gasped for air, the puddle of his blood expanding around his body. I bent down to help him, and just then Anna ran out of the bedroom screaming and yelling some angry laments in Hungarian. She stepped over the bleeding body of her unconscious husband and ran down the stairs. Was she in pursuit of the assailant? Did she try to procure the help of a physician? Why would she not remain with her dying husband? I was about to summon help when I noticed Mr. Mrazek, the party confidant, running quickly out of his flat towards the crime scene. I stepped back and he bent down hissing repeatedly and relentlessly a question into his ear, "Gusto, who did it to you?"

Perhaps he did not realize that the gravely injured man could no longer provide the answer. I knew that he was beyond help. I saw so many moribund and dead in the camp that I had no doubt that Schramm was about to meet his maker. Anna returned within minutes, wailing and lamenting. Her customary down-to-Earth looks were transformed, her white nightgown in disarray, her dark hair covered in a night cap, and she seemed like an aggrieved and heartbroken mourner on a public stage. By then there were so many people around Anna. I was sure that all the help she needed was available. I retreated home carefully. Augustyn Schramm had been shot dead at point-blank range by a handsome young man who looked more like a student than a cold-blooded murderer. It was a strange event in a quiet, unassuming high-rise in suburban Prague, where violence was practically an unknown phenomenon.

In no time the entire area surrounding our apartment house was cordoned off. It was typical of the priorities of a police state: the security forces reached the crime scene in record time, even before any medical assistance was summoned. Uniformed police filled the building, searching for the suspect or some clues to the crime. All tenants were questioned, but most were not even up when it happened. In due time someone knocked on our door, and a burly policeman ordered me to step out for questioning. On our floor, I was the one to be questioned with the utmost intensity. Mr. Mrazek informed the police that I was alone in the hallway when he first stepped out of his flat. Therefore, if anyone could have caught a glimpse of the assassin, it would have been me.

My sense for danger, honed during my concentration camp years, told me I might be in grave peril. I was aware that if I were to admit having seen the young man, I could be harmed by him or any possible accomplices. I vividly remembered his imploring sign requesting my silence. On the other hand, if I didn't divulge what I had seen, I ran a different risk. Apprehended and arrested he might testify that I had seen him as he was running away from the crime scene. In that eventuality I would be guilty of perjury—at any time a major crime—but more so in the days of absolute police power. I was aware that any partial or false testimony would result in a severe penalty, particularly in the investigation of the murder of someone seemingly important to the state. The massive police presence revealed that Augustyn had an entirely different rank than one of an ex-chief of parachutists of the Czech armed forces during the Second World War. This might have been his official title but there was much more to Augustyn Schramm. He also could not have been an ordinary party apparatchik or his death would have warranted far less concern.

All these thoughts raced through my mind; all eventualities seemed fraught with risks and I had so little time for cool deliberation. I heard the angry voice, the word "Jan" and the imploring expression on the face of the assailant. The policeman carefully wrote down my personal data, and when he asked what I had seen in the hallway when I first opened my door, I replied with a resounding "Nothing!" I told him the hallway was empty. The detective in charge decided that I should follow them to the police station for further questioning. I saw that he wavered when he saw that I was about to take my boy with me. They had second thoughts about my accompanying them with a screaming baby who now demanded, in no uncertain terms, his belated breakfast. The policeman suggested that I leave the baby behind, and I recall the feeling of embarrassment at having to admit that my husband was not at home. The policeman did not seem to find this extraordinary; he did not even lift his eyes from his notebook.

Eventually he relented, agreed that I stay put for future questioning. After all I was not going anywhere any time soon. After the tenants were interrogated, the police reopened the area. Arthur returned home, worried about the incident.

The life in a police state was no picnic and Arthur did not want to be a part of it. Long ago he reached the conclusion that we should leave the country one way or another because the conditions were deteriorating at a hazardous pace. I knew that there was no legal way to get out, and I would not risk my child's safety in attempts to cross the border illegally. The border crossings were tightly guarded and any apprehended defector was shot on sight.

The next day, the newspaper carried a brief notice reporting the murder of Augustyn Schramm. His war exploits as the head of the parachutist units were singled out for inordinate praise. The article informed the public that Schramm would be granted a state funeral, an honor exclusively bestowed upon officials of highest importance. His widow would leave the country immediately following the interment for her native Hungary. Who was Augustyn Schramm?

I never saw or heard of Anna again, not even at the trial which took place a few months later. The jurisdiction over the case was in the hands of a military tribunal, presided over by high-ranking officers. The public was excluded. Anyone who is interested in those rocky times of history must be astonished that I devoted so much time to this event: after all, we had just survived a long stint in a Nazi concentration camp where cruelty and death ruled supreme. Surely the violent death of one man was nothing extraordinary for us.

Yes and no. There was a difference.

For starters, we had nourished hopes we could have a new beginning in a civilized society governed by laws. We wanted to stay in this country we loved, respected and considered our home. Though we had just survived the rule of German infamy that shook our faith in the Czech people's probity, we wanted to believe in the new fledgling democracy of postwar Czechoslovakia. But events before and after the coup drove home the point that the Communist dictatorship might not differ much from the German one, although perhaps Jews would not be chosen as the primary target of persecution. With pain in my heart, I came to accept the need to leave, to search for a place where freedom reigned. I did not want my son to grow up and live under the yoke of a police state. Though Jews were not happily, or fully, embraced by the Czech society, we were not subjected to open hatred or lawless persecution. And we, perhaps naively, hoped that with time and education, latent anti–Semitism would vanish. Schramm's demise forced me to focus on reality and the urgency for action. From then on it was only a matter of opportunity and timing. Thus Augustyn Schramm's death brought about the watershed in our lives.

Later we learned that the real Augustyn Schramm had been the head of the Czechoslovak KGB, a man who maintained direct contact with his Soviet counterpart, Lavrenty Beria, from whom he alone took orders. The most infamous order he allegedly carried out was the murder of Jan Masaryk. Czechs were now obsessed with this unsolved crime. There were attempts to shed light on the issue but no clear evidence was produced, and so the official version of suicide was allowed to stand. The tenants of the apartment building at 9 Horni Stromky Street did not enjoy a particularly pleasant spring in 1948. There was the police presence in the building which I for one did not mind. At least I knew who they were and that they probably came to question the tenants or the concierge or find out some obscure detail that might help in the apprehension of the perpetrator. I was more afraid of the numerous civilians loitering around, watching every passerby with a sly curiosity. There was no way to distinguish if they were plainclothes police or perhaps friends of the murderer on the lookout for someone who could identify him. While I climbed up the stairs with my child in my arms, I would turn my head and without exception I would see some man in a gray suit looking up and watching. Every single time I felt a cold chill running up and down my spine, the place where I expected the bullet to hit. I held my boy tightly and hastened my steps.

The newspapers remained silent, not a line about the progress of the investigation. One day, we were informed about the high monetary award offered to anyone who would provide information leading to the apprehension of Schramm's assassin. These few lines revealed the lack of success in the search for the perpetrator. The investigation seemed stalled and the police were under pressure to resolve the crime. The angry cronies of Augustyn Schramm burned with desire to catch the perpetrator and find out who was behind the conspiracy to punish the murder of Jan Masaryk. I kept on wondering and hoping that he had escaped to another country.

A few days later, on my way back from an outing with my son, I saw from a considerable distance that the entire block had been cordoned off by the police. I joined the onlookers, and one of them whispered that they had caught the guy who had killed Schramm; what we saw was the reenactment of the crime.

I froze, my stomach tied in knots. What would the assassin tell them? Would he mention that I had opened the door? Would they torture him, beat him to a pulp to make him confess every little detail? What if he mentioned, perhaps unintentionally, that I had seen him? This would brand me a perjurer and send me to jail for a long time. I stood there, covered in a cold sweat of panic. I looked at my child, overwhelmed with worry about his future, without me to shelter him. I got a glimpse of the handsome young man whose imploring gesture on that Easter morning had caused me so much anguish. He wore the same beige raincoat, only it was now thrown over his wrists, perhaps to conceal the handcuffs. He walked away at a fast clip, encircled by plainclothes men, straight into a police car. I went home, my worries and uncertainties unabated.

The question on everyone's mind was how they uncovered the conspiracy designed to avenge the murder the popular foreign minister. It was the cool one million crown award offered to anyone who would lead the police to the perpetrators. And lo and behold the one who succumbed to the temptation was one of members of the conspiratorial group. He hoped to buy his own safety and get rich all in one swoop.

Nothing happened for the next several days but one morning the bell rang, jolting me into intense apprehension. I opened the door and faced a policeman who delivered the official summons for my appearance as a witness at the trial of Miloslav Choc. That was the first time I had heard his name, for the papers never made a mention of it.

On the appointed day, I left my boy with Lilly. I felt great uneasiness but I pretended to be nonchalant. The moment I reached the building of the military court, I was quickly asked to enter. Following a brief wait, the court clerk called my name. I entered a spacious hall, brightly lit and very quiet. The tribunal consisted of military officers as the public was excluded. I glanced at their shoulder insignias, hoping to identify their military ranks. It did not bolster my confidence for they were all high officers. I did not know why a military tribunal was to decide the fate of Choc and his associates: perhaps because of Schramm's rank as the commander-in-chief of the Czech parachutists?

My testimony began with some confusion. I was asked to take an oath and I was offered a New Testament, still used to swear in those about to give evidence in a trial. I refused to give my oath for religious reasons, secretly hoping that no Old Testament would be found, thus freeing me from perjury. The court clerk scrambled to find one and returned a few minutes later with the requested book.

These were the early days of Communist regime in Czechoslovakia so such religious texts hadn't yet been discarded as obsolete; the society sworn to atheism had no need for Bibles or any religious symbols. I recall that I felt like a lowly criminal, violating my integrity and having to swear to false testimony. I do not know why I felt like riffraff for lying to a tribunal appointed by a criminal government. It must have been my upbringing which emphasized respect for the law of the land. Only now the land was ruled by thugs whose justice was a farce. In reality truth was a dangerous commodity; candor and honesty were the fastest route to jail or worse. The administrators of the laws wished to hear only information that fitted their needs in any given situation. As it was, the verdict was a foregone conclusion, preordained and dictated by the secret service.

During the few minutes it took to provide the Old Testament, I had an opportunity to take in the scenario in front of me: the tribunal, the accused men—it was an intimidating sight. The guards were positioned at the entrance and alongside the walls. The presiding tribunal was on an elevated platform; next to them were the court clerks and the official court recorder. The room was drab: the only adornment was the military insignia above the heads of the tribunal, the Communist banner and the flag of Czechoslovakia. In the prisoner's box sat eight men, all in civilian clothes; the first at the end of the bench was Choc. He was charged with murder and treason, the rest were accused as accomplices in his crime. The silence was absolute. Suddenly Choc uttered one clear word, "Jan!" The presiding general motioned angrily and ordered him to remain silent. The guards approached the prisoner's box and, though they never touched him, their menacing appearance sent a clear message. That was the only time I heard the voice of the man who helped me, albeit unwittingly, with the decision to leave Czechoslovakia forever.

Once more I gazed at Choc. He seemed so young, his handsome face twisted with a crooked smirk. The rest of the men seemed to be broken people; they knew only too well what was in store for them. The only thought of mine was that it was such a shame to die so young.

The moment the Old Testament was brought in, I was asked to take my oath and state my credentials. Having done that, the presiding general directed only one question at me, the one I had been asked so many times in the recent past: "Who and what did you see in the stairway immediately following the murder in the apartment house on Horni Stromky 9, where you lived?" Once again, I denied having noticed anybody or seeing anything extraordinary. I was quickly excused and asked to leave the hall where the proceedings went on. The entire farce did not make much sense—as if anything the Communists did made much sense.

The guards shoved me almost rudely out of the hall but I did not mind; I almost felt as if I just escaped jail. On the street I breathed a sigh of relief. What a load off my mind! I cannot describe the feelings of having that threat removed from my life.

The trial was never even mentioned in the press; only the verdicts were announced. All those accused were found guilty and sentenced to death by hanging. The verdict was carried out forthwith. I was deeply saddened by the deaths of the young men who believed themselves to be the avengers of murder of Jan Masaryk.

In the 1950s, a memorial plaque was placed on the building where Schramm met his fate. The plaque extolled the virtues of a brave man who dedicated his life to the heroic cause of Communism and who courageously led the Czech parachutists to victory over the Nazis in the course of the Second World War. His death was blamed on enemies of the working class. These very same nationals would discard Communism in the 1990s and remove the many commemorative plaques dedicated to faithful Communists, including the one to Schramm.

The year 1949 came and we were no further ahead with our plans to emigrate. Arthur's frustration was heightened by the pressure he felt at his place of employment. Not a word was said, not yet anyway, but it seemed that an invisible hand placed an application for membership to the Communist Party on his desk day after day. Arthur was angry and concerned, worrying about the double bind. He did not want to join the party but he had to consider the consequences of such a decision. Disobeying such a blatant hint was extremely dangerous. There would be any number of consequences if he didn't join the party. It could mean the loss of his job, perhaps a demotion, or a host of other complications, aggravating our already complex, precarious lives.

Czech universities now subjected all students to a background and class check. The screening expelled students from a middle- or upper-class background. Only those whose parents worked in factories or mines or were farmhands received permission to continue—the rest were excluded, regardless of their advancement. Some were driven out literally days before graduation. I realized that I could not return to university, no matter what: my father's position would have automatically disqualified me.

Everything was censured: books, newspapers, radio broadcasts and shows. Everything offered as entertainment was dull propaganda, always extolling the Soviets and their achievements, and denigrating the past and anything Western. It was not much fun to go out anymore. Most relationships became guarded, filled with tension. Who knew who was an informer or could turn into one under some duress? People feared friendships that could turn into liabilities; it became prudent not to cultivate sincere, intimate, amicable relationships. Thus the decay eroded the very fabric of basic human ties.

We weighed the possibility of an illegal escape but soon we had to reject it. It would have been suicidal to try to cross the border with a one-year-old baby in our arms. Moreover, even if we were successful, we had nowhere to go. Still, we wanted to leave. Not only had our lives become unbearable because of the heavy-handed police state's suffocating pressures but we also foresaw the time when the tables might be turned against us Jews. The disgruntled population might blame the handful of Jews for being rich capitalists and, in the same breath, accuse us of having fathered Communism. When it came to Jews, logic was never used. No matter what, the Jews were always the most convenient scapegoat of all. We believed that the Mene Tekel (writing) was clearly on the wall.

This period also marked the beginning of the Cold War. Darkness and gloom blanketed Czechoslovakia along with many other nations—victims of Soviet brutality and the Western powers' impotence. But there was also one fantastic redeeming feature that, for Jews, overshadowed everything else.

Departure from Europe

The State of Israel was proclaimed in May 1948. It was the one miracle Jews had prayed and hoped for during two thousand years of dispersion. The new state was only a part, albeit a small one, of the ancient land of our ancestors, but it would be a home for all Jews and an independent state. Jews everywhere rejoiced in the hope of returning to our roots, having a place we could call home, live free, and cease to be a poorly tolerated minority. In the Jewish state our national experience could be lived to the fullest. The newly emerged state had a mandate to provide shelter for every Jew, regardless of where they hailed from.

Though I knew little of the Zionist struggle, I followed the United Nations' vote on the partitioning of Palestine. When the final results tilted the balance in Israel's favor, it galvanized Jews everywhere, regardless of the depth or intensity of their commitment. The miracle of the creation of Israel helped me to form my own private equation of the Holocaust. From that day on, I perceived the blood spilled as a metaphoric event, as the result of a complex delivery, as a kind of ransom paid for our right to a free state. It was this belief in the purpose of human destiny which enabled me to come to terms with our tragic past.

This is not the place to describe the history of the birth of Israel but it was the politics of the creation of the Jewish state that enabled us to leave Czechoslovakia, and so I must touch on a few details. It became our good fortune that the Soviets had a vested interest in the establishment of a Jewish state in the Middle East. They hoped to expel the British from the Middle East and fill the ensuing power vacuum. Besides, the Jews could have been trusted to form, if not a Communist state, then at least a socialist one in an area where most countries were still ruled by quasi-feudal systems, periodically toppled by military dictatorships. Surely the Jews who were inclined to socialism might usher in a new period of history, opening the back door to the Soviets?

The proclamation of the State of Israel led the Arabs to mount a vigorous attempt to annihilate the fledgling state by their combined military power. At the onset of the hostilities, things looked grim for the Israelis and it was not at all clear or even probable that they would prevail. The Soviets, unwilling to watch their plans thwarted, allowed their proxy, the Czechs, to extend help by shipping arms and providing technical assistance. In fact, the Soviets, even before the decision was reached by the United Nations, allowed the Czechs to train Israel's officers and pilots. This provided an enormous help to the ill-equipped, only marginally trained and inexperienced Israelis.

The Soviets were pleased by the Arab defeat in 1948 and, to increase the number of Jews living in Israel, they decided to allow the few thousand survivors in the satellite states (Poland, Hungary, and Czechoslovakia) to immigrate to Israel. The news spread like wildfire. The Jewish community set up an office that expeditiously registered all potential emigrants. Arthur, filled with enthusiasm, was one of the first to line up. I was somewhat less eager: I feared the dangers in a country torn by war and, even though an armistice was in place, the attacks of terrorist groups continued unabated. I feared for our safety and I was anxious for my child growing up in a place constantly surrounded by danger and threats.

In the end I reached the conclusion that Arthur was right. It was our only chance to leave Europe—perhaps forever. In addition, it was morally correct for a Jew to live in Israel and help to build the new state. None of the emigrants were issued individual passports. The entire group, consisting of several hundreds of people, held a permit for mass departure. The Jewish community appointed a man responsible for the documents, and the rest of us had to apply for permission to take some of our belongings with us. That became yet another travesty. The process was utterly ridiculous. Every item, no matter how trivial, had to be listed separately, entered on special forms in triplicate and submitted to the Finance Ministry.

We began to fill out mountains of paperwork, separating every needle, thread, match, sock—in short, we had to catalogue every household item we wanted to take with us. It consumed hours and Arthur, who always loathed paperwork of any kind, had even less tolerance for government ordinances filled with bureaucratic lingo. He avoided the forms like the bubonic plague. Fortunately, Lilly was always helpful and willing to take care of my son, freeing me to trot back and forth with my avalanche of papers. The early spring months were the last ones our two boys spent time together. Too bad they could not grow up as friends; they seemed so compatible as youngsters. Lilly and her husband decided against emigration. They chose to tough it out, hoping that conditions might improve. Lilly's husband was devoted to his job at the Czech radio station where he had carved a nice niche for himself and was well on his way to the top.

Once all the paperwork was completed and submitted to the department of the Finance Ministry, there was little else to do but wait. Due to xenophobic restrictions, no foreign language textbooks were anywhere in sight. I was nonplussed by my futile search. But I was concerned that I would be leaving for Israel without the command of basic Hebrew. Arthur at least knew how to read and write Hebrew, skill he mastered while attending the religious instruction during his public-school years. I also had misgivings about arriving penniless with a small child to a country where we had no relatives or friends. The Czech government granted an exchange for 2.5 Israeli pounds only, an unconscionable decision, forcing us to leave as beggars.

Although I had received a large sum of money in the final settlement of my father's accounts, I could not purchase much in the way of hard currency on the black market. To begin with, prices were criminally inflated: the ratio was 1,000 crowns to 1 Israeli pound, but worse yet, I feared getting caught with any contraband on me. I could not find answers to my dilemma. I knew that I would not tempt fate the way I had done in the past. Now I concerned myself with the repercussions that any foolish step might have on our future. Several weeks after filling out all those forms, the results were returned to us. We were allowed to take about half of the items we had applied for, the rest had to be left behind.

All electrical, musical, technical, artistic or historical items were rejected. I was not surprised. I expected we would only be allowed to take inexpensive household items and basic furniture with us but Arthur had such a hard time parting with some objects of sentimental value. One of those was a small accordion, a gift from his late father, a record player and a few trinkets. Watching his sadness, I tried to come up with some idea how to help, and I remembered that the present finance minister was once a practicing young lawyer at the Finance Ministry whose name my father had mentioned. I made up my mind to ask a favor. This story would be of little importance were it not typical of the perverted times we lived in.

My request for an interview was promptly granted, and Dr. Fischel greeted me in a friendly and warm manner. I sat in his elegant office and for a while we chatted about trivial matters. He then began to reminisce about my father whom he respected and was very fond of. Eventually he began to show interest in my life and activities, perhaps regarding my wish to see him a social call. Encouraged by his kindness, I began to tell him about our plans to leave for Israel. While I spoke, I could not help but notice that his smile gradually froze and his entire mien darkened considerably. When I asked for permission to take a few items of sentimental value with us, I saw that I had touched a raw nerve. Though he listened to my request, it was obvious that he was controlling his fury with considerable difficulty. His anger reached a boiling point when I fell silent. I readied myself for his rejection. For a while there was silence in the room. Dr. Fischel evidently fought for self-control and, once he had gained the upper hand, he replied in an icy voice: "Your father would have been ashamed of you, if he could hear you. You Jews would take apart the entire Czechoslovak Republic if we Communists would not stand on guard. I shall grant you the singular exception and let you take the few items you spelled out, but do know that I do so to honor the memory of your late father, whom we all admired." He rose, bringing an end to my interview. He stood behind his desk, looking at me as if I were dirt.

At the time I was furious. I nearly reminded him that he too was a Jew, perhaps a different kind, but nevertheless a member of the tribe. To say that I was flummoxed is an understatement. I left his office in a huff, my feelings bruised by his dressing down. Then I was furious by his bitter rebuke and his condescending attitude but later I thought that he might have directed his harangue to the microphones that were installed in all offices. Did he speak his mind or was it all for the benefit of the bugs?

Some three and a half years later while we were living in Israel, I listened to the radio broadcast of some excerpts from Prague's show trials. The arraigned finance minister stood in front of a tribunal accused of Zionist sympathies, an accusation tantamount to high treason. I listened in disbelief to his confessions rendered in a monotonous, unemotional voice. He admitted to crimes he could not have committed, had he wanted to. He was sentenced to death by hanging, right along with the other eleven ministers who were all Jewish. The only non–Jew among the executed ministers was Mr. Vlado Clementis. These men were sacrificed on the altar of the failure of the five-year economic plan. The regime needed scapegoats and who was better suited than the Jewish representatives of the government?

According to the Communist dogma the ideology did not fail, only people erred and thus brought about the failure of the planned economic development. As I listened to the broadcast, I could not help but feel sorry for the misguided man who had an apostolic faith in the righteousness of Communist doctrine. He and others had sacrificed integrity and probity for their fanatic beliefs.

We were in the last stages of preparations for our departure from Europe. Our major acquisition was a transoceanic crate large enough to hold all we could take with us. Police inspectors had to be present to supervise the packing. The day was set and we all went to the loading station, arriving with an armful of documents. There were three tax officials and a uniformed policeman waiting for us. At first they inspected the crate. They looked thoroughly over every beam and crossbar, knocking cautiously on the walls, seeking hollow places or potential locations for hiding or smuggling unauthorized goods. Arthur followed the men, the ubiquitous papers in his hands.

Watching from the outside, I noticed my husband lurking in the shadows of the crate. I watched him deftly ease a beam and tuck a small package underneath. I nearly fainted, watching such folly with potentially suicidal consequences. Similar cases of economic "sabotage" were often punished by death or long-term incarceration. It was hard to understand why an otherwise reasonable man would take such a risk for an insignificant amount of money. Later, I confronted Arthur and he conceded that it was hardly a wise thing to do but he had done it anyway, more out of rage than common sense.

Our departure was set for June 1949. The morning was a lovely one; the weather was sunny and mild. The day before, another picture postcard pretty day, I took leave from all the places which once meant so much to me but later only turned into haunting memories of the past.

We felt a sense of loss as we left many friends. The most difficult parting was with Lilly, the one friend who was such a joy and support to me. It was her warmth and decency that helped restore my faith in human compassion. Even today, decades later, I must admit that I have met only a handful of people who could be compared to Lilly in regard to her special personality and outstanding qualities. I hugged Jan, her two year old, silently wondering if and when we would meet again. Was it only our generation that had to take leave from loved ones as soon as we had established emotional ties? And once again I had no answers, just the nagging pain.

The next day, the three of us arrived at the railway station where men and women boarded separate train cars. Women with babies were assigned to sleeping cars. The train moved slowly from the main railway station on the first leg of our journey to Israel. Though most of us were glad to be on our way out of the "Workers' Paradise" we were apprehensive. All we wished was to cross the border and be free.

The train jerked to a stop at the border railway station of Ceske Velenice, the last terminus before crossing into Austria. Arthur visited our coach once during our ride from Prague, and I sensed that he was in search of a hiding place of sorts. Quietly, I reminded him of all the disastrous consequences of even the slightest transgression of the law and he appeared to agree with me. That only partially alleviated my anxiety because Arthur was at times incredibly stubborn. I knew that I would remain tense until we reached Austria.

Arthur nursed a deep grudge against the continuous state-authorized robbery. Had an individual swindled us that badly he would have been sentenced to a long jail term. Only a powerful government could get away with this type of criminal behavior. I believe that the trivial items Arthur smuggled offered him the pleasure of a symbolic revenge.

At the last stop we would have our documents checked and likely a strip search. The custom officials approved our papers and were about to conduct a final inspection. In the sleeping cars there was no scrutiny whatsoever. The many babies were crying and the air was stuffy, like in an unventilated nursery. All men and women were asked to step out of the train and submit to body searches. While one woman checked our clothes, another made certain that we had no valuables hidden on our bodies. No contraband was found and we were permitted to return to our cars, expecting an imminent departure. Then the shock came. The loudspeaker system began to rumble, and soon a voice announced that the train was being detained for the inspection had unearthed a hidden camera and some jewelry in a ceiling shaft in one of the bathrooms. The voice informed all passengers that the train would be held up until the owner confessed he had attempted to smuggle contraband.

I was overcome with dark foreboding. In my heart of hearts I knew that it was Arthur. I recalled his wish to buy a camera, a Leica—at that time the top-of-the-line model. Was it the one found by the customs people in the bathroom shaft? I put on my best poker face, joining the chorus of women who wondered loudly who could possibly have been so foolhardy and stupid. Most occupants of the car were angry and deeply upset about the untimely complication. We were gripped by panic, expecting the train to remain behind if the culprit did not confess. Few hoped that anyone would step forward to admit such idiocy. The names used to describe the author of the border indiscretion were not taken from any dictionary. All of us wished to be far away from the Czech borders; we had nothing left in the country and suddenly we were in jeopardy by this senseless complication.

Seconds stretched into minutes, minutes into hours. We stood motionless in Ceske Velenice while the customs officials attempted to find the culprit. The man in charge of our group tried to convince the officials that simple confiscation would suffice and that the train should be allowed to continue. He reinforced his recommendation by a bulky envelope stuffed with hidden money collected from the desperate passengers. As was often the case, bribery softened the hearts of the rigid officials. This one brilliant move swayed the officers of the law. All of a sudden the train jerked and we were on our way. Most of us whispered a silent prayer of thanks, grateful that the complication was resolved and we were out of harm's way.

Later that night at the first opportunity, I told Arthur how little we all thought of such behavior and his taste for danger, gambling with his and other people's destinies. Again he agreed with me, conceded that he was foolish, to say the least, but I knew that, given an opportunity, he would do it all over again. He was infuriated by the state's continuous thievery from its innocent citizens.

It took only a few hours to cross Austria and we reached Italy. By midday we arrived in Trani. On the platform of the railway station where the train came to a halt were young boys trying to sell oranges. Exhilarated by the sight of fruit we had not seen for years, I threw all my usual caution to the wind and bought one for my boy who had never tasted any citrus fruit. At first he thought that I had got him a toy, but then slowly, ever so cautiously, he tasted it and, to my delight, he liked it.

We spent the night in a camp in Barri, and the next day we were bused to the port where we were to board a waiting ship. It is difficult to describe our emotions at the sight of the ship. An Israeli flag fluttered on its mast. I stood there mesmerized. I believed that I had never witnessed anything of similar beauty, dignity and glory. The blue and white flag displayed the state's insignia, the Star of David. I could not help but reflect on the years when the Star of David was supposed to designate us as the dregs of society, fit only for the gas chambers. We used to hide our stigma, hoping to be invisible. Now the Star of David waved proudly. The sight of the flag moved me to the very depths of my soul. I was overwhelmed by pride in our Jewish destiny. In spite of all the tragedies and decimation of our past, here we were alive and well, on our way to our very own state.

Neither could I tear my eyes from the crew that manned the ship. The officers and sailors looked very impressive; they wore immaculately white pressed uniforms. They were neat and clean, but above all, they seemed such proud men. They laughed, totally unconcerned that their laughter was noisy and boisterous; none of them looked over their shoulder for anyone's approval or disapproval. They were exuberant and happy. I had never met a Jew so free. These Jews were magnificently diverse, proud, and not distorted by millennia of persecution; their backs were straight, unbent by the force of suffered injustice. I felt honored to be a Jew like them and I whispered a prayer. I beseeched the Almighty to let my son grow up to be a man like the sailors of the *Galillah*.

Steeped in my emotion, I failed to notice that the *Galillah* was not nearly as impressive as the young sailors who manned the old, rickety vessel; her seaworthiness was long gone. Under different conditions, such a ship would not have been allowed to carry human cargo. But these were extraordinary times. The newcomers were flocking in droves to the shores of the new state, enthusiastically hoping to find a haven and a new beginning. Later I learned that our journey was the last hurrah of the *Galillah*. Upon our arrival the responsible naval authorities beached the overused, old ship. But while we boarded her, we were in high spirits, aware of the momentous importance of the hour. Not only were we young but we even felt youthful—another new sensation for the survivors of the camps. We listened to the screeching noises of the ship getting ready for departure and the engines being cranked for our journey. Even this cacophony resembled pleasant sounds. We were jubilant as we set to sea.

The trip was neither comfortable nor easy: the vessel was overcrowded, some passengers were quite ill and scores of crying babies voiced their displeasure. Still, I could not recall the last time I had felt so free and elated. Most of us experienced the same sensation of a burden being removed from our shoulders—one we had carried without knowing. We said goodbye to our joyless lives after the Holocaust and severed our ties to our European roots. Europe had nothing more to offer the survivor who did not fit in.

A powerful storm caught up with us near Sicily, dampening our enthusiasm. Violent winds threw the vessel from side to side; waves battered the old ship. At times we feared that she might capsize, drowning us in the Mediterranean. But the next day brought wonderful sunshine and a mild breeze; the only reminder of the night's storm was the sight of the deck, filled with the many seasick passengers who had tried to escape the dirty, crowded cabins.

Vera in Israel, circa mid–1950s.

Most passengers were sick during the entire voyage for the food on the *Gallilah* was awful. Nevertheless, no one complained. We were aware that we would reach our destination in a short time and we had different matters on our minds.

One early morning when the daylight barely penetrated the shadows of the night, we arrived in port. Finally the moment we were waiting for was here. Shouts and cries of "Eretz Israel!" resounded in every corner of the ship.

Everybody rushed and pushed to reach the deck to see the miracle. And, like a dream come true, in the distance, in the shadows of the morning fog, we could clearly discern Mount Carmel. Haifa was in sight. The sounds of Hatikvah filled the air; most sang with tears streaming down their faces. We were home. At long last we returned home.

Epilogue

We struggled to rebuild our lives and families in Israel and Canada. It was by no means a smooth ride. We never regretted the decision to turn our backs on Europe. Not only did we leave a continent soaked with Jewish blood, we also left the daily reminders of the Holocaust. And though we could not forgive or forget, we still became wrapped up in the enthusiasm of building Israel. The opportunity to leave the Communist police state of Czechoslovakia freed us from the yoke of a brutal dictatorship. Having done so, our sons could grow up as thinking individuals, unencumbered by fear and uncertainty. Their formative years were not marred by an atmosphere of suspicion and denunciation. They were not stripped of the right

Vera and Arthur Schiff, circa 1960.

Vera and Arthur, circa 1970.

to conduct themselves as they wished and voice their opinions. They were privileged to grow up free.

I believe that we took risks and showed courage by leaving our country which at least assured us of a minimal living standard. Although I have never regretted our decision to emigrate to Israel, even I have to admit that our beginnings there were anything but safe or easy. I am convinced, however, that our sons benefited uniquely by spending their formative years in Israel and, subsequently, by living in Canada, a truly free country of boundless opportunities.

In 2011 I traveled back to Theresienstadt for what I believed would be my last visit to a place that changed my life forever. It's been more than 75 years since my incarceration there. With the passage of time I have become concerned that history will wipe the memory of Theresienstadt under the carpet. My sons agreed to accompany me as well as my grandson Ethan, a videographer, who wanted to document our journey.

To return to Theresienstadt was not an easy decision. I am always overcome by dark emotions and endless sadness whenever my mind drifts to those lamentable days of our lives. It's even more difficult to be there physically. On one hand, to revisit the dark times of imprisonment in Theresienstadt was an important step in understanding the horrible years I spent there as a teenager-inmate. I always knew that the years of terror of the Nazis' "Final Solution of the Jewish Question" wrought lasting changes

Schiff family photograph, early 1990s. Standing at back, from left: granddaughter Karen, son David, grandson Matthew, son Michael, granddaughter Sarah. Middle row, from left: daughter-in-law Susan, grandson Ethan, former daughter-in-law Shelley. Front row, from left: Vera, granddaughter Deena, granddaughter Hillary, Arthur.

and damages on the handful of survivors. I wanted some measure of closure.

The Theresienstadt I found this time was in so many ways remarkably unchanged. While I was approaching the one-time garrison town and concentration camp, I felt apprehension—the heaviness of my impending confrontation with our past. I am not quite sure what I hoped to find, perhaps

Vera (center, in white jacket) accompanying a March of the Living tour for educators to Holocaust sites in Germany and Poland, 2010 (photograph by Michael Rajzman for the Sarah and Chaim Neuberger Holocaust Education Centre).

that Theresienstadt had been converted into a teaching center that would memorialize the madness of the Nazi years. It should be a warning to the current and future generations about the need for tolerance.

Today, Theresienstadt is a sad, dilapidated town that neither lives nor is dead. It is a haunted place for those innocents murdered there cannot find repose for their suffering was never punished. Few of the perpetrators were expiated for their crimes.

Of the 1,500 hundred souls who live there, many exist on government subsidies. A number of them wander aimlessly, shabbily dressed; there are

Vera at a memorial service for Holocaust victims in Poland, 2010 (photograph by Michael Rajzman for the Sarah and Chaim Neuberger Holocaust Education Centre).

**Vera with her sons, David (left) and Michael, visiting Prague and Theresien-
stadt, 2011.**

men and women who gave up on life long ago and continue to exist in this
place of despair.

On the main square in one of the few decent buildings in Theresienstadt, the one-time SS officers' headquarters, is a present-day home for
invalids and those with various mental challenges. I am sure that they are
much more deserving of the best built residence in town than their prede-
cessors, the Nazis overlords, but they contribute to the surreal atmosphere
of present-day Theresienstadt.

I have visited other memorial Holocaust sites, often displaying neatly
maintained barracks, and frequently the pathways are strewn with white
pebbles. Many such sites resemble parks and are far from reflecting past
reality. Not so in Theresienstadt of 2011. There are some commemorative monuments attesting to the three and a half years of the Jewish
ghetto-camp. There is a very good museum in the former Jugendheim
(children's home). In the Magdeburg barrack there is a replica of the typical quarters and a modest depiction of the theater, a vital part of the camp's
Freizeitgestaltung (cultural life).

I was deeply affected by the statue erected at the place where the Nazis
ordered the inmates to discard the ashes of the tens of thousands of Jews

Top and above: Vera revisiting Theresienstadt, 2011.

Memorial and graves at Theresienstadt, 2011.

who died in Terezin. The bed of the calm river Ohre is the final resting place of those who died in Terezin. The site at the riverbank is marked today by a monument in the shape of a weeping mourner.

Being at this spot hit me very hard. This is the closest thing I have to a grave for my family. The remains of my parents, sister and many friends rest at the bottom of river Ohre. They are in this wet grave, having been denied their lives and then posthumously refused a decent burial place. I stood there for a long time, looking at the peaceful, enigmatic waters of the Ohre. I tried to recite Kaddish, the traditional prayer for the deceased, but somehow I couldn't utter the words glorifying the Almighty.

There is a steep descent from the bank to the waters of the river. My sons went down, paying their respects to the relatives they never knew. They picked up a few pebbles at the ridge and brought these precious mementos with them to Canada. They too were robbed, for they never met their grandparents, aunt, cousins and many relatives who would have loved them with all their hearts. The crimes committed by the Nazis did not stop with us; they extended their dire consequences into the subsequent generations.

One of the preserved tunnels of the camp resembles the one in which I secretly met with Mr. Bleha so long ago. Perhaps it was the same one, I could not tell. Then I came scurrying in to meet the only friend from the outside world who stood so valiantly by my family. There in the dark casemates he would hand me a parcel with food and I would run back to the camp. Now so many years later, I still could feel the tension and fear of those clandestine meetings. For a moment or two I felt like the 16 year old I was then and I sensed an urgent need to get out of the shaft.

The first barrack we visited was Vrchlabi which had been the hospital, the site where my parents died and where I worked all three years of my imprisonment. The yard was in great disarray, untidy, scattered with debris that lay all around: broken, dried-up branches, randomly discarded old pneumatics and other rubbish.

We climbed the staircase to the upper level of the hospital. I couldn't believe my eyes. The inside appeared much like it had so long ago. All was as I remembered it. Only now it was very dirty, mucky, strewn with waste, and showing marked neglect. Bar the accumulated garbage, the crumbling stairs and neglected halls, most looked as if time passed without leaving an imprint on the face of Vrchlabi.

I am not sure what I hoped to find once I climbed up the stairs. The staircase, like all else around, was in a state of abysmal disrepair; some steps were rickety, the junk strewn around gave evidence of human presence, like discarded condoms and excrement. A thought crossed my mind: our wretched stay in Vrchlabi was marked by shortages of everything except illnesses and death and still we kept the structure more or less clean. Presently nobody worries about the maintenance of the building.

The familiarity of the place came into focus, and all of a sudden, I could immediately orient myself as to the locations of the medical departments. It was an eerie feeling as I stood in the empty room, which was the operating room of the department of laryngology where I toiled every day, endless hours under unimaginably difficult circumstances.

It was not only the feeling of "I"; I felt the heaviness and anxiety of the days so long gone. It was here where we attempted to help the patients and make a difference. I remember it as if it happened yesterday. I saw the faces of those who worked there, and I could recall their voices, our hectic working days and the fearful nights.

I hesitated to enter the adjacent smaller room where so long ago a newborn had to die to give his mother a chance of life. Even now more than seven decades later, a cold shudder ran down my spine remembering the awful night. On this hot morning in Vrchlabi I relived what I couldn't forget. I stood there for a long time.

We walked the long passage of Vrchlabi where various departments had been located. We walked by the rooms where the internal medicine patients had been cared for. I looked away from the department of urology, where Dad died, my boyfriend Max met his painful end and many others slipped into the peaceful embrace of death.

We were not allowed to go up to the attic-level which was once the isolation hall for TB patients. It was there where Mom died. Perhaps I should be grateful for the small mercy that the dilapidated staircase had barred us from climbing there. Not that I can ever forget the hall number 90, the TB ward, but at that moment I had revisited all the pain I could bear.

Because the building was in such a desolate state of repair I couldn't go up to find a happier memory of Theresienstadt, our kumbal (the small crevice) in the attic in Vrchlabi. In 1944 Arthur fixed it up and made it almost cozy for the two of us. I would have loved to visit our kumbal. Without a word or a whisper we left the hospital.

We went to visit the Sudeten barracks next, a place where my poor dad was housed, packed in with hundreds of other men in one huge, drafty, foul-smelling hall. There he slowly withered away. The Sudeten barracks were a jungle where only a predator could prosper.

Today Sudeten is another run-down barrack that was under military administration until 20 years ago. As we visited, the halls of Sudeten were empty, bar the filth, broken glass and a whole lot of unidentifiable detritus. Although I did not want to recall my dad's pathetic suffering there, I couldn't help but remember the large open spaces filled with men crammed tightly in there, each mattress touching another man's, filled with noise, clutter, stench and misery. It is still painful to recall that my dad spent the last two years of his life there.

We also received special permission to visit the Hanover barrack which was once Arthur's "home." The lower level of Hanover is now rented out to carpenters. As we entered they busily banged away, oblivious to our visit.

There was a monotonous, depressing similarity to these barracks. Huge cavernous spaces filled with stale air, mountains of debris, and, in the case of Hanover, a large amount of broken glass. We stepped on shards that crunched under our feet. I am not sure why there were such thick layers of broken glass in Hanover; it seemed as if the floors were covered with it, like wall-to-wall carpeting.

My memories of this place were less ominous. Here was Arthur's bunk. I had to smile, recalling my first visit to his sleeping quarters. There was a ban on women entering men's barracks: in Theresienstadt most everything was forbidden. It was sometime in April 1944 when I, the seasoned inmate, met the camp rookie, Arthur.

In 2011, standing in the shambles of the Hanover amidst the debris, I thought of his confidence and his deep faith. I pondered our chance meeting and falling in love with a man who had such a granite-like inner core.

Left: Vera awarded an honorary Doctor of Letters (D. Litt) from the University of New Brunswick (Saint John) for her contributions to Holocaust education, 2012. *Right:* Vera toasting her fellow graduates, 2012 (photographs by Cheryl Fury).

Dr. Katz-Schiff with Dr. Cheryl Fury and Vice President Robert MacKinnon, 2012.

Would I have survived without his inspirational confidence? His smile took a lot of the dreariness out of the hideous days of Theresienstadt.

Hamburg is the only barrack not defaced. There is no graffiti, broken panes of glass, peeling paint or collapsing walls. Instead, the outer walls are stuccoed in fresh lemon-colored paint, and all waste has been removed. We entered the inner sanctum of Hamburg with its exemplary clean and tidy yard. The well in the center was elevated by handsome stones and quite decorative. Some young saplings had been planted as well.

I passed the guard house where long ago—in 1942, to be exact—I nearly

Vera addresses her fellow graduates at fall Convocation, 2012.

lost my innocence. A Czech gendarme on duty tried to rape me, but I outwitted him. Today I smiled but then I was petrified.

Glancing at the upper level of the top floor, I saw the place where my mom, sister and I lived crammed in a medium-sized hall with some 100 other women. Then I looked at the opposite side of the upper floor; that was where Arthur was hiding when my mom and I were about to get loaded on a train to Auschwitz. Then I was convinced that would be the last time I saw him. I had volunteered to go with my mom in a transport of the doomed TB patients, all of whom would be sent to the gas chambers without selection. If not for the sudden miraculous reversal of our fate by the commandant of the camp, Colonel Karl Rahm, it would have been the end for the tubercular transport headed for the gas chambers. My eyes wandered to the center of the yard where SS Obersturmbannführer Karl Rahm stood, selecting those who at the last minute dared to beg for their lives. It was there that he showed compassion and exempted my mom and me from the transport of the doomed.

Vera Schiff today (photograph by Roy Danics).

Lastly my eyes wandered to the dreadful place which had once been the sickbay. That was the place where my beloved sister Eva suffered for some three months and ultimately lost her battle for life at not quite 18 years of age. Even today I feel the pain like a heavy boulder pushing on my heart.

I came to that concentration camp as a sixteen year old—still a girl—and was liberated at nineteen, aged beyond my years. Then in a fight for the lives of my dearest as well as my own, I never allowed myself the luxury of self-pity. Only now as an old woman I look back at the teenager I was then, her valiant efforts to make life-saving contacts, to please the powers that be, to find or steal food for those who were in such dire need. Coping with many of my own physical problems, I tried desperately to save the lives of those I loved best. Now all of a sudden I felt pity for the teenage me, for the loss of my loved ones, my stolen youth, education, possessions and broken dreams. I would like to believe that all my loved ones died for some purpose but it is the naked, unadorned truth that they died because the Nazis didn't allow them to live. And it hurts today just as much as it did those long years ago.

Final Postscript—2021

Although my memoir was written years ago, I believe it is as relevant now as it was then. Have we learned any lessons from this violent dark period in history?

I worry as I look at our deeply divided world. We still haven't succeeded in uprooting prejudices and biases—a scourge that brought so much misery.

In the aftermath of the Holocaust, we coined a motto: "Never again." We hoped that humans would never commit such heinous crimes ever again. But violence is still rampant. Differing ideologies continue to justify the inexcusable. When will we learn that diversity enriches our lives? Most of us want the same things. We wish our families safety and prosperity in a clean, secure and sustainable environment. Why is there still intolerance to our differences in race, religion and politics? Why do we allow for bloodshed and subjugation of so many all over the world? We have to teach and practice tolerance and strive for broad-mindedness.

I am writing this during the pandemic, when we all are hit by Covid-19. This submicroscopic organism has forced us to face new realities. We have to accept how fragile we are and how uncertain our survival is. I have experienced and witnessed humanity's propensity for evil but I have also experienced human kindness. Will this shared menace go some way to uniting our fractured world? Will humanity rise to the challenge of this global disaster in unprecedented ways?

We still have our work cut out for us these many years after the Holocaust and World War II.

Index

Numbers in *bold italics* indicate pages with illustrations